The MAILBOX®
The Idea Magazine For Teachers®
PRESCHOOL

1997–1998

YEARBOOK

Jayne M. Gammons, Senior Editor
Lori Kent, Associate Editor

The Education Center, Inc.
Greensboro, North Carolina

The Mailbox® 1997–1998 Preschool Yearbook

Editor In Chief: Margaret Michel
Magazine Director: Karen P. Shelton
Editorial Administrative Director: Stephen Levy
Senior Editor: Jayne M. Gammons
Associate Editor: Lori Kent
Contributing Editor: Angie Kutzer
Copy Editors: Lynn Bemer Coble, Mandy Dixon, Karen Huffman, Scott Lyons, Jennifer Rudisill, Debbie Shoffner, Gina Sutphin
Cover Artist: Lois Axeman
Contributing Artist: Lucia Kemp Henry
Staff Artists: Jennifer Tipton Bennett, Cathy Spangler Bruce, Pam Crane, Nick Greenwood, Clevell Harris, Susan Hodnett, Sheila Krill, Mary Lester, Rob Mayworth, Kimberly Richard, Rebecca Saunders, Barry Slate, Donna K. Teal
Editorial Assistants: Mickey Hjelt, Laura Slaughter, Wendy Svartz
Librarian: Elizabeth Findley

ISBN 1-56234-210-X
ISSN 1088-5536

Printed in the United States of America.

The Education Center, Inc.
P.O. Box 9753
Greensboro, NC 27429-0753

Look for *The Mailbox*® 1998–1999 Preschool Yearbook in the summer of 1999. The Education Center, Inc., is the publisher of *The Mailbox*®, *Teacher's Helper*®, *The MAILBOX*® *Bookbag*™, and *The Mailbox Teacher*™ magazines, as well as other fine products and clubs. Look for these wherever quality teacher materials are sold, or call 1-800-714-7991 to request a free catalog.

Contents

Thematic And Contributor Units 5

    A Prehistoric Preschool Welcome 6

    Kangaroo And Company 12

    Get Ready, Get Set, Go! 18

    Under Construction 24

    Monstrous Emotions 30

    Celebrate In Centers 36

    I'm Special! 44

    Snow Foolin' 50

    Clothing With Class 56

    Making Masterpieces 64

    Jelly-Bean Jamboree! 70

    Happy Hands 77

    Bursting Into Bloom! 84

    Sunny-Side Up 92

    Wild About Watermelons! 96

    Footloose And Fancy-Free 102

    A Patchwork Of Fine-Motor Activities 104

Book Features 107

    A *You're Adorable* 108

    Where The Wild Things Are 110

    Chicka Chicka Boom Boom 114

    Caps, Hats, Socks, And Mittens: A Book About The Four Seasons 117

    Snowballs 122

    The Very Hungry Caterpillar 125

Nursery-Rhyme Units 129

    Hickory, Dickory, Dock! 130

    Miss Muffet Goes Modern 134

    Jack Be Nimble; Jill Be Quick 139

    Mary, Mary, How Does Your Garden Grow? 144

    One, Two, Three, Four, Five; I Caught A Fish Alive! 149

    Diddle, Diddle, Dumpling 155

Once Upon A Story 161

It's Circle Time! 177

Head, Shoulders, Knees, & Toes 187

Songs & Such 193

Fingerplays, Poems, And Rhymes 203

Crafts For Little Hands 215

Busy Hands 227

    Squeezin' And Squooshin' 228

    Stack 'Em Up! 230

    Shimmer And Shine! 232

    Swirl And Twirl 234

    Slip And Slide! 236

The Second Time Around 239

Setting The Stage 243

The Magic Of Manipulatives 251

    Rubber Stamps 252

    Cardboard Tubes 254

    Candles 256

    Magnetic Letters And Numerals 258

Explorations 261

    Luscious Leaves 262

    Soapy Science 264

    Dental Magic 266

    The Well-Dressed Nest 268

Building Character 271

    Courage 272

    Friendship 273

    Gentleness 274

Getting Your Ducklings In A Row 275

Building Bridges Between Home And School 283

Bulletin Boards And Displays 297

Our Readers Write 311

Index 316

Thematic And Contributor Units

A Prehistoric Preschool
Welcome

Rumble, rumble. Stomp, stomp, stomp! Could that be the sound of dinosaurs thundering down the hall? No, but it *could* be the sound of excited preschoolers arriving at your door! Calm your Jurassic jitters by using these dinosaur-themed ideas to prepare a prehistoric preschool welcome for your new class. Have a "tremenda-saurus" year!

ideas contributed by dayle timmons and Angie Kutzer

A Prehistoric Present For You!

You can have enormous impact on youngsters' entry into preschool with these pre-preschool fun packs. Before the first day of school, prepare a dinosaur project, a dinosaur nametag, a welcome note, and dinosaur crayons for each child. Then deliver the fun packs during home visits prior to opening day. To prepare a pack for each child, duplicate the dinosaur pattern on page 9 onto white construction paper, the note on page 10 onto colorful paper, and a dinosaur nametag on page 11 onto colorful construction paper; then cut them out. Personalize the dinosaur pattern and nametag. To make dinosaur crayons for each child, put old crayons of the same color in a microwave-safe dish. Microwave on low, stirring occasionally. Pour the melted crayon wax into dinosaur-shaped candy molds (available where cake and candy supplies are sold). Place the molds in the freezer; then pop out the crayon shapes when they're solid. Seal one of each color of crayon in a plastic sandwich bag. Place the dinosaur pattern, note, nametag, and crayons in a lunch bag decorated with dinosaur stickers or dinosaur-themed notepad pages. Later use youngsters' completed dinosaur projects during your first group time, as described in "Getting To Know 'You-asaurus' " on page 7.

These dinosaur paws are on the floor, so you can follow them to Mrs. Timmons's door!

Making Tracks

Encourage independence by creating a "dino-rific" path that your little foot stompers can follow to your class on the first days of school. Make a dinosaur-paw template by enlarging the pattern on page 10 to the desired size. Then trace a supply of the pattern onto colorful Con-Tact® covering. Cut out the paws; then attach them to the floor in a path that leads from the school entrance to your classroom door. If desired, post a sign near the beginning of the path that reads, "These dinosaur paws are on the floor, so you can follow them to [your name]'s door!" Parents and children alike will be making tracks to find out what else you have in store!

Rip-Roarin' Ready To Start The Day!

Once your little ones have arrived at your door, greet each one with a dinosaur hug. Assist each child in attaching the nametag that he received in his fun pack to his clothing; then guide him to your group area. To get youngsters ready to follow daily routines, read aloud *Time For School, Little Dinosaur* by Gail Herman (Random House, Inc.; 1990). After listing Little Dinosaur's steps for getting ready for school, ask volunteers to offer ways that they got ready to come to school that morning, such as brushing their teeth or helping to prepare their snacks. Explain that a routine is also necessary each day once they arrive at school. Demonstrate the routine you would like youngsters to follow that includes activities such as putting belongings in cubbies and choosing centers. Then have each child step out into the hall and reenter the classroom, pretending that he has just arrived. Before you know it, students will be rip-roarin' ready to start the day—just like Little Dinosaur!

Getting To Know "You-asaurus"

Use the *extinct* to discover the *distinct* personalities that make up your new class. Invite youngsters to bring their completed dinosaur projects (see "A Prehistoric Present For You!" on page 6) with them to one of your first group times. Compare the dinosaurs. Then, using the accompanying note as your guide, discuss the similarities and differences that the dinosaurs reveal about your children. Collect the dinosaurs and display them—along with an enlarged copy of the note—on a bulletin board that can easily be seen by parents as they visit your school. This class is "dino-mite"!

An Invitation To A Dinosaur Stomp!

The invitation's out to watch tails wag, scales shake, and horns hoot and holler in Paul Stickland's *Dinosaur Stomp!* (Dutton Children's Books, 1996). Don't miss your chance to read about the dinosaur dance. Then follow up the fun by doing "The Dino Dance-O." To prepare personalized puppets for your little ones to take out on the dance floor, duplicate a class supply of the dinosaur patterns on page 11 onto various colors of construction paper. Personalize each dinosaur with a different child's name, cut out the patterns, and then tape each one to a craft stick. After sharing the story, give each child his puppet and direct him to find his own space in an open area of your room. Encourage your little ones to boogie down with their dinos as you lead them in singing the following song. That's what it's all about!

The Dino Dance-O
(sung to the tune of "The Hokey-Pokey")

You put your dino up,
You put your dino down,
You put your dino up,
And you shake it all around.

You do the Dino Dance-O
And you turn yourself around.
Stomp twice on the ground.
Dino Dance-O!

You put your dino in front,
You put your dino in back,
You put your dino in front,
And you give your knees a slap.

(Repeat chorus.)

You touch your dino to your head,
You touch your dino to your toe,
You touch your dino to your head,
Then you shake it to and fro.

(Repeat chorus.)

You do the Dino Dance-O.
You do the Dino Dance-O.
You do the Dino Dance-O.
That's what it's all about.
Dino Dance-O!

Brontosaurus Behavior

Use the characteristics of two dinosaur opposites, brontosaurus and tyrannosaurus, to discuss appropriate classroom behavior with your little ones. Locate in reference books pictures of a brontosaurus and a tyrannosaurus. Looking at the pictures, have the children compare the dinosaurs' physical features and share any information that they may already know about the two types of dinosaurs. Explain that the tyrannosaurus is thought to have been a mean meat-eater, while the brontosaurus is thought to have been a gentle plant-eater. Make a list of your little ones' suggestions for classroom behaviors that are brontosaurus-like. Then make a list of tyrannosaurus-like behaviors to avoid. Post the lists in the classroom; then refer to them when a rambunctious reptile needs to be reminded to act more like a lovable lizard.

We share.
We say nice words.
We help.

"Tour-ific" Fossils

Introduce your students to their new surroundings and school staff by going on a dinosaur search. To prepare for this activity, enlarge a dinosaur pattern from page 11 onto a piece of poster board. Cut out the dinosaur; then cut it into as many puzzle pieces as there are places and people to visit on your school tour. "Hide" a dinosaur fossil (puzzle piece) at each tour stop, and give one to each person you will introduce to your children on the tour.

Before your dinosaur hunt, explain to your paleontologists that fossils can be the remains of animals that lived thousands or millions of years ago. Read aloud *Bones, Bones, Dinosaur Bones* by Byron Barton (HarperCollins Children's Books, 1990). Suggest that there may be dinosaur fossils throughout your school; then take the group on a dinosaur search. Each time the group finds a fossil, introduce them to the new person or place where the fossil was found. Then return to the classroom to put the fossils together to make the dinosaur. Keep the dinosaur fossils in a puzzle center for youngsters to use independently.

Kim-asaurus

I'm A Preschool Paleontologist!

Chances are your preschoolers are feeling proud of their paleontologic efforts. Top off your day by making these dinosaur headbands. Duplicate a supply of the dinosaur patterns on page 11 onto various colors of construction paper. Cut out the patterns for younger preschoolers. To make a headband, a child chooses a number of the dinosaur patterns, cuts them out if necessary, and decorates them with markers. He then glues them to a personalized sentence strip. Staple the ends of each child's strip together to fit his head. Look at me! I'm as proud as can be!

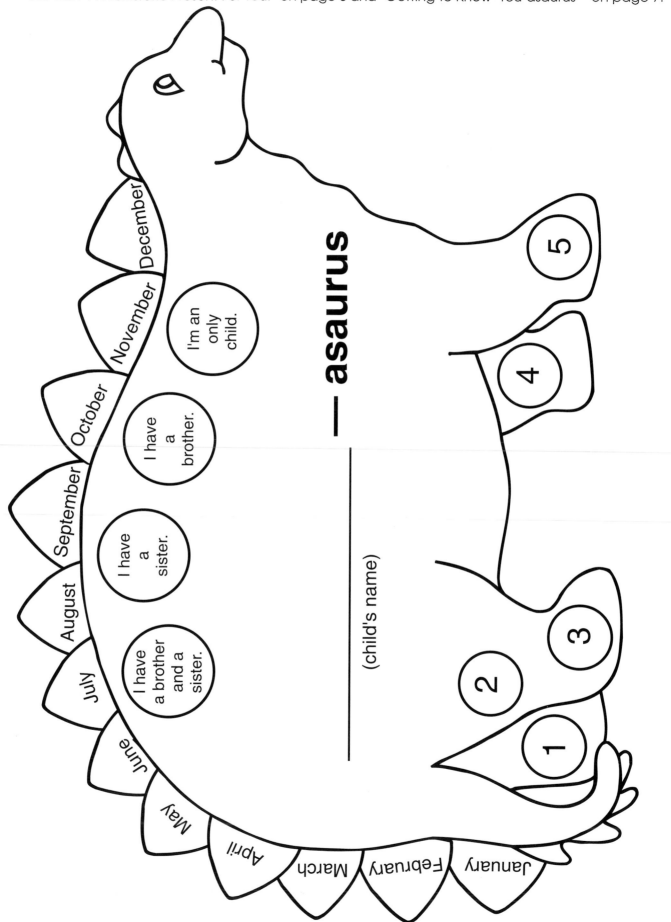

— asaurus

(child's name)

I'm an only child.

I have a brother.

I have a sister.

I have a brother and a sister.

December
November
October
September
August
July
June
May
April
March
February
January

1
2
3
4
5

Note

Use with "A Prehistoric Present For You!" on page 6 and "Getting To Know 'You-asaurus'" on page 7.

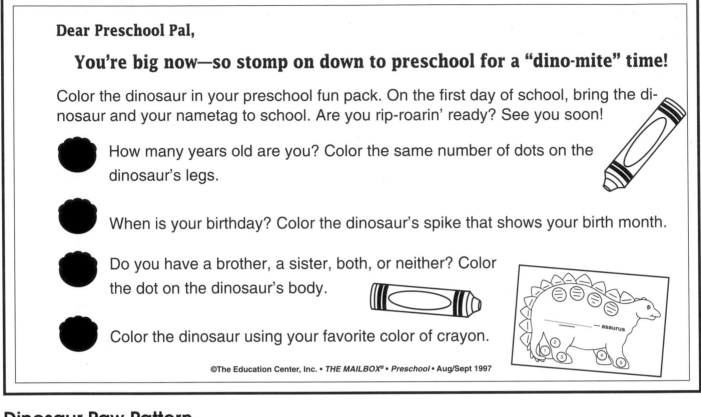

Dear Preschool Pal,

You're big now—so stomp on down to preschool for a "dino-mite" time!

Color the dinosaur in your preschool fun pack. On the first day of school, bring the dinosaur and your nametag to school. Are you rip-roarin' ready? See you soon!

● How many years old are you? Color the same number of dots on the dinosaur's legs.

● When is your birthday? Color the dinosaur's spike that shows your birth month.

● Do you have a brother, a sister, both, or neither? Color the dot on the dinosaur's body.

● Color the dinosaur using your favorite color of crayon.

©The Education Center, Inc. • THE MAILBOX® • Preschool • Aug/Sept 1997

Dinosaur Paw Pattern

Use with "Making Tracks" on page 6.

Use with "A Prehistoric Present For You!" on page 6, "Rip-Roarin' Ready To Start The Day!" and "An Invitation To A Dinosaur Stomp!" on page 7, and "'Tour-ific' Fossils" and "I'm A Preschool Paleontologist!" on page 8.

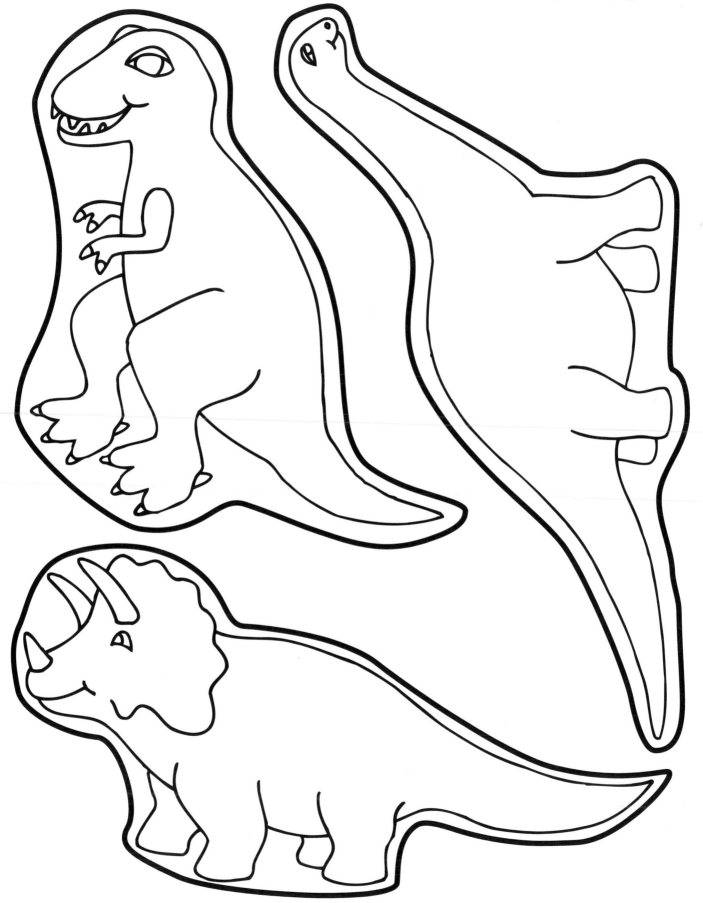

Kangaroo And Company

What's that you say, mate? You're looking for fun ways to help your preschool joeys leave their moms' pockets and meet some new pals? Use the ideas in this bouncy kangaroo unit to introduce your students to a whole new world.

ideas contributed by Bambina L. Merriman

Marsupial Moms

Kangaroo moms are *marsupials.* Marsupial moms carry their young in pouches until their little ones are ready to go out into the world on their own. A kangaroo baby, or *joey,* climbs into its mother's pouch when it is born. For the first four months it stays in its mother's pouch and drinks her milk; then it begins to lean out of the pouch to nibble grass. Soon it is able to hop around and search for food, but returns to the pouch for safety and sleeping. After ten months, the joey is ready to leave the safety of the pocket and explore the world on its own.

After relating this information to your little ones, ask them to name ways that their parents took care of them when they were infants. Next prompt them to suggest things that they can now do by themselves. Congratulate them for being able to do things without their parents present. Then remind them that like mother kangaroos, their parents can still give them safety and security when needed. Mom or Dad is just a hug away!

Little Joey

(sung to the tune of "Have You Ever Seen A Lassie?")

I have a little joey, a joey, a joey.
I have a little joey who lives in my pouch.
I jump up and jump down,
He bumps up and bumps down.
I have a little joey who lives in my pouch.

I have a little joey, a joey, a joey.
I have a little joey who lives in my pouch.
I jump right and jump left,
He bumps right and bumps left.
I have a little joey who lives in my pouch.

Perfect Pockets

Poor mother Katy Kangaroo! *Katy No-Pocket* by Emmy Payne (Houghton Mifflin Company, 1973) is the classic story of a kangaroo who doesn't have a pocket for carrying her baby. Before reading this book aloud, obtain an apron that has pockets. Duplicate a class supply of the joey pattern on page 16 onto construction paper. Cut out and personalize each joey before tucking the set into your apron's pockets. Put on the apron; then read and discuss the story during a group time. As a story extension, give each child the joey labeled with his name, and encourage him to make his own pocket.

To make a pocket, cut off the top 3 1/2 inches of a 6 1/2" x 9 1/2" clasp envelope. Sponge-paint both sides of the envelope brown. When the paint is dry, punch holes in each side of the pocket near the top. Tie a 15-inch length of ribbon to each hole. When each child has made a pocket, help him tie it around his waist and direct him to tuck his personalized joey inside. Then sing the above song. Get ready—it's a tune that requires bouncing!

Five Little Joeys

One little joey with nothing much to do—
Hopped over to a friend; then there were two.

Two little joeys happy as can be—
Bumped into another; then there were three.

Three little joeys wishing there were more—
Bounced around another; then there were four.

Four little joeys, glad to be alive—
Were joined by another; then there were five.

Five little joeys sleepy from their play—
Jumped in their mamas' pouches until another day.

Kangaroo Companions

What do you suppose young joeys do when they've hopped out of their moms' pouches? Ask your little ones what they would do; then suggest that they might like to meet other joeys and have some fun. Using the joey pattern on page 16, cut five joeys from felt. Use a marker to add features; then glue on wiggle eyes, if desired. Place the joeys on a flannelboard as you recite the above fingerplay. When your little ones are familiar with the rhyme, invite them to help dramatize the fun. You'll have your class hopping into friendship in no time!

Colorful Kangas

Give your little joeys a chance to hop around and meet some new pals with this action song. Duplicate a class supply of the joey pattern on page 16 onto various colors of construction paper, making sure that there is an even number of each different color. Cut out the joeys and tuck them into the pockets of the apron worn to introduce *Katy No-Pocket* (see "Perfect Pockets" on page 12). Once you are wearing the apron, ask each child to remove a joey from a pocket and to find his own space in an open area of your room where there is plenty of hopping room. Then sing the following song. As the group sings "Find a partner," each child should find and hop next to a child whose joey is a color match. At the end of the song, collect the joeys, put them in your apron, and begin again.

Jump Little Joeys
(sung to the tune of the chorus of "Shortnin' Bread")

Jump little joeys, joeys, joeys.
Jump little joeys, all around.

Find a partner, partner, partner.
Find a partner; hop around.

Hop with your partner, partner, partner.
Hop with your partner, and then sit down.

Jump Into Learning Centers

Once your little ones are familiar with the activity described in "Colorful Kangas" on page 13, use the song to introduce youngsters to each other and to all of your classroom centers. To prepare this management system for center times, duplicate a copy of the pocket and mother kangaroo patterns on page 17 and a class supply of the joey pattern on page 16 onto a different color of construction paper for each of your centers. Then cut out the patterns. Glue the sides of each pocket onto the corresponding mother kangaroo. Laminate the kangaroos; then cut a slit along the top of each one's pocket. Position one kangaroo in each center. Personalize a set of joeys (one of each color) for each child.

In advance of a center time, select a pair of each color of joey, making sure to have one for each child. Give each child his joey; then sing the song. When each child has found his partner, direct both children to go to the center displaying the matching mother kangaroo and tuck their joeys in the kangaroo's pocket. At the end of a center time, have each pair of children exchange joeys and take them home. Encourage parents to look each day at the names on the joeys and to ask their children about their learning time with new friends.

Kangaroo Pocket Book

Leap into language by creating a class pocket book. Enlarge the mother kangaroo pattern on page 17 onto a piece of poster board. During a center time, take pictures of pairs of children working together, making sure that every child is in one picture. Rotate each developed picture so that the picture is upside down; then flip it over. On the back, write the pictured pair's dictation of their activity. Seal each picture in a resealable plastic bag. Stack the bags so that the pictures are all facing the same direction; then staple them together at the top edge. Attach the connected bags to the center of the kangaroo with a strip of tape. Share the book by showing each picture, then lifting up the pocket to read the dictation. Kids are sure to get a kick out of this kooky kangaroo book!

Jumping Joeys

Youngsters will hop, leap, and jump for joy over this exciting math and movement activity. To prepare, cut a supply of circles from three colors of construction paper. Tape each color of circles in a straight path on the floor, so the three paths are side by side but vary in length. Create a chart as shown, including each child's name and each path's color. Ask a pair of children to stand at opposite ends of a path. Encourage one child to count the number of kangaroo hops it takes to travel down the path to his friend. Record the results. Continue in this manner until the child has hopped down all three paths; then invite his partner to do the same. Hippity-hoppity—math is fun this way!

1, 2, 3...

Kay			
Casey			
Seth			
Kyle	2 hops	6 hops	8 hops
Katie	3 hops	5 hops	10 hops
	red	yellow	blue

Hop-And-Seek

Here's a fun way to build listening skills—kangaroo style! To prepare, you will need one sheet of green construction paper per child. Duplicate the mother kangaroo pattern on page 17 onto one of these sheets; then cut all of the sheets into bush shapes. Before playing the game, lead youngsters to discuss why it is important for young kangaroos to follow grown-up kangaroos' directions. Then introduce the game by spreading the bush shapes on the floor of an open area, making sure the kangaroo picture is facing down. Ask the children to stand among the bushes; then give a series of directions that will lead each youngster to find a bush to stand on. For example, you might say, "Hop forward three times, and then hop onto a bush" or "Tiptoe around a bush, and then hop on it." Then direct the children to step off their bushes and look under them to see whose bush displays the mother kangaroo. Collect that bush and a portion of the remaining bushes. Replace them on the floor, once again hiding the mother kangaroo. Ask the child whose bush displayed the kangaroo to give the directions for the next round of play.

Stuffed Snack

These pizza pocket snacks and the teamwork it takes to make one are yummy stuff! Direct a pair of children to wash their hands. Provide the pair with napkins, one piece of miniature pita bread, a plastic knife, pizza sauce, a slice of mozzarella cheese, and assorted pizza items such as pepperoni and vegetables. Explain to the partners that they will need to work together to make a pizza pocket snack. Then assist the pair as they cut the bread in half, spread some sauce inside the pockets, cut the cheese in half, and stuff their pockets with the items of their choice. Bake the pockets in a 350°F oven or heat them in the microwave until the cheese has melted. Now that's a snack any joey would love!

Bouncy Books

Bounce into reading with these books about kangaroos and their companions.

Little New Kangaroo
Can Little Kangaroo's mother carry all of his new friends? Hold on tight for a lighthearted tale of friendship.
Written by Bernard Wiseman
Illustrated by Theresa Burns
Published by Clarion Books, 1993

Snap!
Joey plays games with his friends the mouse, the snake, the echidna, the platypus, and...the crocodile. SNAP! (Don't worry, Joey and his friends get the last laugh.)
Written by Marcia Vaughan
Illustrated by Sascha Hutchinson
Published by Scholastic Inc., 1996

Joey
The fun begins when Joey invites his friends over to his pouch to play.
Written & Illustrated by Jack Kent
Published by Simon & Schuster
Children's Books, 1987

15

Joey Pattern

Use with "Perfect Pockets" on page 12, "Kangaroo Companions" and "Colorful Kangas" on page 13, and "Jump Into Learning Centers" on page 14.

Award

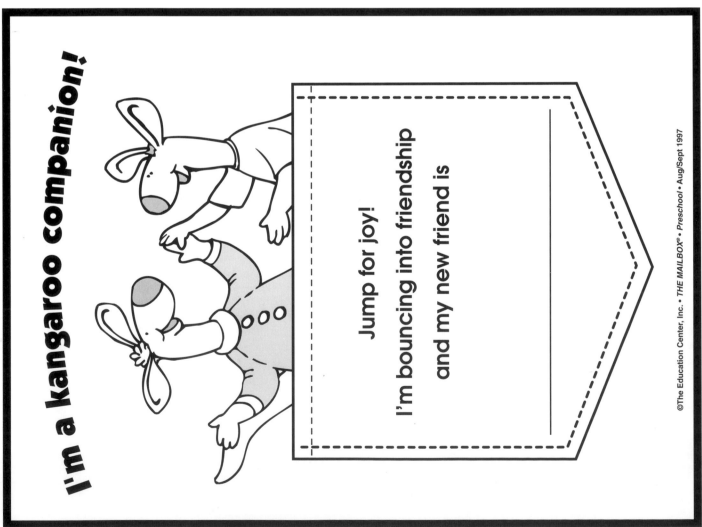

I'm a kangaroo companion!

Jump for joy!
I'm bouncing into friendship
and my new friend is

pocket

Get Ready, Get Set, GO!

Get ready! A new class of preschoolers is on the way. Get set! Use these timely tips from fellow preschool teachers to organize attendance taking, group times, snacktime, learning centers, supplies, and cleanup time. Go, teacher, go!

Taking Attendance

Smiling Faces

To make taking attendance a simple matter and help youngsters practice name recognition, create this management display using pictures of students' smiling faces. Request that a home-supplies store donate countertop samples that are no longer in use. Trim then mount a child's photo onto each sample and label the back of the sample with the child's name. Screw a class supply of cup hooks into a piece of wood so that they are evenly spaced and in rows. At the beginning of the year, hang the samples on the hooks to reveal the sides showing the children's faces. As each child arrives at school, have him locate his picture and turn his name over. Later in the year, request that each child locate his name and turn his picture over. This quick method will tell you at a glance which children are not present.

Lynn Coleman—Preschool, Tumbling Tykes Preschool, Endwell, NY

Hang It Out To Try

Little ones will be quick to recognize their names when you hang this attendance-taking method out for a try. From colorful paper, cut a class supply of T-shirt shapes; then label each shape with a different child's name. Store the shirts in a miniature laundry basket along with miniature plastic clothespins. Secure a length of yarn onto a display board at students' level. As each child arrives at school, request that she find the shirt labeled with her name and clip it to the clothesline. Take a look at your display to see who's hanging out with you each day.

Debbie Quigley—Parent Education, Sweetwater Adult School
National City, CA

Group Time

Have A Seat On A Shape

Use this management tip to provide each child with his own seat on the carpet, and to review shapes and colors at the same time! Using geometric-shaped stencils and colorful paint, paint a variety of shapes in different colors onto your group-area carpet. When it's group time, invite each of your little ones to sit on a shape. Request, for example, that a child "sit on a green shape" or "sit on a shape that is round." Not only are these shapes permanent, but they also add an attractive touch to your group space. Welcome to the group. Won't you please have a seat on a shape?

Lorna Friese—Three-Year-Olds, St. Mark's Nurturing Center, St. Charles, IL

Seasonal Seating

Here's a less permanent, yet long-lasting option for creating a seating arrangement in your group area. Each season or month, write a child's name on a decorative notepad sheet. Tape the sheets to your group-area floor or carpet with several strips of clear, carton-sealing tape. You can vacuum, mop, or sweep over the shapes. What's more, when it's time for a change, the tape won't leave a sticky residue.

Sue DeMoss—Preschool, Maquoketa Head Start, Maquoketa, IA

Transition Tips

Get Your Line In Shape

Little ones will enjoy finding their places in line when you employ this management technique. Duplicate a class supply of several favorite patterns from previous issues of *The Mailbox®* onto different colors of paper. Cut out the patterns and label them sequentially with numerals. Arrange the patterns on the floor in a line; then adhere them with clear Con-Tact® covering. When it's time to line up, direct a child to find a specified shape, color of shape, or numbered shape. Or allow each child to choose his shape and describe it. Everyone in line? Let's go!

Dawn Hurley—Preschool, Child Care Center, Bethel Park, PA

Step Right Up

You'll be able to invite your line leader to step right up when you use this transition tip. Using a permanent marker, trace a pair of foot shapes onto the center of a carpet square. During group activities or transition times, place the square on the floor to indicate where you would like the line to begin; then request that the leader for the day step onto the feet. Once your leader's in line, everyone else can find their places. Now that's the way to get those ducks in a row!

Martha Whitaker—Preschool, Loving Start Preschool
Whitefish Bay, WI

19

Snacktime

Personalized Placemats

These personalized placemats will help you organize snacktime in a snap. Cut half as many vinyl placemats in half vertically as there are children in your class. For each child, attach a strip of masking tape to a placemat half; then label the tape with the child's name and any food allergies. These placemats look spiffy, and they wipe clean in a jiffy!

Lee Turner—Two- And Three-Year-Olds
Chamblee Methodist Kindergarten, Chamblee, GA

A Spot For You

Personalize each child's spot at your snacktime area by making these seasonal nametags. Glue a child's picture to a cutout or decorative notepad page labeled with the child's name. Then use clear Con-Tact® covering to adhere the nametag onto the table at the child's assigned space. If desired prepare a matching nametag to use to label the child's cubbie. Here's a spot just for you!

Chrissy Casey—Preschool, Rocking Horse Child Care Center
Malvern, PA

Ian
Milk Allergy

Learning Centers

Housekeeping

Clip-A-Center

Youngsters can independently choose and change learning centers with this colorful management system. To prepare, cut a different-colored tagboard square for each of your learning centers. Label each sign. Color the same number of clothespins to match a center's sign as you will allow children in that center at one time. Clip the clothespins to the appropriate signs; then place the signs in the centers. When visiting a center, a child removes a clothespin from that center's sign and clips it to his clothing. When no more clothespins are available on a sign, that center is full. When leaving a center, a child replaces the clothespin on the sign.

Susan Burbridge—Preschool
Trinity Methodist Weekday School
San Antonio, TX

Cookie-Cutter Center Tags

If you're looking for a way to organize your learning-center time, then this idea might be cut out just for you! In each center, nail as many picture-frame hooks into the wall—or attach as many self-adhesive hooks onto the wall—as you will allow children in that center at one time. Obtain a class supply of plastic cookie cutters that have hooks for hanging. Give each child a different-shaped cookie cutter. To choose a center, a child simply hangs his cutter on one of a center's hooks.

Dawn Hansen—Preschool, Lasting Impressions Preschool, Kankakee, IL

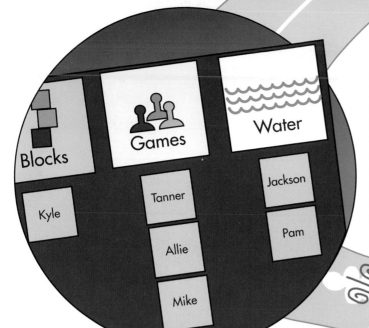

Flannelboard Choices

To make choosing centers a simple matter, set up this color-coded management system. Display a different-colored tagboard square in each of your centers; then cut a smaller square from each different color of tagboard. Back each smaller square with felt for use on the flannelboard. Label each square with the corresponding center's name; then draw a picture to represent that center. Personalize a felt square for each child. To use this system, arrange the labeled squares across the top of a flannelboard. Give each child his personalized square to place on the flannelboard under the square that represents the center of his choice.

Tracy Farrell—Pre-K, St. Columba School, St. Paul, MN

Center Rotation

To establish groups and ensure that youngsters rotate through all of your structured learning centers, try this technique. Label each of the centers in your rotation with a different-colored bird cutout. Prepare a matching set of bird cutouts for each center so that the total number of cutouts equals the number of students in your class. Punch a hole in each cutout and thread it with yarn to make a necklace. Store the necklaces in a container. When it's center time, ask each child to close his eyes and choose a necklace to wear. Group the children by the color of their necklaces and send them to the corresponding centers. During the remainder of your center time, rotate the groups until each group has visited each center.

adapted from an idea by Sandy DiFilippo—Four-Year-Olds
Laurel Park & Recreation Preschool, Laurel, MD

It's easy to see how much I've learned, When I bring home the stickers I've earned.

"Pop-Sticker" Collections

Encourage your little ones to complete learning centers by rewarding them with monthly sticker collections. Personalize a library pocket for each child; then mount the pockets to a piece of poster board. Each month, glue a seasonal shape to an ice-cream stick for each child. Personalize the sticks; then place each child's stick in his pocket on the chart. When a child completes a learning center, attach a sticker to his shape. At the end of each month, send the "pop-sticker" collections home with notes similar to the one shown.

Gloria Whitley—Preschool, G.U.M. Preschool, Mesa, AZ

Supplies

Colorful Crayon Holder

Reinforce visual discrimination and organize crayons with this neat crayon holder. Collect eight plastic cups, a cardboard food-carton container that has eight sections (or two drink carriers with four sections each), and a wrapper from each of the eight different colors of jumbo crayons in a box. Tape a wrapper to each cup; then insert the cups in the sections of the container. Sort a supply of crayons into each cup. If desired tape the cover of a crayon box to a shelf to indicate where you would like the crayon holder to be stored when it's not in use.

Sue DeMoss, Maquoketa Head Start, Maquoketa, IA

Storage Time-Saver

If you often find yourself looking for supplies, save valuable teaching time by using a shoe bag to store items used most often. Hang the bag on the outside of your storage cabinet; then fill the pockets with frequently used items such as stickers, staplers, and glue. Be sure to store items for adult use—such as sharp scissors—out of your little ones' reach.

Melissa L. Epling—Preschool, Panther Creek Elementary, Nettie, WV

Borders Galore

Do you have borders galore? Try this tip for organizing your borders and more. Organize your borders and items such as rolls of stickers by theme or season; then arrange them on extension rods. Position the rods between the walls of a storage closet. Now when you're ready to use these supplies, you'll only have to pull out what you need.

Annette Horton—Pre-K, Frederick Douglass Elementary, Winchester, VA

Perplexing Puzzle Pieces

Here's a way to keep your boxed puzzles organized and improve little ones' counting skills at the same time. Label each of your puzzle boxes with a different numeral; then label the back of the puzzle pieces in each set with the numeral on that puzzle's box. Encourage youngsters to store the puzzle boxes in numerical order when cleaning up. When a stray puzzle piece is found, simply match the numerals and it can quickly be returned to its box.

Carole Watkins—Program Coordinator, Holy Family Child Care Center Crown Point, IN

Puppet Storage

For an attractive way to display classroom puppets, make this puppet holder. Obtain a supply of thick dowel rods that are longer than your puppets. Drill holes as wide as the diameter of the rods into a one-inch-thick piece of wood. Use wood glue to secure a rod in each hole. As a safety precaution, round the corners of the wood holder; then paint it. When the paint is dry, glue felt to the bottom of the holder to prevent it from scratching shelves or carpet. Now you're ready to display your puppets in a child-friendly way!

Joy Wallace—Four-Year-Olds, Home Daycare
Centreville, MS

Cleanup Time

Cleanup Matchup

Here's a transition tip that aids in color recognition, speeds up cleanup time, and promotes cooperation among youngsters. Mount a large paper circle on the wall in each area of your room, using a different color for each area. Cut and laminate a set of smaller circles of each color so that the total number of circles equals the number of children in your class. When it's cleanup time, ask each child to select a laminated circle and clean the area of the room that displays the same color of circle. As a variation for older children, provide cards labeled with color words. Or label the centers with numerals and provide cards labeled with dot sets.

Barbara Wagner—Preschool, Higgelty Piggelty Preschool
Allison, IA

I Spy

Play a quick game of I Spy to facilitate cleanup time. Announce that you spy a mystery item that needs to be put away; then encourage the cleaning to get under way. When cleanup time is over, announce the mystery item and reward the child who put it away with a sticker. Then give everyone a sticker for working together on a job well done.

Debbie Brown—Four- And Five-Year-Olds, Corson Park School
Millville, NJ

Pam Crane

FINISH

Under Construction

Build a firm foundation for youngsters' language, math, motor, and social skills with this construction unit. The following ideas provide a framework for moving youngsters from learning about construction to having fun in your classroom centers. So put on your hard hat, grab your toolbox, and hammer away!

ideas contributed by Linda Blassingame

Build A House

Construct a better understanding of the stages of building a house by singing this song to the tune of "Clap, Clap, Clap Your Hands."

Build, build, build a house,
Build it big and strong.
Build, build, build a house,
Build it all day long.

Draw, draw, draw the plans,
Draw the lines in blue.
Draw, draw, draw the plans,
To tell us what to do.

Dig, dig, dig a hole,
Dig it deep and wide.
Dig, dig, dig a hole,
The house will fit inside.

Pour, pour, pour the floor,
Make the cement splat.
Pour, pour, pour the floor.
Smooth it till it's flat.

Build, build, build the walls,
Build them straight and true.
Build, build, build the walls,
Then put the roof on, too.

Stack, stack, stack the bricks,
Stack them straight and tall.
Stack, stack, stack the bricks.
Cement won't let them fall.

Twist, twist, twist the pipes,
Pipes are big and small.
Twist, twist, twist the pipes,
Then hide them in the wall.

Paint, paint, paint the walls,
Yellow, red, and blue.
Paint, paint, paint the walls,
Then paste wallpaper, too.

Plant, plant, plant the trees,
They'll grow straight and tall.
Plant, plant, plant the trees.
We're finished—that is all!

From The Ground Up

Building a house is a big project! So is helping curious preschoolers understand the stages of building construction. Explain the basics of building by reading aloud the simply written *Building A House* by Byron Barton (Greenwillow Books, 1981) or by discussing the text and illustrations of *How A House Is Built* by Gail Gibbons (Holiday House, Inc.; 1990). Then thrill your little ones by giving them an opportunity to watch the blasting, sawing, pouring, and pounding of real house construction. Show the highly recommended, live-action video *House Construction Ahead*™ by Fred Levine Productions™. (For ordering information call 1-800-843-3686.)

If your youngsters' interests grow bigger than house construction, move up in the world and discuss the building of skyscrapers. Review the illustrations in *Up Goes The Skyscraper!* by Gail Gibbons (Simon & Schuster Children's Books, 1986). Or show *Building Skyscrapers*™ by David Alpert Associates. (For ordering information call 1-800-265-7744.)

24

It Takes Teamwork

Once youngsters are familiar with the steps of building a house, build vocabularies by discussing the workers involved in each stage of the job. The following chant will prepare children to work in the classroom construction zone described on pages 26–29.

Architect, architect, what do you do?
I draw plans; then the builder works, too.

Builder, builder, what do you do?
I build the frame; then the mason works, too.

Mason, mason, what do you do?
I lay the bricks; then the plumber works, too.

Plumber, plumber, what do you do?
I fix pipes; then the electrician works, too.

Electrician, electrician, what do you do?
I wire the house; then the carpenter works, too.

Carpenter, carpenter, what do you do?
I build the walls; then the painter works, too.

Painter, painter, what do you do?
I paint the house; then the decorator works, too.

Decorator, decorator, what do you do?
I make it pretty; then the landscaper works, too.

Landscaper, landscaper, what do you do?
I plant the grass; then the movers work, too.

Movers, movers, what do you do?
We get the house ready for you!

Pam Crane

Construction Zone

Use the following center ideas to turn your classroom into a construction zone. Prepare labeled necklaces to indicate the number and type of workers needed in each center. During center times, ask each child to indicate the job he'd like to take; then provide him with his necklace and send him off to that construction site to get busy!

Builder

Dig Yourself A Hole

It's likely that your little ones will really dig the big machines used at construction sites. Make available at your sand center a variety of toy trucks, such as a bulldozer and a dump truck. Discuss the photos in Tana Hoban's *Construction Zone* (Greenwillow Books, 1997) with children who visit the center. Then encourage your crew to get carried away!

Architect

Learning By Design

Every builder needs a plan. Develop problem solving, shape recognition, and fine-motor skills by turning your art center into an architect's office. Obtain a set of blueprints to share with youngsters during a group time. Then display the blueprints, as well as sketches of house plans (found in house-plan magazines), in the center. Stock the area with blue pencils, large sheets of paper, rulers, and templates of various sizes and shapes. Encourage children to draw plans, then create their designs at a block center.

Billy

All Mixed Up

Youngsters will have a blast at your class cooking center when making these cement shakes. To mix one shake, pour one cup of milk into a one-quart tumbler with a lid. Add two tablespoons of rubble (miniature marshmallows) and two tablespoons of sand (any flavor of gelatin except lemon); then secure the lid on the tumbler. Shake the tumbler for one minute to simulate the action of a cement truck. Pour the mixture into a glass and drink with a straw. Now that's a treat that's sure to fill you up!

The Ins And Outs Of Plumbing

Preschool plumbers will enjoy discovering the mechanics of a plumbing system at your water table. Purchase various sizes of inexpensive PVC pipes and connectors from a home-supplies store. Encourage youngsters to connect and reconnect the pipes, and to pour water through the pipes.

For added fun, place a plunger in a tub of water. Watch the excitement as students learn how to create a vacuum.

Carpenter

Fascinating Fasteners

It's time to get down to the nuts and bolts of building. Place an assortment of large and small nuts and bolts in a manipulatives center. Then encourage young carpenters to strengthen fine-motor and visual-discrimination skills by finding matches. Challenge a child to sort the nuts and bolts by size, then seriate them. Or trace the outline shapes of differently sized nuts onto a piece of cardboard; then have a child place a nut on its matching outline shape.

If I Were A Carpenter

All good carpenters depend on math skills for success. Prepare this center to give your novice carpenters the opportunity to reinforce number concepts. Label blocks of Styrofoam® with different numerals. Provide a pair of safety goggles, a small hammer, and a supply of golf tees. Challenge a child to hammer the correct number of tees into each Styrofoam® piece.

Sam

Topping Out

A flag at the top of a building under construction indicates that the building is *topped out,* or that the framing is complete. Stock a building center with a variety of manipulative toys for building. Personalize a paper-and-craft-stick flag for each child. Then when she completes a structure, encourage her to use a small ball of clay to secure her flag to the top.

A Paint Job

Visit a paint store to request donations of painting hats, paint sticks, and empty paint cans. Add paintbrushes and rollers to the set of props; then invite youngsters to use the props to pretend to cover your room with color! Or fill the paint cans with water and encourage some exterior painting as well.

Decorator

Beautiful Walls

Locate four large identically sized pieces of cardboard. Place a piece on the floor in a center along with scraps of wallpaper, paintbrushes, watered-down glue or paste, and sponges. Encourage a child at this center to use a brush to apply glue to the back of a piece of wallpaper, then place the piece on the cardboard and smooth it with a sponge. When the cardboard piece is covered with paper, replace it with a new one. Then when all four pieces have been papered, tape them together—wallpapered sides facing in—to resemble a house.

Jackson

Make A House A Home

The final touches that a decorator adds turn a house into a home. Stock a center with construction-paper house shapes, an old wallpaper-sample book, paint chips, scissors, and glue. To use the center, a child writes his name on a house shape. He then cuts samples of the wallpaper and paint colors he would like to use in his house, and glues them onto the shape. Display the decorating plans, or bind them together to create a book.

For open-ended decorating fun, encourage children to sort paint chips by color. Or cut pairs of house shapes from wallpaper samples. Encourage children to find the matching shapes.

Building Literacy

For your reading center, fill a toolbox with these additional construction-related titles:

Architecture Animals, Architecture Colors, Architecture Counts, and *Architecture Shapes*
Series Written & Photographed by
   Michael J. Crosbie and Steve Rosenthal
Published by Preservation Press, 1995

Albert's Alphabet
Written & Illustrated by Leslie Tryon
Published by Atheneum, 1991

Machines At Work
Written & Illustrated by Byron Barton
Published by HarperCollins Children's Books, 1987

The Little House
Written & Illustrated by Virginia Lee Burton
Published by Houghton Mifflin Company, 1978

A Carpenter
Written & Illustrated by Douglas Florian
Published by Greenwillow Books, 1991

Blow The Whistle!

It's time for a snack! To prepare this snack for each of your construction workers, fill a personalized paper lunch bag with these supplies for building a healthful house: one graham cracker, half of a cheese slice (triangular in shape), colorful cereal pieces, and a small paper plate. As each child unpacks her bag, place a spoonful of peanut butter on the side of her plate. To build her snack, a child arranges her cracker and cheese on her plate to resemble a house. She then decorates the house by dipping cereal pieces into the peanut butter, and arranging them on the cracker. Mmm...that house looks good enough to eat!

Home-Supplies Scavenger Hunt

Conclude your unit with a scavenger hunt in a home-supplies store. In advance of your class trip, visit the store to take pictures of various items in stock, such as windows, doors, and sinks. Have multiple copies of your photos developed. Divide your class into small groups, arranging for an adult volunteer to accompany each group on your trip. When you arrive at the store, give each group a supply of photos. Encourage each group to tour the store to locate the pictured items. If desired, make arrangements with the store to fill a paper shopping bag for each child with items that display the store's logo, such as a painter's hat, a paint stick, stickers, or pencils. Request home-improvement pamphlets or sale flyers from the store to send home to parents, along with a note containing students' comments about the trip.

MONSTROUS EMOTIONS

Monsters are make-believe, right? Of course! But with some imagination, the monsters in this unit can really teach your little ones a lot about emotions. Ready? Boo! (Sorry, didn't mean to scare you.)

ideas contributed by dayle timmons

HAVE YOU EVER MET A MONSTER?

Well, what was it like? Ask your little ones to share with you what they imagine monsters are like. What makes a monster a certified monster, anyway? Where do monsters live? What do monsters eat? What do monsters do? Ever wonder what *monsters* are afraid of? Record youngsters' comments; then display their answers around the monster masterpieces described in the following activity.

Monsters are very big! Monsters look funny!

Monsters eat everything!

Monsters act silly.

Monsters are awake at night. They're not afraid of the dark!

MONSTER MASTERPIECES

There's something monstrously creative afoot in this group activity. In advance enlarge the outline shapes of several monsters (see pages 34 and 35) onto bulletin-board paper. Divide your class into as many small groups as you prepared monster outlines. Gather each group of children around an outline and ask them what they think a truly magnificent monster would look like. Then provide the group with paint, scissors, glue, and assorted craft materials such as printed paper, shredded paper, crepe-paper streamers, and sequins. Encourage the children to use their creative efforts to bring the monster shape to life. When the projects are complete, cut out each group's monster; then display the monsters on a wall. There now— something you've created can't be all that scary, can it?

WE'RE GOING ON A MONSTER HUNT

Imaginary monsters seem to hide in the scariest places! Leading youngsters in the following chant will help them conquer their fears of sometimes scary places and even introduce them to a friendly monster!

We're going on a monster hunt.
We're going to find a big one!
We're not scared, but...

What if he's under the bed? Better go over it. Squoosh, squoosh, squoosh.
What if he's in the closet? Better close it. Slam, slam, slam.
What if he's behind the curtains? Better open them. Swish, swish, swish.
What if he's in the hallway? Better tiptoe down it. Tiptoe, tiptoe.
What if he's in the garage? Better stomp through it. Stomp, stomp, stomp.

Aahh! It's a monster!
What's that you said?
You're big, but you're friendly, and you want to go to bed?

Now we're not afraid of monsters, so...
Stomp through the garage,
Walk through the hallway,
Close the curtains,
Open the closet,
Jump into bed,
And turn out the lights! Click!

MONSTER MASKS

Here's a creative way for youngsters to learn that some things that scare us aren't what they seem to be. To make her own monster mask, a child embellishes a solid-colored paper plate with her choice of craft materials, such as cotton balls, buttons, pipe cleaners, curling ribbon, Styrofoam® pieces, muffin-pan liners, beans, audiotape from broken cassettes, and more. Tape a personalized craft stick onto the back of each child's mask. Then invite each child to hold her mask in front of her face as she is featured in the following song. The remainder of the group will have a frightfully fun time showing scared faces as the featured child makes her scariest sound.

SCARY MONSTERS
(sung to the tune of "Have You Ever Seen A Lassie?")

[Child's name] is a scary monster, scary
    monster, scary monster.
[Child's name] is a scary monster.
Let's hear [his/her] scary sound!

MONSTERS HAVE FEELINGS, TOO

If thoughts of monsters make children afraid, how do thoughts of children make monsters feel? Use this activity to suggest to your little ones that monsters have feelings, too. In advance enlarge one of each different monster on pages 34 and 35 onto a different color of construction paper. As you show each monster to your group, ask that students look closely at the monster's pose and facial expression to decide how it feels. Ask for reasons based on youngsters' own experiences to explain that monster's emotion. Then have children show similar expressions on their faces. Conclude the activity with a monster parade, marching past a mirror so that each child can review his favorite monster face.

FEELINGS, NOTHING MORE THAN FEELINGS

Woe, woe, woe, feelings. What do you do when you feel the way you do? Discuss natural and appropriate behaviors associated with various feelings. Follow up your discussion with the following rhyme and song. If desired, use the enlarged monsters from "Monsters Have Feelings, Too" as visual cues for each line or verse.

IF I WERE A MONSTER

If I were a happy monster, I'd go ha, ha, ha!
If I were a sad monster, I'd go boo, hoo, hoo.
If I were a mad monster, I'd go stomp, stomp, stomp!
If I were a scared monster, I'd go AAHH! AAHH! AAHH!
But I'm just me, you see, so I'll go [sound or action of child's choice].

MONSTER EMOTIONS
(sung to the tune of "If You're Happy And You Know It")

Happy monsters like to sing and clap their hands.	Clap hands.
Happy monsters like to sing and clap their hands.	Clap hands.
Happy monsters like to sing.	
Happy monsters clap their hands.	
Happy monsters like to sing and clap their hands.	Clap hands.
Sad monsters sometimes frown and start to cry…	Rub eyes.
Mad monsters stop to think, then count to five…	Count to five.
Scared monsters gulp and think of something nice…	Gulp.
Proud monsters stand up tall and say, "Hooray!"	Say, "Hooray!"

NO MONSTERS AT MY HOUSE!

Get ready for big language fun with this book that reviews the many emotions of monsters. Duplicate one of each different monster pattern on pages 34 and 35 onto different colors of construction paper. Cut out the monsters, corresponding colors of house shapes, and a white house shape. Program the pages with text as shown. On the white house, have each class member draw his picture. Laminate the monsters and houses. On the center of each colored house shape, attach the loop side of a Velcro® piece. On the back of each monster, attach the hook side of a Velcro® piece. Bind the pages together so that the illustrated white page is last. During a group time, give each monster to a child. As you chant the text and keep a steady beat for each page, have the child with the matching monster attach it to the page.

A mad monster lives in a red house, red house, red house.
A mad monster lives in a red house. That's where a mad monster lives.

Mad Monster

But no monsters live with me!

MONSTER MATCH

Parents are sure to appreciate the opportunity this take-home game provides for getting in touch with their little ones' feelings. For every child, duplicate each pair of matching monster cards (pages 34 and 35) onto a different color of paper. Cut out the cards; then place them in a resealable plastic bag along with a copy of the parent note on page 35. There's no make-believe here—each family's sure to have fun!

BEASTLY BOOKS

These delightful titles will reassure your little ones that they have the power to turn imaginary beasts into mild-mannered monsters.

The Monster At The End Of This Book
Written by Jon Stone & Illustrated by Mike Smollin
Published by Western Publishing Company, Inc.; 1995

Harry And The Terrible Whatzit
Written & Illustrated by Dick Gackenbach
Published by Houghton Mifflin Company, 1979

Go Away, Big Green Monster!
Written & Illustrated by Ed Emberley
Published by Little, Brown and Company; 1993

There's A Monster Under My Bed
Written by James Howe & Illustrated by David Rose
Published by Simon & Schuster Children's Books, 1986

Monster Patterns

Use with "Monster Masterpieces" on page 30, "Monsters Have Feelings, Too" and "Feelings, Nothing More Than Feelings" on page 32, and "No Monsters At My House!" and "Monster Match" on page 33.

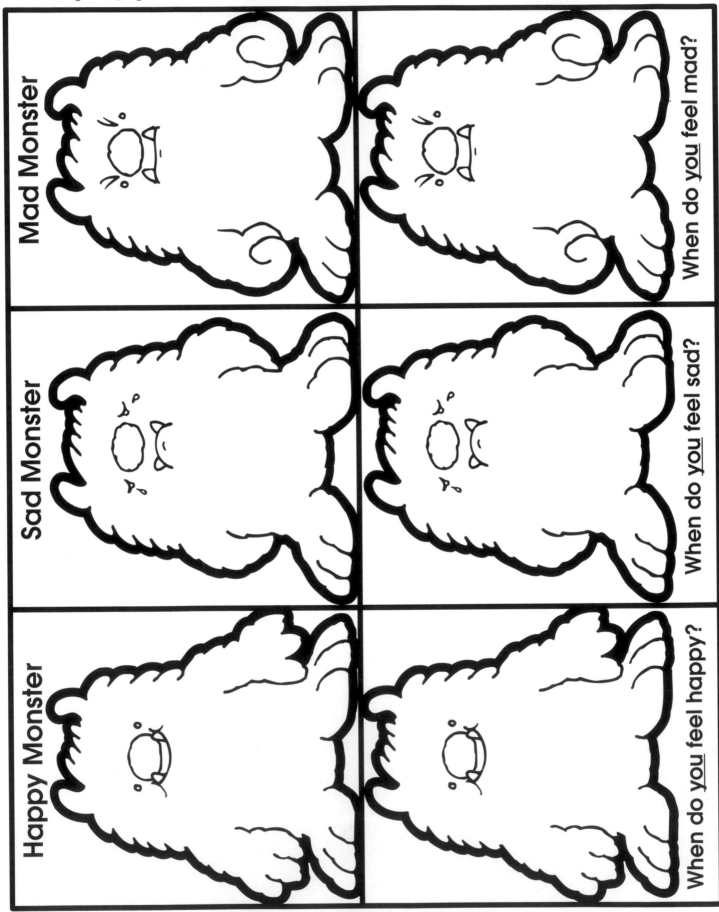

Mad Monster

When do you feel mad?

Sad Monster

When do you feel sad?

Happy Monster

When do you feel happy?

DEAR PARENT,

Get in touch with your "little monster's" feelings with this monster-match game. To play, display all of the monster cards. Ask your child to choose a card, then name that monster's emotion. Challenge your child to find the card with the matching monster. Then ask your child to tell you about a time when he/she felt that monster's emotion. Be sure to share your feelings, too! Have a monstrously fun time!

Proud Monster

When do you feel proud?

Scared Monster

When do you feel scared?

Celebrate In Centers

Celebrate the diversity of our valued traditions with these seasonal centers.

ideas contributed by Linda Blassingame and Lori Kent

Seasonal Center Setup

To fill your classroom with holiday merriment and learning fun, set up the centers described on pages 37–40. Then use this system to indicate which of the centers relate to Hanukkah, Christmas, or Kwanzaa. Reproduce the blank candle pattern (page 41) onto blue paper for each Hanukkah center, red for each Christmas center, and green for each Kwanzaa center. Cut out the candles; then display the appropriate color of candle in each center. What a room full of diverse learning opportunities!

Tyler

Dear Parent,

Happy Holidays!

Play-Dough Center

Menorah Mats

Cooking Center

Kwanzaa Kabobs

Music Center

Bell Exploration

Paint Center

Kwanzaa Flags

Tactile Center

Santa's Beard

Candle Collections

This management system is a bright way to record the centers each child visits, and spark parents' interest in your classroom activities as well! For each child, duplicate a copy of the parent note and booklist (page 41) onto white construction paper. Personalize the parent-note candles; then cut all the candles out. For each center, program a blank candle with that center's name and activity. Then duplicate a class supply of that candle onto the appropriate color of construction paper so that it matches the candle displayed in the center. Cut out the candles; then store each set in its corresponding center.

To use this system, direct a child to take a candle cutout from each center he visits. Tape the candles to his parent note as shown, accordion-folding them to create a booklet. When he has visited the desired number of centers, tape the booklist to the last candle in his collection. Your little ones will shine with pride when they take these candle collections home to share with their families.

Hanukkah

These centers focus on the Jewish holiday Hanukkah—the Festival of Lights.

Dramatic-Play Center

Lots Of Latkes

Your little ones can cook up lots of Hanukkah latkes when you stock your dramatic-play area with a few frying pans, bowls, spoons, spatulas, an empty container of oil, and some aprons. Cut out brown construction-paper circles to resemble latkes; then laminate them. Encourage your youngsters to make pretend latkes while playing in this center.

Play-Dough Center

Menorah Mats

This play-dough center will have your little ones rolling with delight! Reproduce the menorah pattern (page 42) onto construction paper several times. Laminate each page; then place the mats in your play-dough center. Invite a child to roll play dough into candle shapes, then arrange them on a menorah mat. Challenge the child to count the number of play-dough candles on the menorah.

Cooking Center

Menorahs To Munch

Youngsters will get a tasty Hanukkah treat after making these munchable menorahs. Stock your cooking center with marshmallows, pretzel sticks, and resealable sandwich bags. Invite a child to make an edible menorah by counting out nine marshmallows onto a napkin, then pressing a pretzel into each one. Have him line up the marshmallows side by side to resemble a menorah. Encourage him to eat a few of the marshmallow and pretzel pieces. Direct him to place the remaining pieces in a resealable bag to take home and eat later.

Pam Crane

37

Christmas

Your little elves will have a "ho, ho, ho" lot of fun celebrating Christmas in these jolly centers!

Woodworking Center

Santa's Workshop

Turn your woodworking center into Santa's workshop with the addition of Styrofoam® pieces, empty spools, craft sticks, glue, and markers. Provide toy catalogs to help your busy workers gather ideas. Encourage a child visiting this center to make a toy for Santa's sleigh using the materials provided. To add a little touch of elfin delight, provide students with felt Santa hats to wear while they are hard at work.

Tactile Center

Santa's Beard Is Soft And White

Your little merrymakers will get a real feel for Santa's beard when visiting this tactile center. Enlarge the Santa pattern (page 43) onto a large sheet of white paper. Color the pattern. Tape it onto a tabletop; then cover it with clear Con-Tact® covering. Squirt a dollop of nonmenthol-scented shaving cream onto Santa's beard. Invite a child to use her fingers to give Santa a beard that is fluffy and white.

Gross-Motor Center

Holiday Beanbag Toss

Use this idea to toss some gross-motor fun into your holiday centers. Use an X-acto® knife to cut a Christmas-tree shape out of a piece of green foam board. Cut circles from the tree to resemble ornaments. Hot-glue the tree shape to a cylindrical container filled with sand. Place the tree on the floor in an open area. Place several beanbags in a gift-wrapped box near the tree. Invite one child in a pair to toss a beanbag through a hole in the tree. Have his partner stand near the tree, righting it if it falls. When all the beanbags have been tossed, have the pair return them to the box. Then direct the pair to change roles.

Shelly Dohogne—Early Childhood Special Education
Scott County Central, Sikeston, MO

Christmas

Invite your little angels to celebrate the Advent season in these centers.

Away In The Manger

Youngsters will have lots of opportunities to build on their understanding of the first Christmas when you stock your block area with the figures from a nativity set, some straw, and fabric scraps. Encourage children to work in small groups to create a nativity scene using the materials provided.

Sensory Table

Angels All Around

Your little cherubs will enjoy this heavenly sorting experience. Fill your sensory table with Styrofoam® packing pieces and a quantity of cotton balls. Cut angel shapes from each of three different colors of construction paper. Laminate the angel shapes; then hide them in your sensory table. Make sorting pockets by cutting three cloud shapes from construction paper in corresponding colors to the angels; then glue each one onto a separate white paper bag. Tape the bags to the edge of your sensory table. Challenge a child visiting this center to find the angels, then sort them by color into the cloud pockets.

Music Center

Hear The Bells

The ringing of bells is a universal signal to call people together, announce news, and celebrate important events. Stock your music center with a wide variety of bells and some recorded Christmas music featuring bells. Invite a child to explore the sound of each bell, then shake his choice of bells as he listens to the recorded music. Now that's some jolly jingling!

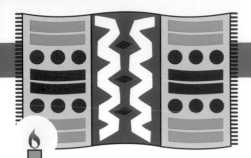

Kwanzaa

At these centers students can celebrate the values and traditions of African-Americans.

Paint Center

Kwanzaa Flags

Your little ones will learn the colors of Kwanzaa when making *benderas,* or flags. Stock your easel with large sheets of white construction paper and red, green, and black paint. Encourage a child to paint a flag as shown. When the paint is dry, tape his flag to a paint-stirring stick for a handle. When each child's flag is complete, lead students in a parade around the classroom as you play some traditional African music. Happy Kwanzaa!

Cooking Center

Kwanzaa Kabobs

Students will love preparing these delicious fruit kabobs to remind them of the bountiful harvest celebrated during Kwanzaa. In your cooking center, place a variety of fruit pieces such as pineapple, apples, bananas, oranges, and maraschino cherries. Add black paper plates and a supply of red and green toothpicks. Invite a small group of children to visit the center. Direct each child to skewer her choice of fruits onto red and green toothpicks to make kabobs. Then have her place her kabobs on a plate. When each child has prepared her kabobs, invite the group to sit together to celebrate the harvest.

Manipulative Center

African Trading Beads

To prepare this center, dye quantities of penne pasta red and green. Mix several drops of red or green food coloring with enough rubbing alcohol to soak the amount of pasta you would like to dye that color. Soak the pasta; then drain it before spreading it out to dry. Place the dry pasta and lengths of black yarn in a center. Encourage a child to string the pasta onto the yarn; then knot the ends together to form a necklace.

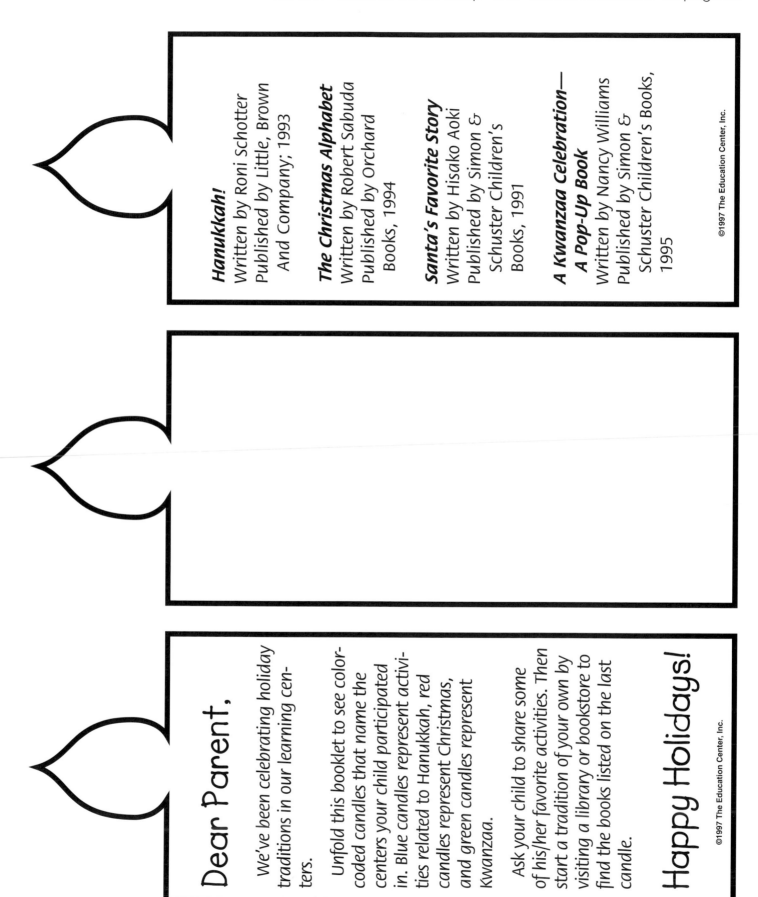

Hanukkah!
Written by Roni Schotter
Published by Little, Brown
And Company; 1993

The Christmas Alphabet
Written by Robert Sabuda
Published by Orchard
Books, 1994

Santa's Favorite Story
Written by Hisako Aoki
Published by Simon &
Schuster Children's
Books, 1991

**A Kwanzaa Celebration—
A Pop-Up Book**
Written by Nancy Williams
Published by Simon &
Schuster Children's Books,
1995

©1997 The Education Center, Inc.

Dear Parent,

We've been celebrating holiday traditions in our learning centers.

Unfold this booklet to see color-coded candles that name the centers your child participated in. Blue candles represent activities related to Hanukkah, red candles represent Christmas, and green candles represent Kwanzaa.

Ask your child to share some of his/her favorite activities. Then start a tradition of your own by visiting a library or bookstore to find the books listed on the last candle.

Happy Holidays!

©1997 The Education Center, Inc.

Menorah Pattern

Use with "Menorah Mats" on page 37.

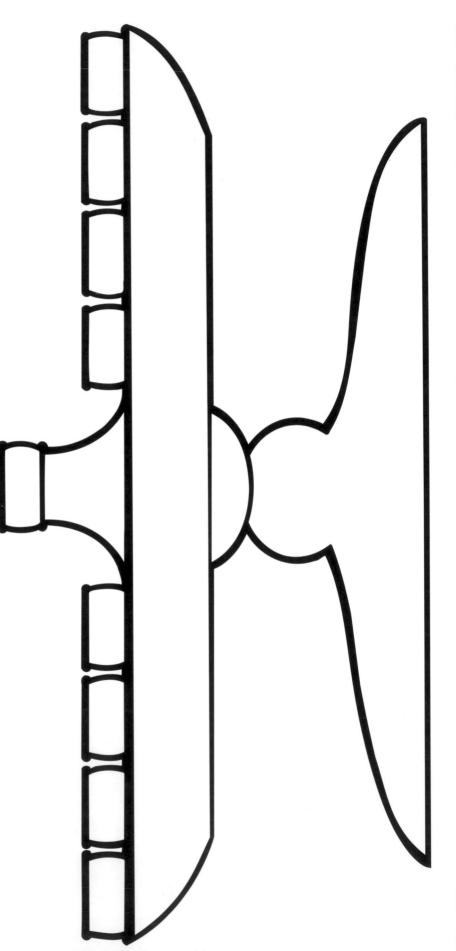

Santa Pattern
Use with "Santa's Beard Is Soft And
White" on page 38.

I'm Special!

Like Rudolph, children who believe in themselves can rise to any occasion. Sometimes it just takes a Santa Claus to point out a child's potential and lead her in the right direction. Use these self-esteem boosters to keep your little "deers" glowing!

ideas contributed by Kerry Rogers

The Most Famous Reindeer Of All

You'll go down in history when you don a pair of paper antlers (see the directions on page 46), tape a red circle on your nose, and read aloud a version of Rudolph's well-loved story. If possible, share the original story by Robert L. May. Then lead your group in singing "Rudolph The Red-Nosed Reindeer" as made famous by Gene Autry. Help your little ones understand that even though we're different on the outside, it's what's inside—the attitudes we have about ourselves—that makes us really special!

We all are special as can be;
You are you, and I am me.
Looking different matters not;
It's what's inside that counts a lot!

susan hodnett

Everyone Is Special

Use this song to make each and every child feel special. Seat youngsters in a group circle. In turn, place the previously used antler headband and nose on a child in the group. Then sing the first verse of the following song to point out one of that child's special characteristics. For example, you could sing, "…who has curly hair," "…with a dimple in her chin," or "…who likes to use paint." Then ask the group to join you in singing the second verse. Be careful not to compare children's abilities, but to bring out each child's unique traits. Yes, we know somebody special!

Somebody Special
(sung to the tune of "Have You Ever Seen A Lassie?")

Do you know somebody special, so special, so special?
Do you know somebody special [child's unique trait]?

Yes, we know somebody special, so special, so special.
Yes, we know somebody special, (and) his/her name is [child's name].

Unique Reflections

One sure way to make a child feel special is to ask her to spend some time with you! In turn, invite each child to stand with you near a full-length mirror. Ask her to name an aspect of her appearance that makes her special. Write "I'm Special!" and her response on a sheet of construction paper. Next help her identify some aspect of her personality or an ability that makes her special. Record this thought on the paper also. To complete the page, ask the child to sit near the mirror as she draws her self-portrait.

Darling Deer

Your little dears' portraits will look darling when posted with these reindeer projects. Ask each child to cut a heart shape out of tan construction paper. Next trace the child's hands onto a sheet of brown paper; then cut them out. Direct the child to glue the hand shapes to the heart as shown to resemble antlers, draw a smile, and add wiggle eyes and a pom-pom nose. Invite each child to personalize her deer by decorating it with her choice of materials, such as ribbons, wrapping paper, or holiday decorations. Finally, glue a spring-type clothespin to the back of the deer. Secure the child's portrait in the clip before displaying both projects.

I'm special!

I have dimples!

Charles

I know just when you need a hug!

Rudolph and I are both special, you see;
My hands and feet only match me!

Lizzy

Reindeer Roundup

When Rudolph got a chance to guide Santa's sleigh, he put his best foot forward. Give your little ones a chance to put their best *feet and hands* forward with this class mural. To make a Rudolph print, a child dips his foot in a shallow pan of brown paint, then presses it onto a length of bulletin-board paper. After washing his foot clean, he then dips the palm sides of both hands into the paint, then presses them above the footprint as shown to resemble antlers. When his hands are clean, he dips a thumb in red paint, then presses it onto the footprint to resemble a nose. After washing his hand once again, he glues paper or wiggle eyes to the reindeer. Write his name or attach his picture near his print. When the mural is complete, display it within children's reach along with the rhyme shown. Encourage youngsters to find their classmates' handprints on the mural.

Won't You Guide My Sleigh Tonight?

It's time to follow the leader—reindeer style! In advance of this movement activity, locate a recorded version of "Rudolph The Red-Nosed Reindeer." Then prepare an antler headband for each child. To make one, trace both of a child's hands side by side near the top of a large piece of brown paper. Cut on the resulting outlines, leaving a strip of paper below the hand shapes as shown. Fit each child's antler headband on his head; then staple the ends of the band together.

During a group time, ask each child to don his headband; then line up the reindeer in an obstacle-free space. Together try various types of reindeer movements such as walking, running, leaping, jumping, galloping, and prancing. Invite a child to lead the group in any movement of his choice as you play the song. After an appropriate time, stop the song, and invite a different child to be the leader. Repeat until each child has an opportunity to lead the herd. Hey, Santa! Can I guide your sleigh in my own special way?

Pockets Of Praise

Help each child make one of these dashing reindeer pockets; then use your sharing times to fill each child's pocket with praise for all his special traits. Have each child paint the front of one paper plate and the back of half a plate brown. When the paint is dry, staple the plates together to create a pocket. Trace the child's hands onto construction paper; then cut out the resulting outlines. Have him glue the hands onto the back of the pocket to resemble antlers. Glue large paper or wiggle eyes to the plate, along with a paper nose. Add a smile; then personalize each child's reindeer's nose. Display the pockets near your group area. Further prepare by duplicating a quantity of the "I'm Special!" note on page 49.

During a group time, select a child to be the focus of attention. Begin by suggesting several ways in which that child is special. Then request that several classmates add to the list. Write each characteristic on a separate "I'm Special!" note. Then drop the notes in the child's pocket. Continue for several group times, until you have filled each child's pocket with notes. If desired, add additional notes to the pockets as you and the class continue to observe each other's uniqueness. Finally, send each child's pocket home along with the parent note (page 49) and a supply of blank "I'm Special!" notes.

Hidden Talent

This circle-time activity is so much fun, your reindeer will shout with glee! In advance, prepare a Rudolph mask by painting a large paper bag as shown. Cut two antlers from tagboard; then attach them to the back of the bag. During a group time, ask youngsters to close their eyes. Then place the paper-bag reindeer over a child's head and shoulders. Ask the group to open their eyes; then give clues about the mystery student by describing ways that he is special. Play until each child's hidden talent is discovered!

A "Pear" Of Reindeer

Invite a pair of children to visit a cooking center to prepare a pair of reindeer. In the center, place pretzels and a variety of small items, such as colorful candy pieces, raisins, gumdrops, grape halves, cherries, and miniature marshmallows. Provide each child with a pear half on a plate. Direct each child to put two pretzel pieces into his pear. Then invite him to put his choice of the items on the pear to resemble eyes and a nose. Before the partners eat, compare the treats. They might look different, but they're both delicious!

Success Stories

Fly away with these additional stories about characters with star appeal.

Tacky The Penguin
Written by Helen Lester
Illustrated by Lynn Munsinger
Published by Houghton Mifflin Company

Dumbo
(Share your favorite version.)

Otto Is Different
Written by Franz Brandenberg
Illustrated by James Stevenson
Published by Greenwillow Books

The following suggestions for making kids feel special have been teacher tested and Rudolph approved!

No Two Are Alike

This creative project is a reminder that no two snowflakes—or children—are alike. Prepare a shallow tray of white paint. Direct each child to dip a hand into the paint, then press his hand onto a sheet of blue construction paper so that his palm print is in the center of the page. Have him continue in this manner, printing his palm in the center each time, while moving the location of the fingerprints to create the six points of a snowflake. Have him sprinkle the flake with clear glitter. When the paint is dry, cut around the shape of the flake; then use white chalk to personalize the back of it. Punch a hole in each flake; then hang the flakes from the ceiling with clear fishing line.

Bonnie McKenzie—Pre-K And Gr. K
Cheshire Country Day School
Cheshire, CT

Royal Abilities

This musical game is sure to make every child feel like a king or queen. To prepare, make a crown and decorate a chair to resemble a throne. Arrange the same number of chairs (including the throne) as there are children playing the game in a large circle. Begin play by directing the students to walk in a line inside the circle in a manner similar to Musical Chairs. Stop the music and direct the children to be seated. Place the crown on the child seated on the throne. Then request that several children in the group say a positive thought about that child. For example, a child might say, "You're a king at painting pictures," or "You're a queen at building with blocks." Continue play until each child has had an opportunity to sit on the throne. Now that's the royal treatment!

Sharon Wicklein
Belleville, IL

I Can!

You can really boost a child's self-esteem with this idea! Cut a supply of construction-paper strips that measure 1 1/2" x 7". Keep the strips and some small stickers handy. Then, when you observe a child doing something special, label a strip "I can!" and describe the achievement. Suggest that the child choose a sticker to decorate the strip. Wrap the strip around his wrist to resemble a bracelet; then tape the ends together.

Jennifer Casstevens—Preschool
West Yadkin Headstart
Hamptonville, NC

"I can!"
Miriam can help clean up!

"I can!"
Miriam can help clean up!

I'm Special!

©The Education Center, Inc. • *THE MAILBOX*® • *Preschool* • Dec/Jan 1997–98

Dear Parent,
   Like Rudolph, children who believe in themselves can rise to any occasion. Inside this pocket you'll find notes describing ways that your child's classmates and I believe she/he is special. Please write more special characteristics on the blank notes. Then watch your child GLOW!

Up, up, and away,
I can fly so high!
Just believe in me,
And I'll reach for the sky!

©The Education Center, Inc. • *THE MAILBOX*® • *Preschool* • Dec/Jan 1997–98

Snow Foolin'

If the weather where you are is delightful, finding ways to help young children experience winter can be somewhat frightful. These ideas are dedicated to teachers and children in the sunny South!

by dayle timmons
Jacksonville, FL

Oh, The Weather Outside Is...Delightful!

This year begin your winter wonderings by helping your little ones visualize what winter weather looks like. Spread a portion of white quilt batting on the floor in your group area. Settle youngsters on the snow-covered floor to view the wintry portions of *Which Way, Weather?* This must-have video shows a diverse group of children as they follow the cycle of the seasons, playing in many forms of weather including winter's snow and ice. (Ordering information available from Bo Peep Productions™: 1-800-532-0420.) As you watch, be sure to encourage lots of comments and questions. Later provide time for children to share any snow experiences they have had. To further introduce the season to your group, read about and discuss the scenes in these snowy stories.

Southern winters are so nice,
Even without snow and ice,
For we can run and jump and play,
In the warm sunshine all day!

Snowy Stories

The First Snowfall
Written & Illustrated by Anne and
   Harlow Rockwell
Published by Simon & Schuster Books
   For Young Readers

Rainsong, Snowsong
Written by Philemon Sturges
Illustrated by Shari Halpern
Published by North-South Books Inc.

Snow On Snow On Snow
Written by Cheryl Chapman
Illustrated by Synthia Saint James
Published by Dial Books For Young Readers

There's No Business Like Snow Business

If you live in a warm climate, it's likely that many of your youngsters haven't had the opportunity to bundle up in winter wear. To introduce children to winter apparel and increase vocabularies, cut out catalog and magazine pictures of people dressed for winter weather. In addition collect an assortment of winter apparel from parents or thrift stores. During a group time, arrange the items on the floor. As you look at the pictures, ask children to comment on the pictured apparel and to find matches from among the real items.

Follow your discussion with this fantasy photo opportunity. Take pictures of several children at a time, dressed in winter clothes and pretending to be very cold. Mount the photos on a blue background that students have sponge-painted or splattered with white paint. Title the board "Brrr…It Snowed In Our Classroom!"

Snow Or Sun?

Develop thinking skills with this hands-on addition to a discovery area. Cut pairs of squares from an assortment of fabrics—some suitable for cold-weather clothing, such as wool and fake fur; and others suitable for warm-weather clothing, such as thin cotton and sheer fabrics. Place the squares in a center along with a paper sun cutout and a snowflake cutout. Encourage a child to compare the look and feel of the fabrics and to pair matching squares. Then challenge the child to sort the squares, arranging those fabrics most appropriate for winter clothing by the snowflake, and those more suitable for warm weather by the sun.

A Cool Center

Use this hands-on center to help youngsters understand why people wear mittens. Fill your water table with crushed ice. Add small shovels and containers. Invite each child to play with the ice. After a few moments, suggest that he dry his hands and put on a pair of mittens, then continue play. How about a scarf, too?

On With The Snow!

Continue to help your little ones visualize winter weather by displaying a snow dome. Then make this snow box that is sure to create a flurry of excitement. Cut a viewing window from one side of a large appliance box. Along the inside of the box, tape a piece of clear cellophane wrap over the window. Fill a smaller box with Styrofoam® packaging pieces or a quantity of white tissue-paper pieces. Lift a child and gently place her inside the box. So that she can experience a moment of winter wonder, sprinkle the fantasy flakes into the box. Invite other children to watch through the window. It's snowing!

Winter Magic

These makeshift snow domes are full of winter magic! Collect a class supply of clear plastic bottles, such as those used to bottle water. Gather an assortment of white, clear, and silver materials such as Mylar® confetti, beads, plastic confetti shapes, pieces of garland, glitter, and sequins. Personalize a bottle for each child. Then invite each child to put his choice of the materials in his bottle. Have him fill his bottle with water; then secure the lid with hot glue. To make a winter wish, a child gives his snow dome a swirl as he recites the following rhyme. For a variation, invite your group to shake their domes while singing the song below.

Winter Wish

Winter, winter, come our way.
Bring us snow for just one day.
Make it cold and make it white.
Snow would be a lovely sight!

Let It Snow!
(sung to the tune of "Let It Snow!")

Oh, the weather outside is sunny,
But wouldn't it be funny,
If snowflakes said, "Hello!"
Let it snow! Let it snow! Let it snow!

Banana Blizzards

If you're not able to make snow cream in your part of the country, banana blizzards are the next best thing! To make a blizzard that serves about ten children, blend together one cup of cold milk with two or three bananas in a blender. Ask the children to count aloud as you add ten snowballs (scoops of vanilla frozen yogurt) to the blender. Then invite each child to turn the blender on and off again to help create the blizzard. Serve the frothy drinks in five-ounce cups.

There's Snow Substitute!

This fingerpaint recipe makes a super substitute for snow. Mix 1/2 cup of liquid starch with two cups of Ultra Ivory Snow® detergent. Use an eggbeater or electric mixer to beat the mixture until it is thick. Add two cups of crushed ice. (If desired use a rolling pin to crush ice cubes in a resealable plastic bag.) Drop a dollop of the snow substitute onto a baking pan. Invite a child to fingerpaint on the pan. Or put an amount of the mixture in an empty water table for several children to enjoy together. When youngsters have had enough hands-on winter fun, warm them up with a hot-cocoa treat!

Snow Bright, Snow White

These white collages are sure to delight! Stock your art center with white construction paper, scissors, and an assortment of white items—such as cotton balls, Styrofoam®, doilies, buttons, beads, lace, wedding-themed wrapping paper, curling ribbon, sequins, snowflake-shaped confetti, and more. Pour white glue onto plastic lids to make gluing easy. Invite each child to use the items of her choice to create a white-on-white collage. These projects make a lovely sight!

53

I'm Melting!

By now your little ones are probably wondering why snow is a no-show, or why it stays so briefly in the sunny South. Explain that because of the sun's warmth, moisture in the air does not get cold enough to freeze and result in snow. Play this game to reinforce that the sun's heat quickly melts any snow that might occasionally appear in your climate. Prepare a melting wand by taping a sun cutout to a pointer or ruler. Lead the class in a movement related to winter, such as shivering, putting on boots, or skating. Then announce, "Freeze!" When everyone has stopped, move about the group, gently tapping each child with the melting wand. Once tapped, a child may continue his movements until a new movement is suggested.

No-Melt Snow Dough

The sun won't melt this shimmering snow dough! Make several batches using the provided recipe. Then store the dough in an airtight container. If desired place the dough in a center along with pictures or illustrations of snowfolk. Provide youngsters with items such as aquarium rocks, toothpicks, buttons, and coffee stirrers. Suggest that youngsters use the dough and items to make miniature snowfolk. Display the creations along with the previous pictures and a sign stating "Snow foolin'—Our snowfolk don't melt!"

No-Melt Snow Dough

1 cup flour
1/2 cup salt
1 cup water
1/4 cup white powdered tempera paint
2 tablespoons vegetable oil
1 tablespoon cream of tartar
1/3 cup clear or silver glitter

Mix all of the ingredients together. Cook over medium heat, stirring until a ball is formed. Knead the dough as it cools.

From People To Puddles

Of course snowfolk are welcome in the South—but they might not want to visit very long! Before this group activity, prepare ten necklaces—each one displaying a different numeral from one to ten. Also prepare a necklace displaying a tagboard sun shape. Invite ten children to wear a numeral necklace; then arrange the children in numerical order in front of the group. Ask another child to wear the sun necklace. As the group sings the following song, each snowperson poses when her number is sung. When the chorus is sung, the child wearing the sun dances among the group. Finally the snowfolk "melt" to the ground. Oh pooh, a puddle!

Melting In The Sun
(sung to the tune of "Angels In The Band")

There was one, there were two, there were three little snowfolk,
There were four, there were five, there were six little snowfolk,
There were seven, there were eight, there were nine little snowfolk,
Ten little snowfolk in the sun.

Ohhhh....
Wasn't that a day, melting in the sun?
Wasn't that a day, melting in the sun?
Wasn't that a day, melting in the sun?
Now there's just a puddle!

Welcome To The South!

Snowfolk might not pick the South as a vacation site, but your feathery friends certainly will! Have youngsters welcome birds that migrate to your warmer climate with these welcome wreaths. To make a wreath, cut a plain doughnut in half as shown. Set one half aside for snacking; then spread smooth peanut butter over the flat side of the second half. Sprinkle birdseed onto the peanut butter. Tie a yarn loop onto the doughnut. Hang the welcome wreaths on trees and other outside items. Then invite youngsters to snack on the remaining doughnut halves as they prepare to greet the bird travelers. Hi, y'all!

Clothing With Class

If you look "clothes-ly" at this unit, you'll see that we've strung together group activities, songs, learning-center ideas, and storytime ideas that pile up to a load of clothing fun. Still hanging around? Get dressed for success!

ideas by Elizabeth Fritz and Lisa Leonardi

Group Activities

A Clothing Drive

Organize a clothing drive that will collect items for the activities in this unit and benefit others as well. Request that each child's family clean out their closets in search of clothes that can be donated. Use the items during your clothing unit; then ask youngsters to help you box or bag the clothes. If possible, plan a class trip to donate the clothes to a local shelter, charity organization, or church.

Global Fashion

Add a multicultural flair to your show-and-tell with this worldly idea. While you're soliciting clothes for donation (see "A Clothing Drive"), ask parents to send or bring to school international clothing collected on vacations or used by family members. You may be surprised at the collection of Mexican sombreros, Indian saris, or African dashikis you can borrow. Be sure to ask permission before allowing the children to try on the items. Or invite interested parents to model the attire during visits to your classroom. Finally have your little ones compare and contrast the variety of clothing worn by children in other cultures by sharing a book with photos of children worldwide, such as *Children Just Like Me: A Unique Celebration Of Children Around The World* by Barnabas and Anabel Kindersley (Dorling Kindersley Publishing, Inc.).

Suit Up And Go!

Give students a flair for fashion and fitness with this relay idea. To prepare, collect two large jackets, two hats, and two pairs of adult shoes. Attach two strips of tape on the floor so that there are two parallel lines several yards long. Place each set of clothes at the end of a tape strip. Divide your class into two teams; then direct each team to form a line behind the pile of clothes. To play, the first member of each team puts on the clothes as quickly as possible and makes his way down the strip and back. When he returns, he removes the clothes. The next child then puts the clothes on and repeats the process. Continue until each child has put on the clothes, run the course, and taken off the clothes. Finally have all of the teammates congratulate each other on a race well dressed.

Fashion Flash

Monday—Favorite Frocks Day
Wear your favorite items from tip to toe.

Tuesday—Silly Socks And Shoes Day
Wear unusual or mismatched shoes, socks,
boots, slippers....

Wednesday—Inside-Out Day
Go ahead...put it all on backwards!

Thursday—Mom And Dad Day
Dress in adult clothes! Wear Mom's jewelry
or Dad's necktie.

Friday—Fancy-Pants Day
Dress spiffily today. (We'll plan for neat-
and-clean activities.)

shorts

PAM

TYLER

Weekly Wearables

Fashion trends come and go. So
during your clothing unit, invite your
little fashion bugs to participate in a
different fad each day of the week!
Send home a newsletter similar to the
one shown to help parents stay on top
of the trends. To step up the fun with
style, have a fashion show each day.
Using a toy microphone, announce
each youngster and describe his attire
as he parades down a bulletin-board-
paper runway. Now that's a fashion
statement!

Favorite Frocks

If you'd like to find out which frocks
your little ones prefer to wear, then
hang this graphing idea up to try! In
advance, enlarge the clothing patterns
(pages 62–63) onto poster board. Cut
the patterns out; then label them.
Secure heavy yarn across a bulletin
board to resemble a clothesline. Use
clothespins to attach the cutouts to the
line. Personalize a clothespin for each
child. On Favorite Frocks Day (see
"Weekly Wearables"), give each child
her clothespin to attach to the item
she most prefers to wear. Write as
you discuss the results; then display
the information on the bulletin board.

When you have completed the
graphing activity, remove the personalized clothespins and store them. On
the remaining mornings of your unit,
ask each child to find her clothespin
from the collection when she enters
the classroom. Direct her to attach the
clothespin to a pattern that matches
one of the items she is wearing.

"Sew" Much Fun

Invite a seamstress or parent who
sews to visit your class to demonstrate how clothes are made. Along
with her basic sewing supplies,
suggest that your guest bring a
pattern that would fit a stuffed toy and
enough fabric to make the item. Invite
her to set up her sewing machine and
make the item in the classroom so
that youngsters can see how an item
is made from start to finish. Follow up
the visit by setting up the learning
center on page 59 titled "Stitched-Up
Shirts."

Songs

Fashion-Bug Jitterbug

This song reinforces classification skills as your little ones show off their clothes. Substitute a different movement—such as *jump, stomp,* or *clap*—and a different article of clothing each time you sing the song.

Show Off Your Clothes

(sung to the tune of "The Farmer In The Dell")

[Dance] if you're wearing [pants];
[Dance] if you're wearing [pants];
Show off your clothes
From head to toe;
[Dance] if you're wearing [pants].

Best-Dressed Class

You'll have the best-dressed class in the school—and a well-spoken one, too—at the end of this circle-time song. Seat your group in a circle. Place a pile of clothing in the center of the circle, making sure you have one article for each child. Ask a volunteer to select an item from the pile to describe and then put on. Sing the song, modifying it accordingly. Sing until each child is wearing an item from the collection.

We All Wear Clothes

(sung to the tune of "The Farmer In The Dell")

A [hat] goes on my [head];
A [hat] goes on my [head];
Clothes, clothes, we all wear clothes.
A [hat] goes on my [head].

Dawn Spurck, Papillion, NE

It's Laundry Time

(sung to the tune of "The Mulberry Bush")

Here's a song that youngsters will enjoy singing while playing in the laundry center described on page 60. It just might take all week to take care of all those clothes!

This is the way we wash the clothes,
Wash the clothes, wash the clothes.
This is the way we wash the clothes,
So early Monday morning.

This is the way we dry the clothes…
So early Tuesday morning.

This is the way we iron the clothes…
So early Wednesday morning.

This is the way we mend the clothes…
So early Thursday morning.

This is the way we fold the clothes…
So early Friday morning.

This is the way we hang the clothes…So early Saturday morning.

This is the way we wear the clothes…So early Sunday morning.

Terry Steinke—Preschool
Emmaus Lutheran School, Indianapolis, IN

Learning Centers

Designer Duds

At this writing and art center, youngsters can create clothing items with designer labels. Use the patterns on pages 62 and 63 to create tagboard templates; then label each one. Stock the center with pencils, markers, scissors, glue, construction paper, wallpaper scraps, and wrapping-paper scraps. Encourage a child in the center to trace the patterns onto paper, cut them out, decorate, and label them. Add students' work to the clothesline prepared for "Favorite Frocks" (page 57).

Stitched-Up Shirts

Invite your little ones to try their hands at sewing when visiting this fine-motor center. Using the shirt pattern on page 62, cut a supply of felt shirt shapes. Punch holes around the edges of the shirts. Wrap a piece of masking tape around one end of each of a supply of yarn lengths. Tie the opposite end of each length to a felt shirt. Invite each child to stitch some shirts. Your budding tailors are sure to have "sew" much fun!

Shoe "Matcheroo"

When it comes to piquing students' interest, this activity's a "shoe-in"! Collect several old pairs of shoes. Using a kitchen sponge or small paint roller, paint tempera paint onto the bottom of each sole; then press it onto a tagboard card. When the paint is dry, place the cards in a center along with the shoes. Challenge a child to find the matching shoes, then find the cards that match the shoes' soles. Youngsters will put their best feet forward in this center!

shirt

Storytime Ideas

Animals should definitely <u>not</u> wear clothing because clothes on a fish would float away.

Cori

What A Bargain!

Here are two exciting dramatic-play ideas for the price of one! To set up a pretend clothing store, place an assortment of the clothes you collected in a dramatic-play area. Hang some of the clothes, and fold others to arrange on tables. Add a toy cash register, old telephones, toy money, and paper bags. Obtain a supply of blank price tags from an office-supply store. Encourage youngsters to price the items by writing a numeral from one to ten on each of the tags. Shoppers can count out corresponding amounts of money to pay for their selections. At this center, youngsters are sure to shop 'til they drop!

Next turn your water-table area into laundry central. Provide small items of clothing and doll clothes, along with a drying rack and clothespins. Set up a retractable clothesline. Finally cut two large boxes to resemble a washer and a dryer. Your little ones will line up to hang the laundry!

Animals In Clothing?

Here's a book that will keep your little ones in stitches! Read aloud *Animals Should Definitely <u>Not</u> Wear Clothing.* by Judi Barrett (Simon & Schuster Children's Books). Then have your little ones make a similar class book that is sure to make them laugh out loud. In advance, duplicate a supply of the clothing patterns on pages 62 and 63; then cut them out. To make a page, a child cuts out a picture of an animal from a nature magazine and then glues it on a piece of construction paper. He then selects a clothing pattern, colors it, and glues it onto the animal picture. Ask the child to explain why his animal should not wear clothing and record his response on the page. Bind the pages between titled covers. Even your little ones know that clothing was made for man, not beasts!

Totally T-Shirts

Ask your children if they have a favorite item of clothing. Then read aloud *Aaron's Shirt* by Deborah Gould (Simon & Schuster Children's Books). Talk about the reasons that Aaron's shirt became his favorite. Then invite your children to design their own lucky T-shirts. Enlarge the shirt pattern on page 62 onto tagboard to create templates and cut them out. Have each child trace a shirt template onto white construction paper, then cut it out. Next encourage him to paint the shirt as desired. When the shirts are dry, use clothespins to hang them on a clothesline hung from your class ceiling. As a group, discuss how the special shirts are alike and different.

Tailor-Made Books

Jesse Bear, What Will You Wear?
Written by Nancy White Carlstrom
Illustrated by Bruce Degen
Published by Simon & Schuster Children's Books

"Charlie Needs A Cloak"
Written & Illustrated by Tomie dePaola
Published by Simon & Schuster Children's Books

Max's Dragon Shirt
Written & Illustrated by Rosemary Wells
Published by Dial Books For Young Readers

The Jacket I Wear In The Snow
Written by Shirley Neitzel
Illustrated by Nancy Winslow Parker
Published by Mulberry Books

Shoes From Grandpa
Written by Mem Fox
Illustrated by Patricia Mullins
Published by Orchard Books

Whose Shoe?
Written & Illustrated by Margaret Miller
Published by Greenwillow Books

Shoes, Shoes, Shoes and *Hats, Hats, Hats*
Written by Ann Morris
Photographed by Ken Heyman
Published by Lothrop, Lee & Shepard Books

Amanda wore her pink hat,
pink hat, pink hat.

Amanda wore her pink hat
all day long.

Colorful Clothing

Seeing themselves in a book will never wear thin on your youngsters! If you plan to have a Favorite Frocks Day (see "Weekly Wearables" on page 57), this class project and your day make a perfect fit. As a group, sing together the text of *Mary Wore Her Red Dress And Henry Wore His Green Sneakers* adapted by Merle Peek (Clarion Books). Take an instant picture of each child. Attach the picture to a piece of construction paper; then program each page as shown, using corresponding colors of markers to write the color words. If desired, laminate the pages and covers before binding them together. After singing your class song to-gether, send it home with a different child each night.

Pam Crane

Clothing Patterns

Use with "Favorite Frocks" on page 57, "Designer Duds" and "Stitched-Up Shirts" on page 59, and "Animals In Clothing?" and "Totally T-Shirts" on page 60.

Clothing Patterns
Use with "Favorite Frocks" on page 57, "Designer Duds" on page 59,
and "Animals In Clothing?" on page 60.

Making Masterpieces

The Fine Art Of Teaching Preschoolers

Introducing your little ones to fine works of art can improve their visual-discrimination skills, increase their verbal abilities, and inspire them to communicate through the language of art themselves. As your guide through this gallery of ideas, I'll give you information about some famous artists to share with your children; then you'll find creative ideas from the real masters: teachers. Enjoy!

Private Collection

To use the ideas in this unit, you'll need a print of van Gogh's *Sunflowers,* prints of Monet's water-garden paintings, examples of Matisse's collages, a print of da Vinci's *Mona Lisa,* and pictures of paintings by Michelangelo, Pollock, and Mondrian. To find these prints and more for your children's viewing, check out books of collections from your local library. Consider requesting that parents send in used calendars and notecards showing works of art. Posters can be purchased at framing stores, or inexpensive postcards of prints can be purchased at museum shops. Before long and without much expense, you'll have a private collection worth valuable learning opportunities.

Vincent van Gogh

* Sometimes van Gogh was very sad, and other times he was very angry. But when he was happy, he painted *a lot.* Some people like to look at his paintings and decide how he was feeling. Ask, "How do *you* feel when you paint?"
* Van Gogh liked to use bright colors to paint pictures of things outside, such as the starry sky and fields. Consider occasionally moving your easel outside.
* No one wanted to buy his paintings while he was alive. Now many people love them!

Van Gogh's Sunflowers

A good look at Vincent van Gogh's *Sunflowers* provides a review of the colors yellow and orange, and gives you an opportunity to introduce the letters *V* and *S.* Explain to your little ones that sometimes van Gogh would paint so fast, the paint on his paintings would be very thick. Encourage each child to use yellow, orange, brown, and green paint to quickly paint some sunflowers. Then ask her to slowly paint some flowers. Compare the paintings when they are dry. Label the paintings with the child's name as shown.

Beth Riley—Four- And Five-Year-Olds
Precious Moments Nursery School
Gloucester, NJ

64

Suzie van Gogh's Sunflowers

Monet's Garden Collage

Have your little ones work together to create a mural that resembles Monet's garden. Explain that when Monet was old, he lived in a house in the country and painted very large pictures of his garden. Direct your youngsters to cut out pictures of flowers from seed catalogs; then have them glue these pictures to a length of bulletin-board paper. Mix white paint into blue, green, and pink paint so that the colors resemble those used by Monet. Have students paint the empty spaces on the mural with the paint. Display this project along with examples of Monet's famous paintings.

adapted from an idea by Louise Anderson—
    Four-Year-Olds
Community Cooperative Nursery School
Norwalk, CT

Claude Monet

✸ Monet liked to draw pictures of his teachers. Sometimes they looked funny! Invite your students to draw pictures of you.
✸ Like van Gogh, Monet liked to paint pictures of things outside, such as boats and water lilies.
✸ Monet used a lot of short brush strokes, so his pictures look different up close than they do farther away. Ask each child to stand very close to your easel while painting in this manner. How does the picture look different when the child stands back to view it?

Henri Matisse

✸ Most of his life, Matisse was a painter. Painting helped him feel better when he was worried. Consider playing relaxing music near your easel. Ask students how they feel when they paint.
✸ Matisse and his painting buddies called themselves "the wild beasts" *(les fauves)*. Have the children talk about what they like to paint, then give their group a name.
✸ When Matisse was older, he got very sick and was too tired to stand at the easel. He sat in his wheelchair and cut shapes out of colored paper. Friends helped him arrange, pin, and then glue the shapes to make large collages.

Matisse's Paper Cutouts

Recycling and creativity go hand in hand with this cut-and-paste project. During the year, save construction-paper scraps. Show your class examples of Matisse's collages. Invite each child to cut shapes out of the paper scraps of her choice; then have her glue them on a large piece of bulletin-board paper. Ask each child to title her collage. As a variation, pair youngsters. Ask one child to sit in a chair and tell his partner where on a sheet of paper to glue his cutouts.

Peggy Witman—Pre-K
Willow Creek Learning Center, Poland, OH

"Man in the Grass"
Alex

Want spagetti for dinner?

Mona Lisa Look-Alikes

Ask your little ones if they can tell what their parents or friends are thinking just by looking at their facial expressions. Then show them a picture of da Vinci's most famous painting, the *Mona Lisa.* Ask each child to share what he thinks the woman is thinking about or what she might say. Record his thought on a paper speech bubble. Take a picture of each child posed like the woman. Display the developed photos along with the quotes. Later glue each child's photo and his quote onto a piece of paper. Bind the pages together to make a book. A penny for your thoughts!

Kathy Barlow—Preschool
Southern Elementary, Somerset, KY

Leonardo da Vinci

- Da Vinci liked art, but he also liked music, science, and math. He drew pictures that explained how to build buildings, bridges, and towns. Consider putting pencils and paper in your block center so your little ones can draw buildings, then build them.
- Oops! Bad things happened to some of da Vinci's paintings. The paint flaked off his painting of a famous meal, the bottom of one was cut off, one painting was used for a tabletop, and the sides of his most famous painting were trimmed. Remind youngsters to be careful when looking at each other's projects—especially near the easel!

Michelangelo's Pain In The Neck

This idea will give youngsters a new perspective on painting masterpieces. Show your group pictures of the ceiling of the Sistine Chapel, pointing out that the paintings tell a story. Explain that people once believed that Michelangelo lay on his back on a tall platform to paint the pictures. Now they know that he stood up, but he still complained about his neck hurting! Tape a piece of art paper to the underside of a table. Invite a child to use markers to draw a scene on the paper while sitting under the table. Write as the child dictates a story to accompany the illustration.

Peggy Witman—Pre-K
Willow Creek Learning Center, Poland, OH

Michelangelo

- Sometimes Michelangelo painted on walls and ceilings! His paintings told stories. Ask your children to predict grown-ups' reactions if they painted stories on buildings.
- Because some of Michelangelo's most famous paintings got very dirty, people thought that he liked dark colors. Then the paintings were cleaned, and they found out he liked bright colors after all!
- Michelangelo liked sculpting better than painting. Ask your children to pose like statues made out of rocks.

One time, an angel that lived in a cloud...

Jackson Pollock

Sometimes Pollock got very frustrated because he didn't think he could draw or paint perfectly.

Pollock put his paper (canvas) on the floor instead of on the easel so that he could walk around it as he painted. Then he poured paint from a can and painted using sticks and other items instead of brushes. Provide lots of painting tools at your painting center, such as kitchen tools, sponge mops, sticks, and more.

Because Pollock moved a lot as he painted, his very different style is called *action painting*.

Splatter-Painting

At first glance, this painting project might seem like a mess! But if you look closer, you'll see that children have opportunities to learn about cause and effect, develop muscle control, and become aware of color patterns. On a warm day, take large containers of watered-down tempera paint, lengths of bulletin-board paper, and paintbrushes outside. To splatter-paint Pollock-style, a child drips, dribbles, and splatters the paint onto the paper. Encourage the child to move his whole arm and body, and to walk around the painting as he works.

Piet Mondrian

Mondrian seemed to really like geometric shapes, especially rectangles. He used math to help him understand things about his world.

The colors he liked are red, yellow, blue, black, white, and gray.

Primarily Boxes

Show your little ones a picture of a painting by Mondrian. Ask them to help you find the shapes and to name the colors in the painting. If the picture or print is large enough, invite each child to use his fingers to trace the outlines of the shapes. Then use this art project to explore rectangles and the primary colors: red, yellow, and blue. Prepare various sizes of rectangle templates. To paint a picture, put one or two small rolls of tape on the back of each template. Lay a template on a piece of art paper, taped side down. Paint around the outline with black paint. Remove the template. Repeat as desired using various sizes of templates. When the black paint is dry, paint the insides of the rectangles using the primary colors.

Art Auction

Invite parents to an evening of art appreciation. Parents will leave the event with priceless treasures, and you'll have funds for class projects—such as a trip to an art museum. During the year ask each child to save several of his favorite works. Or save students' projects from the ideas described in this unit. If desired, display these works in matte frames donated by a framing store or in frames cut from tagboard. Be sure to label each piece with the artist's name, his age, and his title for the work.

On the night of the auction, provide refreshments for parents and children as they look at the art. Ask a parent volunteer to serve as the auctioneer, beginning the bidding at small amounts, such as 50 cents. "Going once. Going twice. Sold to the highest bidder: the proud parent of a young artist!"

Lesley Armstrong—Preschool
Sunrise Valley School
Lawrence, KS

Art Appreciation

Help parents appreciate the little masterpieces you send home by attaching these helpful notes. Duplicate and cut out a supply of the frame pattern on this page. Before attaching the frame to a child's work, write a note explaining either the process used or the art concept that the child learned about. If the project relates to your study of a famous artist, give some information about that person. Now that's an idea worth framing!

Peggy Witman—Pre-K
Willow Creek Learning Center, Poland, OH

Use this frame with "Art Appreciation" above.

©The Education Center, Inc. • *THE MAILBOX*® • *Preschool* • Feb/Mar 1998

A Gallery Of Good Books And Products

I Spy Two Eyes: Numbers In Art, I Spy A Lion: Animals In Art, and *I Spy: An Alphabet In Art*
Devised & Selected by Lucy Micklethwait
Published by Greenwillow Books

A Child's Book Of Play In Art
Selected by Lucy Micklethwait
Published by Dorling Kindersley Publishing, Inc.

Getting To Know The World's Greatest Artists
Series Written & Illustrated by Mike Venezia
Published by Childrens Press®, Inc.
The editor recommends the titles in this series as fun and interesting for young children.

Matthew's Dream
Written & Illustrated by Leo Lionni
Published by Random House, Inc.

Camille And The Sunflowers: A Story About Vincent van Gogh
Written & Illustrated by Laurence Anholt
Published by Barron's Educational Series, Inc.

The Art Lesson
Written & Illustrated by Tomie dePaola
Published by G. P. Putnam's Sons

Puzzle Gallery: Pets, Puzzle Gallery: Children, Puzzle Gallery: Food, Puzzle Gallery: Games
Series Published by Alfred A. Knopf, Inc.
Each book contains five 12-piece puzzles of five great paintings, along with questions to encourage critical and creative thought.

Art Image Preschool
Written by Christine Thompson
Published by Art Image Publications
Art Image Preschool is an art-based curriculum that provides ideas for incorporating works of art into your existing units, such as pets, shapes, and colors. For a catalog, call or write Art Image Publications, P.O. Box 568, Champlain, NY 12919 (1-800-361-2598).

Jelly-Bean Jamboree!
Sweet Ways To Learn Colors

Jumping jelly beans! Here's an assortment of ideas for teaching colors in a most delicious way—with jelly beans, the favorite candy of the season.

ideas contributed by dayle timmons

Bet You Can't Eat Just One!

Jelly beans might come in a variety of pretty colors, but they weren't made to admire. They were made for eating! Open a bag of jelly beans and invite each child in the group to take one. Ask each child to hold up his jelly bean when you name its color. Once each child is sure of his bean's color, have him eat it! Then sing this silly song. As each different color word is substituted, encourage the children who ate a bean of that color to stand up and rub their tummies. Ready for Round Two?

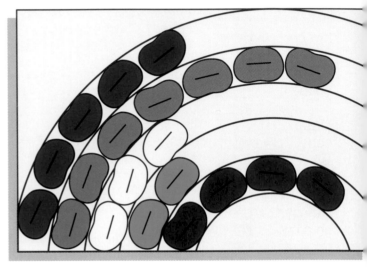

Jelly Beans In My Tummy!
(sung to the tune of "Skip To My Lou")

[Red] jelly beans—yum, yum.
[Red] jelly beans—yum, yum.
[Red] jelly beans—yum, yum.
Jelly beans in my tummy!

A Rainbow Of Colors

After several rounds of the previous song, your youngsters might have picked favorite flavors. Use this graphing idea to find out what they are. To prepare a graph on a length of white bulletin-board paper, draw a rainbow that has a segment for each different color of jelly bean in your package. Duplicate a supply of the jelly-bean patterns (page 76) onto construction paper that corresponds to each of the colors of your jelly beans. Cut out the jelly-bean shapes. Ask each child to pick a paper jelly-bean shape that represents his favorite flavor; then personalize the shape.

During a group time, return the shapes to the children. Sort the children by the colors of beans they selected; then help each child glue his shape to the rainbow to create a graph. Discuss the results. Celebrate your findings by eating—what else?—more jelly beans!

Colorful Stamping

Your little ones will be amazed—and you will be, too—over these stamps made from real jelly beans. To make two stamps, cut a large jelly bean in half lengthwise. Hot-glue each half to the bottom of a separate film canister so that its flat side can be used for printing. Make the desired number of stamps or make a pair of jelly-bean stamps for each different color of beans in your package. Provide shallow containers of paints that correspond to the colors of the beans. Using the outline shape of the book page on page 75, cut out a large, white construction-paper jelly-bean shape for each child. Encourage each child to use the stamps to make prints on a cut-out shape.

As Colorful As Jelly Beans

Have interested children who are also fellow jelly-bean lovers help you make this book describing the variety of jelly-bean colors. In advance, duplicate a supply of the book page (page 75). Cut out the shapes. During a group time, ask your children to help you make lists of items that are the same colors as the colors of jelly beans in a package. When the lists have been made, give each child one of the bean-shaped pages. Ask him to choose a crayon that corresponds with one of the jelly-bean colors; then have him use the crayon to draw an item from the list or a different item of his choice. Write as he dictates his completion to the programmed sentence. When each child has completed a page, sort the pages by color. Bind all the pages between similarly shaped tagboard covers. (If desired, use the printing method described in "Colorful Stamping" to decorate the covers of the book before assembling the pages.) Title the book. Soon your little ones will be hungry to read it all by themselves!

A __blue__ jelly bean is as __blue__ as __eyes__ .

Jelly-Bean Countdown

Real jelly beans are so colorful, it doesn't take long for them to get eaten! Have your little ones help you count down the disappearing colors of jelly beans in this flannelboard rhyme. To prepare, use the patterns on page 76 to cut five different colors of felt jelly-bean shapes. Get ready! Count down!

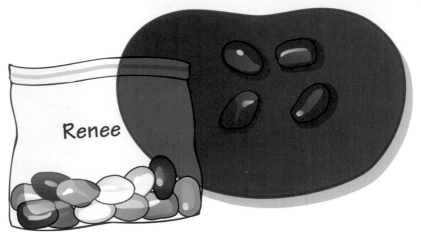

Five little jelly beans;
I wish I had more!
I'll eat the [color word] one;
Now there are four.

Four little jelly beans;
Tasty as can be.
I'll eat the [color word] one;
Now there are three.

Three little jelly beans;
Only a few.
I'll eat the [color word] one;
Now there are two.

Two little jelly beans;
Eating them is fun.
I'll eat the [color word] one;
Now there is one.

One little jelly bean;
The last one for me.
I'll eat the [color word] one;
I'm as happy as can be!

Assorted Colors

Tempt youngsters' taste buds with this colorful sorting activity. For each different color of jelly bean in a package, duplicate a jelly-bean pattern (page 76) onto a corresponding color of construction paper. Cut out the shapes; then place them in a center along with a class supply of personalized resealable plastic bags filled with jelly beans. To use the center, a child finds his bag of beans. He then places one of each different color of paper jelly-bean shape in front of him and sorts the matching real beans onto the shapes. No need to put *all* of those beans back in his bag when he's finished! Nibbling on the manipulatives is the treat for a sorting job well done.

Spilled Beans

A tisket, a tasket; fill a basket with colorful jelly beans! Here's a movement game that keeps youngsters actively identifying colors. To prepare, duplicate the jelly-bean patterns (page 76) onto various colors of construction paper so that the total number of beans is about three times the number of children in your class. Cut out the shapes; then laminate them for durability. To play, arrange the shapes on the floor in a circle. Put a basket in the middle of the circle. Invite your class to hop, tiptoe, or otherwise move beside the circular jelly-bean path as you sing the first verse of the following song. At the end of that verse, direct each child to place a foot on the nearest bean. Then sing the second verse to direct those children whose feet are on the named color of bean to drop those beans in the basket. Continue singing until all of the beans are in the basket.

Pick Up The Beans
(sung to the tune of "The Pawpaw Patch")

Moving around our jelly-bean circle.
Moving around our jelly-bean circle.
Moving around our jelly-bean circle.
What color jelly beans do you see?

Pick up the [color word] beans; put them in the basket.
Pick up the [color word] beans; put them in the basket.
Pick up the [color word] beans; put them in the basket.
Let's count the [color word] beans—you and me!

Soda Surprise

Plop, plop, fizz, fizz. What a thrill this soda is! Pour clear carbonated drink (such as Sprite® or 7-Up®) into as many ice-cube tray sections as you have children in your class. Ask each child to choose a color of jelly bean, name its color, and drop it into a section. Freeze the cubes. (The jelly beans' colors will tint the liquid to create colored cubes. Jelly Belly® jelly beans will not work for this activity.) During a snacktime, put a cube into a clear plastic cup for each child. Have each child find a cube that corresponds to the color of bean he selected; then assist him in filling his cup with the same type of clear soda used to make the cubes. As they watch the ice melt, youngsters will be surprised to see the clear soda blush with color. Using a spoon, remove the colorless bean from each child's drink. Wow! Drinks that taste like jelly beans!

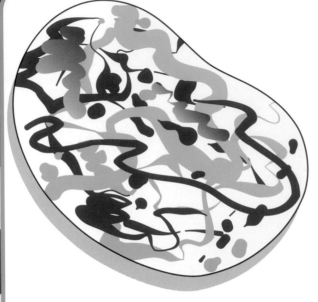

Roly-Poly Beans

What happens when jelly-bean colors collide? Use jelly beans in this variation of marble painting to find out! To paint with jelly beans, select two different colors of jelly beans. Place a large, white construction-paper bean shape (pattern on page 75) inside a tray. Carefully dip each jelly bean into a corresponding color of paint; then drop it onto the tray. Roll the jelly beans around the tray to create a design on the bean shape. Roly-poly jelly beans create cool art!

Jelly-Bean Stew For Me And You!

Colorful jelly beans are the main ingredient in this stew that reviews colors. Obtain several bags of jelly beans that include the colors listed in the following poem. Sort the beans by color; then divide them into sandwich bags so that each child has a bag of same-colored beans. Place a large pot in the center of your group. Introduce the poem to the children; then invite them to help you make jelly-bean stew. As you slowly repeat the poem, have each child pour his beans into the pot when his color of beans is named. Invite volunteers to stir the stew as you continue to repeat the poem. Using a soup ladle, fill a small cup with beans for each child. Let's all eat stew!

Jelly-Bean Stew

Jelly-bean stew,
Jelly-bean stew,
Red and yellow,
And purple, too!
Orange and pink,
And black and green,
It's the prettiest stew I've ever seen!

poem by Gloria Trabacca, Portland, OR

Book Page
Use with "Colorful Stamping" and "As Colorful As Jelly Beans" on page 71,
and "Roly-Poly Beans" on page 74.

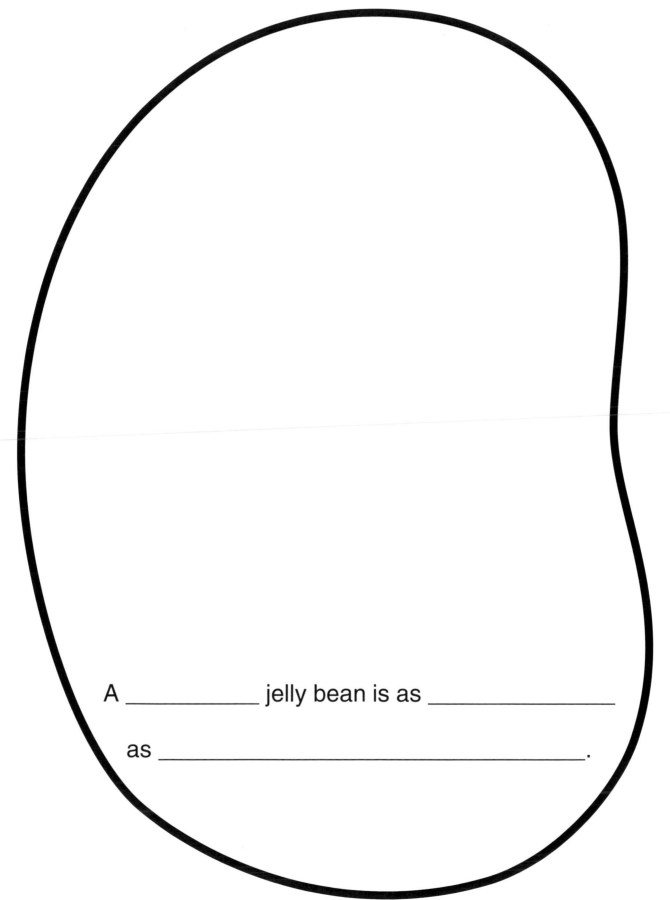

A _____ jelly bean is as _____

as _____.

Jelly-Bean Patterns

Use with "A Rainbow Of Colors" on page 70, "Jelly-Bean Countdown" and "Assorted Colors" on page 72, and "Spilled Beans" on page 73.

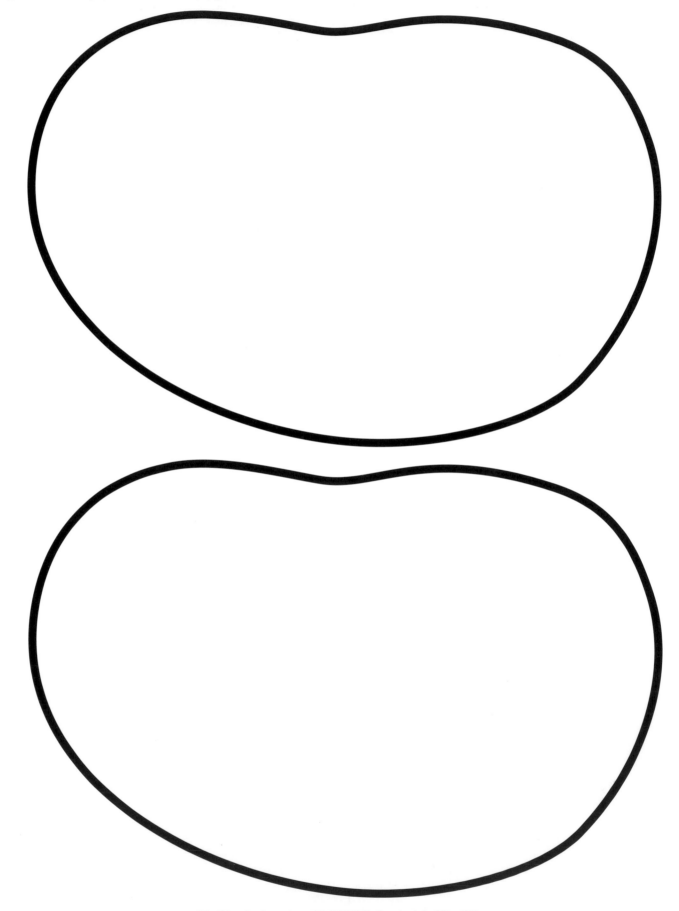

Happy Hands

We've got to hand it to you! When we asked for your favorite projects using handprints and hand shapes, we got more than a handful. Thanks, teachers, for lending a hand!

How Old Are You Now?

A child wearing this birthday crown is sure to feel like a queen or king. To make a crown, trace the birthday child's hand onto construction paper; then cut around the resulting outline. Glue the appropriate number of fingers to the palm so that the hand is displaying the child's age. Glue the hand onto a paper band. Program the band with a message similar to the one shown. Invite the birthday child to use markers and stickers to decorate his headband. Staple the band to fit the child's head. What a handsome crown!

Kathleen Savage—Pre-K, Mountainland Head Start, Provo, UT

A Handful Of Headbands

Need a quick way to add pizzazz to storytime or creative play? If so, then these versatile headbands are sure to please!

Dog

Glue construction-paper hand cutouts to either side of a paper band to resemble ears. Add spots to the headband, if desired. Staple the band to fit a child's head. Once a child dons this canine cap, use face paint to paint his nose black. Woof-woof!

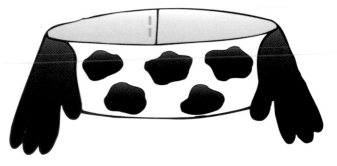

Reindeer

Outline two tan construction-paper hand cutouts with glue; then sprinkle them with gold glitter. When the glue is dry, glue the cutouts to a brown construction-paper band to represent antlers. Staple the band to fit a child's head. Have one of your little deer wear the headgear; then use red face paint to paint her nose, if desired.

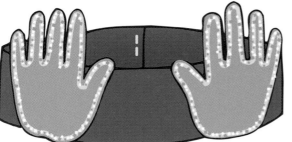

Bunny

Glue pink construction-paper hand cutouts to a white band. Staple the band to fit a child's head. Glue a cotton-ball tail to the back of the band.

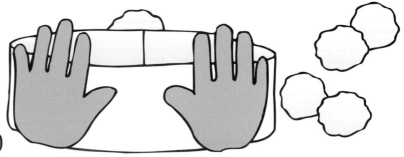

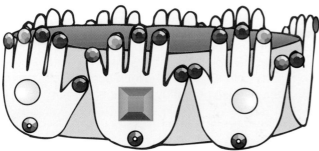

Crown

Glue gold or yellow construction-paper hand cutouts to a construction-paper band. Decorate the cutouts with fake jewels, glitter, and sequins. Staple the band to fit a child's head. Your students will feel like royalty when wearing these pretty crowns.

Sherry Cook, Glenwood Springs, CO

77

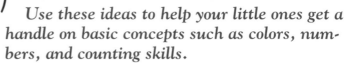

Use these ideas to help your little ones get a handle on basic concepts such as colors, numbers, and counting skills.

I Can Read My Colors

These handsome books are just right for helping youngsters recognize colors and color words. For each separate page, paint a child's hand a different color; then have him press his hand onto a sheet of construction paper. When the paint is dry, write the corresponding color word on each page. Bind the pages together between covers; then title the book "I Can Read My Colors."

adapted from an idea by Tina Marie Cotterell—1- to 12-Year-Olds
Tender Moments Care, Sumner, IL

Number Fish

You won't have to travel to the depths of the ocean to find this school of nifty numbered fish. To make a class book, program sheets of construction paper as shown, substituting a different numeral and color word on each page. Enlist the help of your little ones in painting the corresponding number and color of handprints onto each page. When the paint is dry, have students use markers to add details to the fish. Bind the pages between covers; then place the book in your classroom reading center. One fish, two fish. Oh, what cool fish!

Monica D. Raymer, Gavin Cochran Elementary, Louisville, KY

Color Combos

Pair children up for this activity that gives them an opportunity to discover new colors, share, and create a colorful group mural. Working with two children at a time, paint each partner's hands with a different primary color. Invite the pair to share their colors by rubbing their hands together to create a new color. Then have them press their hands onto a sheet of bulletin-board paper to create a handsome rainbow collage of color!

Lori Secor—Preschool, Children's Corner Daycare
Albany, NY

Are you right-handed or left-handed?

left — Curtis Amelia Joseph Maggie

right — Gretchen Ty Eric Jamal Spencer Keesha James Allie Jackson Tyler

Left Or Right?

Use this graphing activity to introduce your little ones to the concept of left- and right-handedness. Prepare a graph by labeling a length of bulletin-board paper similarly to the one shown. Invite a child to press his dominant hand into skin-toned paint, then onto the appropriate row on the graph. Write the child's name under his print. Students will enjoy locating their friends' handprints when you display this graph in your classroom.

Barbara Meyers, Fort Worth Country Day School, Fort Worth, TX

Holding Hands

Your little ones will give this counting booklet the high five! For each child reproduce the same number of the booklet pages (page 83) onto construction paper. Staple the pages together to make a booklet. Personalize the top page as shown. Fill at least as many small bowls as there are pages in each booklet with different manipulatives.

To complete each page of his booklet, invite a child to grasp a handful of one type of manipulative, then count them. Write the corresponding numeral and manipulative on the page. Have the child draw a picture of the manipulative in the hand outline on the page. Encourage each child to share his completed book with a friend. Now that's hands-on learning!

Barbara Meyers

My hand can hold...
by Emily

My hand can hold...
5 Legos

©The Education Center, Inc. • THE MAILBOX® • Preschool • April/May 1998

"I Can" Hands

While completing this project, your little ones will discover that there are many things they can do with their hands. For each child, program a sheet of construction paper with the phrase "Things I can do with my hands…" Have a child press her hands into skin-toned paint, then onto her paper. When the paint is dry, label each print "left" or "right." Ask the child to draw pictures of things she can do with her hands. Write as the child dictates descriptions of her pictures. When each child has completed a project, display these minimurals on a wall or bulletin board along with the graph described above.

Barbara Meyers

Things I can do with my hands...

build with blocks

color

pet my cat

left   right

79

Take a look at these creative craft ideas—handpicked for showing off your youngsters' handiwork and perfect for gift giving.

Handy Air Freshener

These air fresheners make super gifts for Mother's Day or Father's Day. To make one, trace a child's hand onto craft foam; then cut on the resulting outline. Glue a picture of the child onto the middle of the hand shape; then use a permanent marker to write the child's name and the date on the opposite side of the hand. Using a needle, insert a length of gold elastic thread through the hand and tie the ends into a knot. Add a few drops of potpourri oil onto the hand to complete this "handy-dandy" air freshener.

Dianna Bruckner—Two-Year-Olds
Winter Park Day Nursery
Winter Park, FL

Tiles To Treasure

These unique handprints make lovely keepsake plaques or coasters that parents are sure to treasure for years to come. To make one, paint a child's hand with acrylic craft paint. Have her gently press it onto a square ceramic tile, being careful to avoid smearing the paint. When the paint is dry, use a permanent marker to write the child's name and date on the tile. Spray the entire tile with clear acrylic sealer (available at craft stores). Allow the tile to dry overnight.

As a variation, paint a child's fingertip; then have her press it onto a one-inch square ceramic tile. Finish the project as previously described. When the tile is dry, hot-glue a magnet onto the back to make a nifty refrigerator magnet. This project is a keeper!

Mary Kay Steffey—Preschool, Noblesville Head Start, Noblesville, IN

May 1998
Lori

A Handful Of Thanks

Each student's handprint will give this thank-you gift special meaning. Using dimensional fabric paint, write "Thanks for lending a hand!" onto a sweatshirt, an apron, or a canvas tote bag. When the paint is dry, decorate the item with the children's handprints. What a handsome gift to give to parent volunteers, classroom assistants, and other helpers who deserve a hand for their hard work.

Joy Gompah—Pre-K
Little Lambs Child Care
Lockport, NY

Thanks for lending a hand!

Don't let these handprinted critters slip through your fingers!

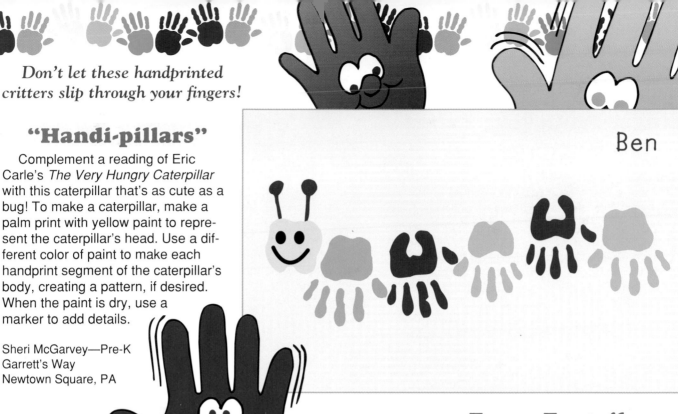

"Handi-pillars"

Complement a reading of Eric Carle's *The Very Hungry Caterpillar* with this caterpillar that's as cute as a bug! To make a caterpillar, make a palm print with yellow paint to represent the caterpillar's head. Use a different color of paint to make each handprint segment of the caterpillar's body, creating a pattern, if desired. When the paint is dry, use a marker to add details.

Sheri McGarvey—Pre-K
Garrett's Way
Newtown Square, PA

Fancy Fantails

Youngsters will be proud as peacocks after creating these fancy fantails! To make one, press both hands in blue or green paint; then press them onto a sheet of construction paper so that the thumbs overlap. Paint a craft stick black. When the paint is dry, glue small wiggle eyes to the stick; then glue it to the center of the handprint feathers. To complete the peacock, glue jewels and sequins to the finger feathers. How fancy!

Karen Bryant—Pre-K
Miller Elementary School
Warner Robins, GA

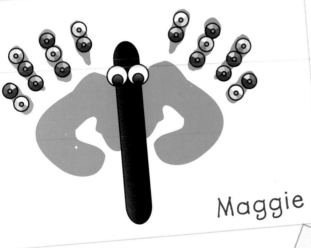

Tiger Paws

These terrific tigers are sure to make your little ones roar with applause! To make a tiger print, paint a child's hand with orange paint. Paint black stripes over the orange paint on the palm and several fingers. Have the child press her hand onto a piece of construction paper. When the paint is dry, have the child use orange and black markers to add a tail and facial features. Looks like you've got a pattern there, Tiger!

Jennifer Harrison—Pre-K
Hawthorne Elementary
Baltimore, MD

81

Put your hands together to celebrate spring!

Finger-Frolicking Tulips

Excitement is sure to bloom when your little ones create these fingerpainted tulips. Fingerpaint with a desired color onto fingerpainting paper. When the paint is dry, cut out a tulip shape. Next trace both hands onto green construction paper; then cut on the resulting outlines. To assemble the flower, glue the tulip to a green construction-paper stem; then glue the hand shapes to either side of the stem to resemble leaves. Personalize and write the date on the hand shapes. Cultivate these pretty posies on a bulletin board or window for a colorful display that's hands above the rest!

Lida Mills—Preschool, Hodgkins Park District, Hodgkins, IL

Pam Crane

Chloe   May '98

You Are My Sunshine

This idea is sure to add a handful of sparkle to your classroom! To make a sun, cut an eight-inch circle from white construction paper. Have a child repeatedly press one hand into yellow paint, then around the edge of the circle. Sprinkle glitter onto the wet paint. To complete the project, mount the child's photo in the center of the circle. What a sunny delight!

Nanci Alley—Preschool
First United Methodist Wee Care Center
Alamosa, CO

A Spring Garden

With some hands-on help from your center's staff and children, this display will really take flight! Make green handprints along the bottom of a length of bulletin-board paper to resemble grass. In the center of the paper, use brown and green handprints to make a tree. Paint green flower stems and leaves; then press a colorful handprint flower at the top of each stem. Create a bit of butterfly fancy by dipping two hands into paint; then press them onto the paper so that the thumbs overlap. Decorate the butterflies with painted dots and antennae. What a spring delight!

Denise Turetsky—Assistant Teacher
Temple Judea Nursery, Massapequa, NY

Hands Up For Spring!

My hand can hold...

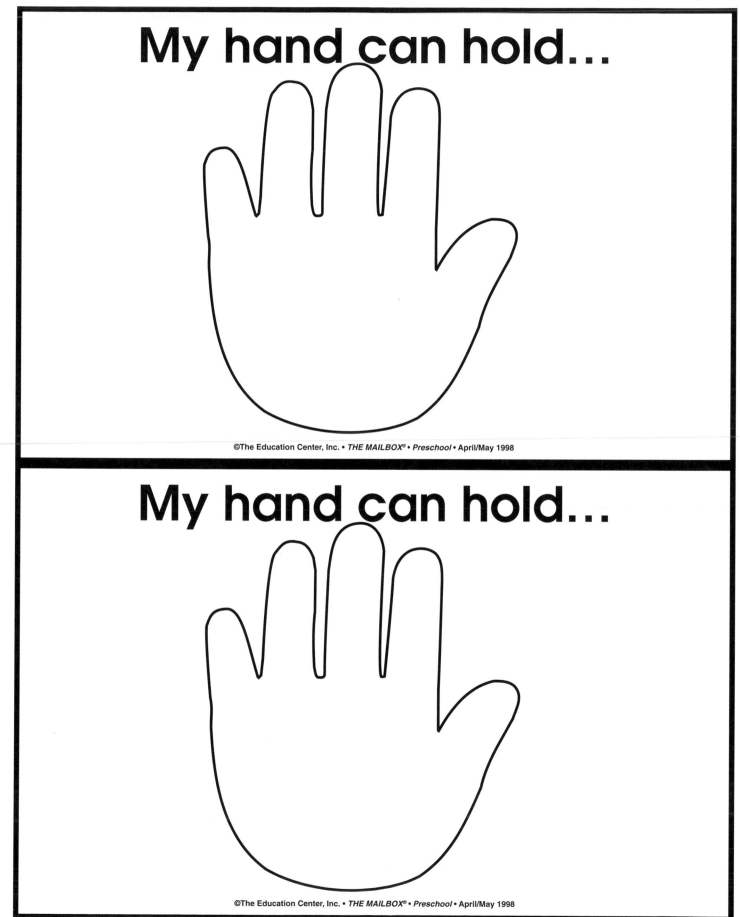

©The Education Center, Inc. • *THE MAILBOX*® • *Preschool* • April/May 1998

My hand can hold...

©The Education Center, Inc. • *THE MAILBOX*® • *Preschool* • April/May 1998

Bursting Into Bloom!

Your little sprouts are sure to blossom as you dig into this bouquet of flower-themed learning ideas.

ideas by dayle timmons

Down And Dirty

Get your flower unit started by getting down and getting dirty—really! To prepare to grow a garden of marigolds this spring and summer, first locate a plot that is away from active playground areas, close to an outdoor water source, and in a sunny area. Prior to asking your children to join you at the spot, outline the section and loosen the grass and soil if necessary. Request that parents dress their children for several consecutive days in clothes that can be soiled. During your outdoor times on those days, supervise children as they freely dig in the soil to prepare it for gardening. After several days of laying the groundwork (better known as playing in the dirt!), rake the soil to smooth the dirt and prepare for planting the seeds. This is the way we dig the dirt, dig the dirt, dig the dirt. This is the way we dig the dirt; we're learning about gardening!

Bordering On Beautiful

Now that the field of your dreams is ready, you need a cool kid-made border for your garden. Border the area with large rocks or prebuilt wooden fencing (available at home-supplies stores). Invite children to use various colors of acrylic paints to paint the rocks or fence. Not only does this project give each child more input into creating your garden; it also adds color before the flower festival even begins!

Planting The Seeds

To help your gardening project "suc-seed," ask parents to send varieties of marigold seeds to school. Carefully open the packages; then empty the seeds into labeled resealable plastic bags. Laminate the packages. Staple one package of each variety to a tongue depressor to prepare labels for your garden. Place the remaining packages in your writing center or in your math center for sorting practice. Then take the seeds, the labels, some gardening tools, and your gardeners out to the garden to plant some seeds.

Garden Snakes

No need to be afraid of these garden snakes! To keep birds and small critters away from your newly planted garden, have youngsters paint these colorful reptiles. Provide pictures of real snakes. If possible, have each child find his own stick to paint using acrylic paints. Or give each of several groups of children a stick to paint. When the paint is dry, alternate putting each different snake in the garden. Ssss, gotcha!

A Blooming Surprise

Use this song to reassure youngsters that with some "TLC," water, and sunlight, their flowers will one day bloom.

Will My Flowers Bloom?
(sung to the tune of "The Wheels On The Bus")

The seeds from the pack go in the ground,	*Pretend to plant.*
In the ground, in the ground.	
The seeds from the pack go in the ground.	
Will our flowers bloom?	*Palms up, questioning.*
The rain from the sky goes drip, drop, drip.	*Wiggle fingers downward.*
Drip, drop, drip; drip, drop, drip.	
The rain from the sky goes drip, drop, drip.	
Will our flowers bloom?	*Palms up, questioning.*
The sun above is bright and hot,	*Form circle with arms overhead.*
Bright and hot, bright and hot.	
The sun above is bright and hot.	
Will our flowers bloom?	*Palms up, questioning.*
Our little seeds are sprouting fast,	*Slowly wiggle fingers upward.*
Sprouting fast, sprouting fast.	
Our little seeds are sprouting fast.	
Look! Our flowers bloomed!	*Palms open beside face.*

MARIGOLD

50¢

Marigold seed,

marigold sprout,

Seeds sprout.

marigold buds,

marigold flowers,

marigold seeds!

Watch What Develops

So what are we waiting for? Make a marigold timeline to help youngsters know what to watch for throughout the gardening project. Also use the display to document the garden's growth with real photos and youngsters' thoughts and illustrations. To prepare the timeline, duplicate a copy of the booklet pages (page 91). Color and cut out the pages; then glue them sequentially onto a length of bulletin-board paper. Refer to the illustrations as you discuss the stages. Take pictures of your garden in each of the corresponding stages. Display the real photos on the display along with youngsters' comments and artwork. After your project, laminate the photos; then place them in a science center to encourage discussions and sequencing practice.

Pretty Maids (And Masters) In A Row

In addition to your outdoor garden—or in place of it if outdoor space is limited—plant these windowsill gardens. Provide each child with a small, recycled container such as a yogurt cup or milk carton. Direct each child to fill the container with soil; then plant several marigold seeds. Provide a magnifying glass for close observations and a water bottle for misting the sprouts.

Identify each child's planter with these floral labels. Prepare a tracer from the smallest pattern on page 90. Direct each child to trace the pattern onto yellow or orange construction paper, then cut it out. Personalize each child's flower; then attach his picture to it. Next have each child paint a tongue depressor green. When the paint is dry, glue his flower to the depressor; then insert it into his planter. At the end of your gardening project, send these flowers home to be shared with families.

Kara

Isaac

Marigold Merriment

Flowers won't be the only things emerging when you use this booklet idea to develop your little ones' prereading skills. Using the largest flower pattern on page 90, cut a flower shape from orange or yellow tagboard for each child. Duplicate a class supply of the booklet pages on page 91. Have each child color a set of booklet pages; then cut them out. Have him assist you in sequencing the pages; then staple them to the center of a flower shape. Merry reading!

Marigold Merriment!

"Scent-sational" Flowers

While your little ones are waiting for their gardens to bloom, fill their time with a bouquet of flower-themed learning ideas. For starters, mix up several batches of flower-scented play dough. Store each scent of dough in a separate container labeled with flower pictures cut from a seed catalog. Place the doughs in a center along with flower-shaped cookie cutters, small plastic flowerpots, and painted green craft sticks for use as stems.

Scented Play Dough

3 cups flour
3/4 cup salt
3 tablespoons cream of tartar
1/8 cup powdered tempera paint (any color)
2 cups water
3 tablespoons oil
approximately 10 drops of potpourri oil (any floral scent, such as rose, gardenia, lavender, or jasmine)

In a large pot, mix together all of the dry ingredients. Stir in the water and oils until the mixture is smooth. Stir the ingredients over medium heat until the mixture forms into a ball. While the dough is warm, knead it on a floured board until it is silky smooth. When the mixture has cooled, store it in an airtight container.

Stop And Smell The Flowers

Let your school and parents know about your flower studies with this display that smells as good as it looks. To make a flower, use the middle-sized flower pattern (page 90) to cut a flower shape from a small, white paper plate. Use watercolors to paint the shape. When the paint is dry, glue a cupcake liner to the center of the plate. Add a few drops of floral-scented potpourri oil to a pastel-colored cotton ball. Glue the cotton ball to the center of the liner. Tape a length of green curling ribbon to the back of each child's flower. Attach the flowers to a wall or display so that they resemble a bouquet. Tie the ribbons together with a ribbon bow. Add the invitation "Stop And Smell The Flowers!"

Delicious Dirt

Now that your little ones have admired and smelled flowers, invite them to taste them, too! In advance, fill one ice-cream cone for each child three-fourths full of chocolate cake batter (prepared from a mix). Stand the cones in cupcake baking pans; then bake them according to the package cupcake-baking directions. Also cut off the pointed end of a supply of wooden skewers. To make one flowerpot snack, frost one of the cakes with chocolate frosting. Crush one chocolate-sandwich cookie in a bag; then sprinkle the crumbs over the frosting. To make each flower, put one gumdrop, a butter cookie, and then another gumdrop onto a skewer. Insert the flowers into the pot. Dig in!

A Rainbow Of Color

Isn't it amazing that flowers come in all the colors of the rainbow? With your class, look through a seed catalog or a reference book with photos of flowers. Encourage volunteers to identify the flowers by their colors. Then share the festive book *Planting A Rainbow* by Lois Ehlert (Harcourt Brace & Company). Use this crafty idea to find out which colors of flowers are your children's favorites. From shades of red, orange, yellow, blue, and purple construction paper, cut a quantity of the three sizes of flower patterns on page 90. Ask each child to find three different sizes of one color of flower shapes. Help him sequence the shapes, and then glue the centers together. Provide scraps of various colors of paper so that students can embellish their flowers, if desired. As a class sort the flowers by color; then arrange them on a green background for a display that's blooming with color.

Picking Flowers

Continue to cultivate color-recognition skills with this circle-time game. Using the smallest pattern on page 90, cut a class supply of flower shapes from various colors of construction paper. To play, seat the group in a circle; then ask a volunteer to stand inside the circle. Give each seated child a flower. Lead the group in the following chant as the volunteer moves around the circle. Direct the volunteer to pick a flower by the end of the chant. Then ask the child whose flower was picked to trade places with the first child. Continue until each child has picked a flower.

Pretty flowers grew out in the sun.
[Child's name] came to the garden;
She/He picked the [color] one.

Flower Child

Cultivate cutting skills with this crown of flowers. Use the smallest flower pattern (page 90) to prepare tracers. Invite each child to make a crown by tracing the desired number of flower shapes onto various colors of construction paper. Have him cut out the flowers, and then glue them onto a sentence strip. Staple the strip to fit the child's head. It's a crown of glory!

Youth Garden Grant

The National Gardening Association would like to help you cultivate young gardeners of the 21st century. If you have an outdoor school garden or plan to start one, request an application for the 1999 Youth Garden Grants Program. Three hundred schools and youth groups will be chosen for awards consisting of hundreds of dollars worth of tools, seeds, garden products, and educational materials. Consideration is given for innovative programming, sustainability, community support, strong leadership, and need. To receive an application, call 800-538-7476; send a request to: Garden Grants, National Gardening Association, 180 Flynn Ave., Burlington, VT 05401; or E-mail the association at nga@garden.org. Download an application from the web site at: http://www.garden.org. Deadline for completed applications is November 15, 1998.

Offshoots

Has your patch of marigolds got you hooked on gardening? For more ideas, request a complimentary issue of *Growing Ideas: A Journal Of Garden-Based Learning* (published by the National Gardening Association) by writing to National Gardening Association, 180 Flynn Avenue, Burlington, VT 05401. *Growing Ideas* provides instructional ideas, horticultural information, and a forum for exchange among teachers using plants to stimulate learning. Also check out the "Kids And Classrooms" section of the National Gardening Association's World Wide Web site: http://www.garden.org.

Digging Deeper

Flower Garden
Written by Eve Bunting
Illustrated by Kathryn Hewitt
Published by Harcourt Brace & Company
(See page 31 for teaching ideas.)

Alison's Zinnia
Written & Illustrated by Anita Lobel
Published by William Morrow & Company, Inc.

The Flower Alphabet Book
Written by Jerry Pallotta
Illustrated by Leslie Evans
Published by Charlesbridge Publishing

Counting Wildflowers
Written & Photographed by Bruce McMillan
Published by William Morrow & Company, Inc.

Flower Patterns

Use with "Pretty Maids (And Masters) In A Row" and "Marigold Merriment" on page 86, "Stop And Smell The Flowers" on page 87, and "A Rainbow Of Color," "Picking Flowers," and "Flower Child" on page 88.

marigold sprout,

marigold seeds!

Marigold seed,

marigold flowers,

Marigold Merriment!

marigold buds,

Sunny-Side Up

Warm up your summer days with these sunny ideas that are so bright your little ones will need to put on their shades!

ideas contributed by dayle timmons

Family Fun In The Sun

Get your summer off to a blazing start with this take-home project that shines the light on family participation. Provide each child with a yellow tagboard sun shape. Send the shape home along with a note requesting that families share their favorite outdoor summertime activities by writing them on the shape, gluing photos on the shape, or by gluing magazine pictures on the shape. As each child returns his project, give him a chance to shine by sharing those things that his family likes to do in the sun. Display the suns from your ceiling for a room that's sunny-side up.

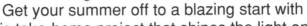

We go to the beach.

Sing A Song Of Sunshine

Once your class is beaming with pride over their family projects, make a list of the outdoor summertime activities that your children and their families enjoy. Use the ideas on the list to modify the following song. You'll be singing all summer long!

All Summer Long
(sung to the tune of "The Wheels On The Bus")

The people in the sun <u>swim in the pool</u>,
<u>In the pool, in the pool</u>.
The people in the sun <u>swim in the pool</u>,
All summer long.

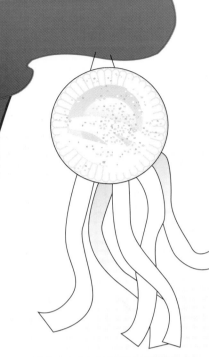

Moving Ways With Sunny Rays

With this craft and movement activity, each of your little ones can spread some sunshine all over the place. To make a sunbeam streamer, paint the bottom of one small paper plate and the top of a second paper plate yellow. Sprinkle on gold glitter. To the back of the plate that is painted on the top, tape a number of yellow and white crepe-paper streamers. Glue the plates together so that both yellow sides are facing out. Get youngsters warmed up by inviting them to find sunny outdoor spots in which they can move their streamers. Locate the following Raffi favorites and play them on a portable tape or CD player outside while your little sunbeams move. Ready to catch some rays?

"Rise And Shine"
sung by Raffi
Rise And Shine; Kimbo Educational

"One Light, One Sun"
sung by Raffi
One Light, One Sun; Kimbo Educational

Solar Power Snack

Power up with these sun snacks! To make one, spread cream cheese that has been tinted yellow onto a round cookie. Place the cookie on a small paper plate; then arrange candy corns around it. It's a treat that's simple and "sun-sational"!

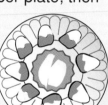

Some Like It Hot

What is the sun, anyway? Your little ones will be fascinated with the idea that the sun is really a star and that means it's a ball of very hot, glowing gases. The sun gives us heat and light. To help satisfy your little ones' curiosity about the sun, find a sunny outdoor spot for your class and share *Sun Up, Sun Down* by Gail Gibbons (Harcourt Brace & Company).

Follow up the story by finding out who enjoys the sun's heat and who does not. Prepare a graph with two columns, one labeled "Hot, hot, hot!" and the other "Not, not, not!" Ask each child to tell you whether he likes it hot or not; then draw the outline of a sun on the appropriate side of the graph. Have the child color his sun with a glow-in-the-dark yellow crayon. Discuss the results; then turn off the lights for a shining solar surprise!

Hot, hot, hot! | Not, not, not!

93

Celebrate The Sun

Here's a cheer that's full of reasons for celebrating the sun. Review the information shared in *Sun Up, Sun Down* (see page 93). Then teach youngsters the phrase repeated in each verse. Invite them to cheer and keep a steady beat as you chant.

You're Our Star

You're super, sun, and you're our star,
Even though you're very far.
You give us heat; you give us light.
When you're around it's day, not night.

You're super, sun, and you're our star,
Even though you're very far.
We need you in so many ways.
Your long, hot rays make summer days.

You're super, sun, and you're our star,
Even though you're very far.
Because of you the flowers grow.
You make the rain and bright rainbows.

You're super, sun, and you're our star,
Even though you're very far.

You Scream, I Scream, We All Scream For Sunscreen!

As helpful as the sun is, too much exposure to the sun can result in damage to our skin. Use this idea to demonstrate the importance of clothing and sunscreen to protect our skin and keep it healthy. Cut two brightly colored paper dolls for each child. (Use a gingerbread-man cookie cutter as a pattern, if desired.) Trim one of the dolls as shown to resemble clothing. Personalize the clothing. Help each child tape the clothing to his doll. Then secure the dolls to a flat surface and place them outside so that the clothing shapes are facing the sun. After several hours, remove the dolls from the sun and lift off the clothing shapes. Discuss the difference in color between the paper exposed to the sun and the paper that was covered by the clothing shapes. Explain that even though the paper was lightened by exposure to the sun, our skin is darkened by the sun's rays. Complete this activity by applying sunscreen to each child before sending him out to play.

Geraldine B. Nemirow, Reading, PA

Liquid Sunshine

Have you ever wished you could soak in the sunshine and save it for a rainy day? If so, try this fun activity that's part fact and part fantasy. To help your young scientists understand light absorption, explain that dark colors like black "save" (absorb) sunlight and get hot, while light colors like white send back (reflect) sunlight. Then offer to make a box for saving sunshine for rainy days. Cover a box and its lid with black paper. Remove the label from a can of powdered lemonade; then empty its contents into a separate container. Prepare a new label titled "Sunshine" for the can. Put the can in the box; then set the box outside in the sun for a day. Upon bringing the box inside, explain that the sunshine is invisible but will become visible overnight. When the children are gone, return the powder to the can. Next time you have a rainy day, bring out your can of sunshine. Just add water and enjoy!

Reading On The Sunny Side

These titles will keep you reading from sunup to sundown.

What The Sun Sees, What The Moon Sees
Written & Illustrated by Nancy Tafuri
Published by William Morrow And Company, Inc.

Sun Song
Written by Jean Marzollo
Illustrated by Laura Regan
Published by HarperCollins Publishers, Inc.

The Sun's Day
Written & Illustrated by Mordicai Gerstein
Published by HarperCollins Children's Books

Following The Sun
Written & Illustrated by Jenny Stow
Published by Carolrhoda Books, Inc.

The Wind And The Sun
Retold & Illustrated by Tomie dePaola
Published by Silver Burdett Press

Wild About Watermelons!

Now that it's summer, you'll need juicy, mouthwatering, fresh-picked ideas to keep the learning growing. We think these ideas will be just "ripe"!

Pam Crane

Learning Your Way Around A Watermelon

It turns out that there's a lot of learning to be done with a watermelon. Watermelons aren't just for eating anymore—they're for learning about opposites, too. Take your children outside on a sunny day. Put a watermelon on newspaper on the ground. Begin your discussion about opposites by describing the *outside* of the watermelon. Ask volunteers what the *inside* will look like. Invite each child to thump the outside and try to pick up the watermelon. Next cut each child a slice. Compare the *soft* flesh of the inside to the *hard* rind of the outside. Discuss that while the whole watermelon was *heavy,* each slice is *light.* Best of all, eat your juicy slices. (Save those seeds and rinds! You'll need them for activities in this unit.) Mmmm, delicious and messy! Isn't *wet* better than *dry?*

LeeAnn Collins—Director, Sunshine House Preschool, Lansing, MI

Can A Watermelon Grow In My Tummy?

What's that? Someone swallowed a seed? Have no fear! The following song reminds little ones that a watermelon can't grow in there! Invite the children to echo you as you shout, "Oh, no!", then sing each verse.

Watermelon Echo Song
(sung to the tune of "Frère Jacques")

Oh, no! *(Oh, no!)*
I just swallowed *(I just swallowed)*
A watermelon seed. *(A watermelon seed.)*
Will I grow a watermelon *(Will I grow a watermelon)*
Deep in me? *(Deep in me?)*

Shout phrase, hands on face in alarm.
Begin singing slowly as with fear.

Oh, no! *(Oh, no!)*
That seed won't grow *(That seed won't grow)*
In my tummy. *(In my tummy.)*
There's no rain or sunshine *(There's no rain or sunshine)*
Deep in me! *(Deep in me!)*

Shout phrase.
Sing faster with joy.

LeeAnn Collins

A Tale Of Many Tendrils

Of course watermelon seeds can't sprout in tummies, but what *do* they need to grow vines and produce melons? Make this prop to describe the sequence of how a watermelon grows. Paint the bottoms of two paper plates green to resemble watermelons. Tape one end of a five-foot, green crepe-paper streamer to the inside rim of one plate. Starting near the opposite end of the streamer, glue a construction-paper yellow flower, then a green melon bud. Staple the rims of the plates together several times, leaving an opening opposite the end where the streamer is attached to the plate. Tuck the streamer into the watermelon pocket. As you share the following song or poem, gently pull the streamer vine out of the watermelon pocket, revealing the flower and then the melon bud.

Growing Melons

(sung to the tune of "The Farmer In The Dell")

Watermelon seeds, watermelon seeds,
On the ground and all around,
Watermelon seeds.

The vines begin to grow…

The yellow flowers bloom…

The melon buds appear…

Big and green and round, big and green and round,
The melons grow until they are all
Big and green and round.

Sharon Nichols, Madison Primary, Madison, FL

The Watermelon Story

A farmer plants a seed one day
And waits for it to grow.
Rain and sun and sandy soil
Are sure to help, you know.

A sprout pops up from underground,
Green as green can be.
It grows and grows so very long,
It's now a vine, you see.

A flower grows upon the vine,
Big and bright and new.
And right behind each lovely flower
Grows a watermelon, too!

The melons grow and grow and grow
Until they're big and grand.
They sit upon the farmer's field,
The best in all the land.

LeeAnn Collins—Director
Sunshine House Preschool
Lansing, MI

"Melondramatic" Play

Now that your little lip smackers have whet their appetites for watermelon and know what it takes to make one grow, prepare this patch for some dramatic play. Set the scene with props, such as a toy wheelbarrow, a watering can, three-foot lengths of hose, gardening gloves, garden tools, and straw hats. Label laundry baskets with pictures and signs labeled "small" and "large." Cover the patch with crepe-paper-streamer vines. What about the watermelons? Follow these instructions (right) for making papier-mâché melons. Be sure to invite each of your farmers to join you in the melon-making mania!

LeeAnn Collins—Director
Sunshine House Preschool, Lansing, MI

Mix warm water into an amount of flour until you have a thick, soupy paste.

Tearing along the grain, tear newspaper into one-inch-wide strips.

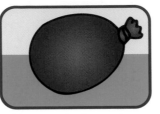

Blow up a balloon; then tie the end in a knot.

Repeatedly dip strips of newspaper into the paste; then press them onto the balloon.

Cover the balloon but not the knot.

When the paper is dry, cut off the knot; then remove the balloon.

Paint the shape to resemble a watermelon.

Surprise Me With Seeds

It's harvesttime at the play-dough center! Wash a number of the leftover seeds from your introductory eating experience. Use your favorite recipe to prepare a batch of bright-red play dough. (To add a watermelon scent to your dough, add a package of sugar-free, watermelon-flavored gelatin to the dry ingredients before cooking the dough.) Hide the seeds in a batch of the dough. Encourage youngsters to finger through the dough in search of the seeds. To encourage youngsters to sculpt their own watermelon slices, make a batch of green play dough to add to the center along with circular cookie cutters and plastic knives. This fine-motor melon center is sure to be picked over and over again.

LeeAnn Collins

A Slice Of Summer Art

That play-dough center sure did make good use of the leftover seeds. If you don't mind, we'll also use the rinds! To prepare a painting center, layer three plastic plates with moistened paper towels. Brush green, red, and black paint onto the towels to create three colors of paint pads. Provide small sponges and watermelon rinds. Encourage a child to dip a rind onto the green pad, then press it onto a large sheet of paper to create designs. If desired, a child may press a rind print, then use the sponges to add red and black paint until his prints resemble a watermelon.

LeeAnn Collins—Director, Sunshine House Preschool, Lansing, MI

Mighty "Vine" Visors

Keep slicing and dicing the fun with this fresh-off-the-vine visor idea. To make one, paint a paper-plate half to resemble a watermelon slice. Laminate a 1 1/2" x 16" paper strip. When the paint is dry, staple the ends of the strip to the plate to create a visor. If a child is feeling especially wacky in his watermelon hat, offer to use face paint to paint small black seeds on his cheeks. You're really wild over watermelons now!

Mary Ledyard—Preschool, Holy Rosary Central Steubenville, OH

Ornamental Melons

These melons are fun to make and can be used as necklaces, magnets, or ornaments. To make two melon slices, roll some Crayola® Model Magic® nontoxic, air-drying modeling compound into a ball. Press the ball flat. Use a knife to cut the pancake shape in half, creating two slices. Poke a hole in each slice that will be a necklace or an ornament. Allow the slices to dry overnight. Then color the slices with markers or paint them. If desired, glue real seeds to the slices. Thread appropriate ribbon lengths through the holes to make necklaces or ornaments. Or glue magnets on the backs of the slices.

Rae Warfel, Youngworld Children's Center, Wexford, PA

Watermelon Hopscotch

Use these ideas indoors or outdoors to inspire some melon movement and patterning practice. To prepare an outdoor hopscotch game, use chalk to draw a number of watermelon slices in a row on a sidewalk. Alternate drawing one, then two seeds in each slice. Encourage a child to hop along the slices as in hopscotch, landing on one foot where there is one seed in a slice, then on two feet where there are two seeds in a slice.

To prepare an indoor version, prepare a number of construction-paper watermelon slices with one or two seeds. Laminate the slices; then secure them to the floor in a row, alternating the one-seed slices with the two-seed slices. A child hops along the slices as described. One, two, one, two, one, two…

Amy Reynolds, Merry Moppet Preschool, Belmont, CA

What A Site!

Perhaps you'd like some tasty watermelon treats. Or maybe you've been pondering how to grow a patch of melons. Here's an Internet site we recommend: All About Watermelons *(http://www.watermelon.org/welcome.html)*— a watermelon Web site posted by the National Watermelon Promotion Board. When you visit this site, you'll find lots of tasty recipes for kids, a pattern for a watermelon puppet, information about how to grow watermelons, and even information about watermelon festivals that may be taking place in your state this summer. Check it out!

Refreshing Reading

"What-a-melon!" That's what folks will say when they see this interesting addition to your reading center. Fill a wading pool with pink or red shredded paper or tissue paper. Toss in a handful of black paper seed shapes; then wind crepe-paper-streamer vines around the pool. Invite youngsters to settle in for some seedy reading. See the book titles on page 101 for some refreshing reading ideas.

Beth Bonow, Hollywood, FL

Watermelon-Seed Maracas

Introduce some rhythm into your watermelon unit with these marvelous maracas. Collect a class supply of empty film containers. To make a maraca, use a black marker to draw seeds on a 1 7/8" x 4" piece of red paper. Tape the paper around a container. Put a number of watermelon seeds in the container; then secure the lid. Encourage each child to experiment with the sound of his maraca by adding or taking away seeds. Shake your maracas to the beat of your favorite summer songs. Or invite your little ones to shake their maracas to the beat as you sing Raffi's "Down By The Bay" *(Singable Songs For The Very Young)* or read the book (published by Crown Books For Young Readers).

LeeAnn Collins—Director, Sunshine House Preschool, Lansing, MI

Worth The Wait

Jesse waited and waited and waited for a watermelon day. At the end of the summer, the day arrived. *Then* she had to wait some more—a ripe watermelon has "a whole summer's worth of heat inside it" and takes a while to get good and cold. Read aloud *Watermelon Day* by Kathi Appelt (Henry Holt And Company, Inc.). Then have a taste-test to determine if your youngsters agree that cold watermelon is worth waiting for. In advance cut enough bite-sized watermelon pieces so that each child can have several. Put half of the pieces in the refrigerator and keep half at room temperature. When the pieces have chilled, have each child eat some cold and some warm watermelon; then take a vote to discover which youngsters prefer. Chances are, either way they'll prefer to keep eating watermelon!

LeeAnn Collins

You're Invited To
A Watermelon Day!
Join us after lunch on
Friday for a
slice of summer!

Everybody's Yellin' For Watermelon

Why wait all summer for a watermelon day? Begin planning a gathering today and invite youngsters' parents to join in the fun. Prepare a class supply of construction-paper invitations similar to the one shown; then send them home to parents.

On your day, simply gather together to enjoy a cool summer snack. Or encourage children to share with their parents those centers and activities they have enjoyed during your watermelon unit. To make a watermelon piñata for your festivities, follow the papier-mâché directions on page 98. Fill the papier-mâché watermelon with watermelon-flavored candies. Seal the hole with tape. Suspend the piñata for play. When the piñata is broken, distribute the candies among the group. Everybody's yellin', "We love watermelon!"

Nancy M. Lotzer, Farmers Branch, TX

FOOTLOOSE AND FANCY-FREE

Summertime is barefoot time. So take off your shoes and let your little piggies loose!

GOODNESS KNOWS! I SEE YOUR TOES!

Invite your little ones to bare their soles—the soles of their feet, that is—with this fun storytime activity. Seat your children in a circle; then turn off the lights. Invite each child to take off her shoes and socks and put the items behind her back. Use a feather duster to tickle the children's little toes as they make their appearances. Then use a flashlight to point out each individual child's feet. When each set of feet has been spotlighted, shine the light on one of the following book selections and read it to your class by flashlight.

Katy Zoldak—Pre-K Special Education
Metzenbaum School
Parma, OH

BAREFOOTIN' BOOK PICKS

Tiny Toes
Written by Donna Jakob
Illustrated by Mireille Levert
Published by Hyperion Books For Children

Beach Feet
Written & Illustrated by Lynn Reiser
Published by Greenwillow Books

Foot Book
Written & Illustrated by Dr. Seuss
Published by Random House Books
For Young Readers

PITTER-PATTER PAINTING

The frolicking foot fun really begins when your little ones' painted feet walk all over a bulletin-board-paper canvas. On a warm day, put a wading pool or large tub outside near a sidewalk. Fill the pool with water and place some towels nearby. Secure a length of bulletin-board paper to the sidewalk. Finally fill several shallow pans with washable paint. Invite one or more children at a time to remove their shoes and socks, step into the paint, and then walk over the paper. Direct them to wash the paint off their feet by wading in the pool. If desired, label each trail of feet with the artist's name.

Katy Zoldak

Rodney Luck

Christine Robinson

FASCINATING FEET

Parents and little ones alike will find this display fascinating and will enjoy matching each pair of feet with a face. In turn, invite each child to remove his shoes and socks; then paint the bottom of his feet. Have the child step onto a length of bulletin-board paper to make a pair of footprints. Beside his prints, write the child's name. Then, on a separate piece of paper, record several interesting facts about the child. Tape the paper over the child's name so that it can be lifted to read the facts. Mount the display at students' eye levels so that they can guess the owners of the prints. Encourage parents to read the descriptions aloud and ask their own children to assist them in identifying the described person before lifting the paper to read the name.

L. Marisol Buitrago—Preschool, Mt. Vernon Preschool
Alexandria, VA

LET'S GO BAREFOOT!

Let's go barefoot in our bare feet!
No shoes, no socks, out-in-the-air feet!

Let's go barefoot in our bare feet!
Wet feet, wet toes, wet-underwater feet!

Let's go barefoot in our bare feet!
Tickle bare toes, on-green-lawn feet!

Let's go barefoot in our bare feet!
Hot feet, hot toes, sidewalk-hot feet!

Let's go barefoot in our bare feet!
Lovely summer, warm-fresh-air feet!

Lucia Kemp Henry

PIGGIES IN THE POOL

To give your little ones a "toe-tally" terrific sensory experience, fill a wading pool with water and soil, shaving cream, or slime. (To make slime, mix one part water with two parts cornstarch. Add a small amount of green washable paint, if desired.) Invite youngsters to let their piggies wallow in the fun.

If you prefer to keep water in your pool, add a number of marbles or plastic manipulatives. Challenge youngsters to use their toes to catch and remove the objects. Those toes are jammin' now!

FOOT PHOTOS

Capture all that summertime, barefoot fun in photos. Then mount the photos on a display along with the barefoot chant (above). Or write each verse of the chant on a separate piece of construction paper. Combine the pages and the photos to create a class book. Youngsters' toes will surely be tappin' as you read the book aloud. Be sure to send it home for parents' enjoyment as well!

A PATCHWORK
Of Fine-Motor Activities

Your youngsters will have lots of opportunities to strengthen fine-motor skills when you piece together these ideas to fit your daily curriculum needs.

Wraparounds

Youngsters will get into the groove with this fun activity that gives little fingers a fine-motor workout. Use pinking shears to cut out a variety of seasonal or geometric shapes from tagboard. Tape a length of yarn to the back of each shape. Invite a child to make a design by repeatedly wrapping the yarn around a shape, securing it in the shape's grooves. When he has completed his design, have him unwrap the yarn and begin again. Or make the yarn design permanent by securing the end of the yarn with tape. That's a wrap!

Amy Barsanti—Four-Year-Olds
St. Andrew's Preschool
Nags Head, NC

Confetti Collages

Surprise! This gluing activity is sure to give your little ones plenty of prac-tice using their finger muscles. Use seasonal or thematic hole punchers to punch out a supply of construction-paper confetti. Provide each student with a supply of shapes on a Styro-foam® tray, a sheet of construction paper, and a bottle of glue. To make a collage, a child repeatedly squeezes drops of glue onto her paper, then picks up shapes and presses them onto the glue. What a festive way to improve fine-motor skills!

Amy Reynolds—Four-Year-Olds
Merry Moppet Preschool
Belmont, CA

104

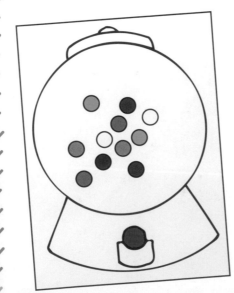

Gumballs Galore

Your little ones will become familiar with colors, as well as exercise their fine-motor muscles, when they make these colorful gumball machines. Supply each child with a sheet of colorful circle stickers and an outline of a gumball machine. Encourage her to peel the stickers from the sheet, then press them onto the paper. When she has peeled and pressed all of her stickers, ask her to point to each gumball and name its color.

Dana Smith—Noncategorical Preschool
Donaldsonville Elementary
Donaldsonville, LA

Ribbon Weaving

Plastic ribbon holders and fabric strips or ribbon are all your youngsters will need to weave up some fine-motor exercise. Visit a fabric store to request discarded ribbon holders. To use the items, a child weaves fabric strips or ribbon through the lattice in the center of a holder. Now that's a center looming with fine-motor fun!

Lynn Cable—Pre-K Special Education
Crystal Lake Elementary
Stuart, FL

Clipping Coupons

Save the coupons in your Sunday newspaper for use with this finger-strengthening activity that will meet the needs of all your preschoolers. Invite younger students to tear out the coupons. Provide older students with scissors and invite them to cut out the coupons using the dotted lines as cutting guides. This idea really makes "cents."

Carri Pawlyshyn—Four-Year-Olds
Boston College Children's Center
Chestnut Hill, MA

Here A Clip, There A Clip

Strengthen little fingers in this center that is a pinch above the rest. Stock a center with clothespins, yogurt containers, plastic plates, and discarded vertical blind samples. Encourage a child to fasten the clothespins to the rims of the items of his choice.

Michele Carter—Pre-K
    Exceptional Education
University Park Elementary
Melbourne, FL

It's Feeding Time!

You'll hear cries of delight as youngsters sharpen their cutting skills in order to feed these hungry characters. Obtain a large, rectangular cardboard box. Stand the box on one end; then cut a slot near the top. On separate sheets of tagboard, draw characters with large mouths. Cut slots out of the mouths; then tape one of the characters to the box so that the slots align.

To use the box, a child cuts appropriate colors of construction paper into shapes, then "feeds" the shapes to the character by inserting them into its mouth. For example, a child might cut leaf shapes from green paper to feed to a dinosaur character or cut cheese shapes from yellow paper to feed to a mouse character. Bon appétit!

Sally Nault-Maurer—Four- And Five-Year-Olds
Learning Readiness Preschool
Anoka, MN

Peg Box

Got It Pegged!

Hand-eye coordination is the skill your little ones will peg with this activity. To make pegs, cut one-inch-diameter dowels into three-inch lengths. Use nontoxic paints to paint the pegs bright colors. Cut several holes slightly wider than the pegs in the top of a baby-wipes container. To use the items, a child inserts the pegs into the holes, then lifts the lid to remove the pegs. For a variation, collect a supply of colorful milk-jug lids. Cut a slot larger than a milk-jug lid in the top of a baby-wipes container. Invite children to insert the lids into the slot. "Kerplunk!"

Ramona Wilson—Preschool
Berry Patch Daycare
Loveland, OH

Minimotor Obstacle Course

Youngsters will be eager to show off their fabulous fine-motor skills with this minimotor obstacle course. Set up several fine-motor stations around your classroom, such as clipping clothes-pins to the rims of cups, picking up beads with tweezers, transferring water using an eyedropper, and others. Direct each child to complete each station before crossing over a desig-nated finish line. Award each child who completes the course with a sticker or other small prize for his efforts.

Tracey Rebock—Preschool
Temple Emanuel
Cherry Hill, NJ

Munching Marbles

Munch, munch, crunch! Youngsters will love feeding this hungry caterpillar as they strengthen their finger muscles. To make one, remove the lid and label from a green two-liter soda bottle. Use pipe cleaners, pom-poms, and paint pens to decorate the bottle to resemble a caterpillar. Put the caterpillar and a container of marbles into a center. Invite children to feed the caterpillar by dropping marbles into the bottle. For an added challenge, have a child count the marbles as he feeds them to the caterpillar. How many marbles can your caterpillar eat?

Rebecca K. Buss—Preschool
St. Luke's Child Day Care Center
Lehigh Valley Child Care
Bethlehem, PA

Squirmy "Wormies"

Transform your water table into a fishing pond where fine-motor skills and sorting practice are the catches of the day! Tint the water in your water table blue; then add a quantity of colorful rubber worms (used for fishing) to the water. Invite a child to use tongs to catch the worms, then sort them into bowls. As an added challenge, have her use her fingers to return the wet worms to the water.

Amy Laubis—Preschool
The Children's Garden
  Preschool
Kenton, OH

Book Features

You're Adorable

A You're Adorable

Words & Music by Buddy Kaye, Fred Wise, and Sidney Lippman
Illustrated by Martha Alexander & Published by Candlewick Press, 1994

A, this book's adorable. *B,* the illustrated children are beautiful. *C,* your little ones are sure to be charmed. Use this book to reinforce a variety of alphabet skills from *A* to *Z.* (For ordering information call Penguin Books at 1-800-253-6476. Or look for it at your library or bookstore.) It won't be long before youngsters are commenting in an alphabetical way, "Teacher, you're A-OK!"

ideas by Carrie Lacher

Singing Through The Alphabet

Start your lyrical journey through the alphabet by first gathering your little ones together to sing a snappy rendition of "The Alphabet Song." Then introduce your students to the lovable text and bright illustrations of *A You're Adorable.* Read the book aloud or sing it (music provided on the inside covers). During subsequent readings, encourage each child to stand up when the letter that begins his name is called. Follow up the letter fun with the following activities that introduce each child to the alphabet and specifically emphasize the letter that begins his name.

Stick With These Letter Puppets

Help your little ones get a real handle on letter skills with these simple stick puppets. Cut letters from tagboard that correspond with the first letters of the children's first and last names. So that you'll have a complete set of alphabet puppets, prepare puppets for any remaining letters. Write each child's name on two craft sticks; then glue each of his letters to the top of a stick. Encourage each child to embellish his letter puppets with the craft items of his choice, such as markers, stickers, plastic jewels, or paper scraps.

During a group time, give each child his puppet that corresponds to the first letter of his name. As you sing the song for the text together, encourage each child to wave his puppet in the air as that letter is named. Later repeat the activity using the letters that correspond to youngsters' last names. As a final variation, provide each child with a different letter of the alphabet, and arrange children in a line by the alphabetical order of their puppets. Let's hear it for the alphabet! Hip, hip, ABC, hooray!

Gee, These Names Look Good To Me

Zoom from letter skills into name recognition with this smart alphabet chart. To prepare the alphabet chart, visually divide a 13-foot length of bulletin-board paper into 26 six-inch-wide columns. Alphabetically label each column with a letter cutout. Mount the chart onto a wall at the children's level. Personalize a 3" x 5" index card for each child. Attach a sticker that corresponds to the first letter of that child's name to the card, if desired. During a group time, gather your little ones by the chart. Give each child her card. As the class identifies the letter in each column, invite each child whose name begins with that letter to attach her card to the chart. When the chart is complete, read all of the names together, identifying the columns with the most and the least names.

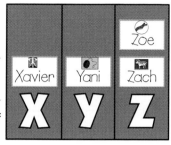

Adorable Adjectives

If your little ones are beginning to recognize the letters that begin and make up their names, then introduce them to the kind and loving words in the book—one letter at a time. Have the group help you make an alphabetical list of the superlative adjectives used in the story's song. Then ask your little ones for additional words that describe someone special, such as *terrific, super,* and *wonderful.* Prepare a center for making love notes by stocking an area with colorful paper, markers, stickers, stamps, and more. Post the list in this center. Encourage each child who visits the center to decorate a note for someone special. Then review the list of adjectives for the child, and ask him to select several for you to write on his note. Challenge older preschoolers to copy their choice of words onto their notes. Now there's a language idea that's *adorable, beautiful, charming, darling, exciting,....*

A Is For Alphabet, *B* Is For Books, *C* Is For Children

It's fun to wander through the alphabet with these additional titles that also feature photographs or illustrations of children.

Action Alphabet: A Is For Arching And Action, Too!
Written & Photographed by Shelley Rotner
Published by Athenuem Books for Young Readers, 1996

AFRO-BETS® ABC Book
Written & Illustrated by Cheryl Willis Hudson
Published by Just Us Books, Inc.; 1987

F Is For Friend

Celebrate the fun of preschool friendships with this class book. Program each letter of the alphabet and the phrase "[Letter] is for..." onto a colorful sheet of construction paper. Arrange the sheets on a large table; then ask each child to find the letter that begins her first name. Photograph each child holding her letter; then take a group picture with each child holding a different letter. When you have a picture of each child, group the photos by the letters that begin the children's names; then cut each group of photos into shapes of objects that begin with that group's letter. For example, cut the pictures of the children whose names begin with the letter *B* into balloon shapes. Mount the photo cutouts on the corresponding pages. Complete each page by writing the name of each pictured child after the phrase, as shown. Embellish the pages with stickers, if desired. Mount the group photo onto a construction-paper cover and title it "*F* Is For Friend." Bind the pages together to prepare the book for sharing during group times and with families. "ABCDEFGee!" What a collection of special friends!

Where The Wild Things Are

Written & Illustrated by Maurice Sendak
Published by HarperCollins Children's Books

Take a walk on the wild side with mischievous Max and his monster friends when you read aloud the 1964 Caldecott Medal winner *Where The Wild Things Are.* Follow up with these activities that are sure to make imaginations soar and leave your little wild things roaring for more!

ideas by Lisa Leonardi

Mischief To Magic

Mischief of one kind and another led to magic with the help of Max's imagination. Prior to this activity, collect a box of household items such as a lamp shade, a stool, a pot lid, and others. Have youngsters reexamine the story's first illustration. What items were inspiration for Max's jungle vines, tent, and wild things? Ask for suggestions and children's help in setting up a similar play setting. For example, you might drape a blanket over a clothesline and add stuffed toys and crepe-paper vines. Place the box of collected items in the center—then stand back and watch your youngsters' imaginations come to life!

Roar Of The Wild

If your wild things are getting restless, the following chant will give them something to roar about! Provide each child with ten Bugles® corn chips to slip onto clean fingertips to represent claws. When the chanting is done, sit down for a snack that's finger-lickin' fun.

Teacher: Wild things, wild things,
Look at you!
Wild things, wild things,
What can you do?

Class: We can roar our roars!   *Roar.*
Gnash our teeth at you!   *Show teeth.*
We can roll our eyes!   *Roll eyes.*
Show our claws, too!   *Extend fingers.*

(Repeat teacher's verse.)

Class: We can eat you up,
'Cause we love you!

Barry Slate

A Wild Rumpus

Do your wild things like to jump, hop, and stomp their feet? If so, a wild rumpus is in order! Provide a volunteer "Max" with a crown and scepter made by inserting a dowel in a Styrofoam® ball. Play some lively music as the group follows Max around the room, copying his movements. When the child is ready to step out of the role of Max and join the group as a monster, he commands, "Now stop!" Select a new Max; then let the rumpus begin again!

Count Those Terrible Teeth

Since Max bid farewell to his ferocious friends, the wild things surely need something to smile about! Using construction paper, wiggle eyes, and the patterns on page 112, prepare ten wild things for a counting center. Label each wild thing with a different numeral from one to ten. To brighten a wild thing's smile, a child arranges the designated number of candy-corn "teeth" on a monster's mouth. Youngsters will smile, too, when you reward their work with a candy-corn snack. Now that's a center your little ones can sink their teeth into!

Wild-Creature Features

Max's creatures certainly have unique features! Have youngsters carefully examine the illustrations and describe the wild things. Then prepare an art center where each child can create his own wild thing. Duplicate onto white construction paper a supply of the wild-creature feature patterns (page 112) and a wild-thing pattern (page 113) for each child. Cut out the patterns; then place them in the center along with a variety of art supplies. To make a wild thing, a child glues his choice of features onto a wild thing, then decorates it as desired. Display the wild things, but beware. They just might come to life!

Monstrous Measuring

Continue to build math skills with this measurement activity using monster feet and jungle vines. Enlarge one of the foot patterns on page 112; then trace the outline a number of times onto heavy paper. Cut out the feet. Cut varying lengths of green crepe-paper streamers. Encourage a pair of children to extend a streamer vine on the floor, then measure its length by placing feet alongside the vine.

WHERE THE WILD THINGS ARE

STORY AND PICTURES BY MAURICE SENDAK

Cover of *Where The Wild Things Are* by Maurice Sendak. ©1963 by Maurice Sendak. By permission of Harper & Row, Publishers.

Wild-Creature Features

Use with "Wild-Creature Features," "Count Those Terrible Teeth," and "Monstrous Measuring" on page 111.

nose

horn

foot

webbed foot

ear

claws

beak

mouth

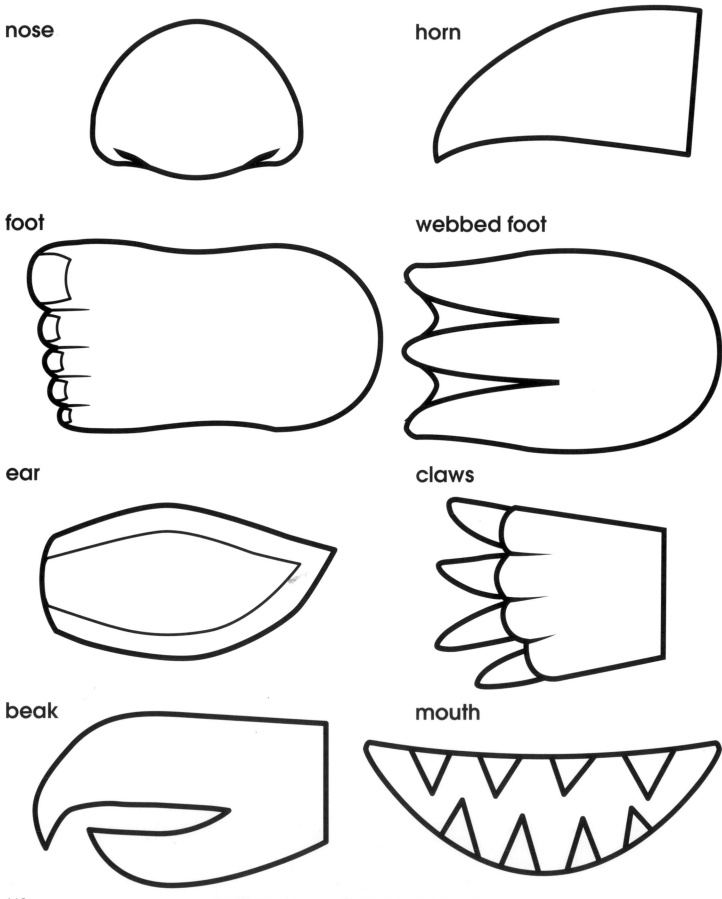

Chicka Chicka

Written by Bill Martin, Jr., and John Archambault
Illustrated by Lois Ehlert
Published by Simon & Schuster Books For Young Readers

"Skit skat skoodle doot. Flip flop flee." Here's a book that's just as fun as can be! Because of the rhythm, rhyme, perky art, and predictable plot, *Chicka Chicka Boom Boom* is sure to be an instant class hit. As you read the story or listen to the tape (tape available with the hardback from Simon & Schuster: 1-800-223-2336), invite youngsters to shake maracas or tap drums for a real "chicka chicka boom boom" effect. Then follow up the reading fun with the following ideas from teachers who are fans of the title. Chicka chicka boom boom!

Class Coconut Tree

There's sure to be enough room for everyone's help when your group makes this coconut-tree mural. Cut out a bulletin-board-paper coconut tree; then mount it to the center of a length of bulletin-board paper. Lay the paper length on newspaper layers on the floor. Provide shallow pans of tempera paint and alphabet sponges. Invite each child to sponge-paint his choice of letters on the paper. Look at all those letters racing up the tree!

Kathleen Tebbe—Preschool
Preston Head Start
Preston, IA

ABCs Up A Tree

Invite each of your little ones to explore the alphabet by making his own letter-filled coconut tree. Put brown and green construction-paper scraps, white construction paper, glue, scissors, magazines, and alphabet stickers in an art or literacy center. Encourage each child to tear the green and brown paper to resemble a coconut tree, then glue the scraps onto a sheet of white paper. Have him arrange alphabet stickers around the tree or cut out letters from magazine pages to glue around the tree. *A, B, C, D, E, F, G.* What letters are up *your* coconut tree?

Keitha-Lynn Stewart—Four-Year-Olds
Little Kids Day Care, Sissonville, WV

Boom Boom

Pam Crane

A J Q L P

I'll Meet You At The Top

This attractive center provides plenty of alphabet learning possibilities for children working independently, with a teacher, or in small groups. Mount a bulletin-board-paper coconut tree to a large magnetic surface (such as one side of a filing cabinet). Cover the tree with clear Con-Tact® covering. Label two sets of 26 index cards with one letter of the alphabet on each card. Store the cards and a set of magnetic letters in containers. Try these activity suggestions:

- Encourage a child to put his choice of magnetic letters on the surface.
- Have the child select a card, find the corresponding magnetic letter, and put it on the surface.
- Select those cards that spell the child's name. Have him arrange the corresponding magnetic letters on the surface.
- Challenge two children to "race" the letters to the top of the tree. Have both children simultaneously select cards and find the matching magnetic letters to put on the surface. The first letter to the top wins.

Look for more ideas for using magnetic letters and numerals in "Magic Of Manipulatives" on pages 258–259.

Tammy Bruhn—Pre-K, Temperance, MI

Is That A Real Coconut?

We know kids learn best from first-hand experiences. Send your little ones up a coconut tree? Certainly not! Bring the coconut to them for some sensory exploration. As a group, explore the feel of a coconut. Listen as you shake it. Use a hammer and nail to drill a hole in the top of the coconut; then drain the milk. Wrap the coconut in a towel; then use the hammer again to crack it open. Use a potato peeler to scrape off small pieces of the meat for tasting. If the taste of the coconut is not quite what your little ones were expecting, invite them to taste shredded baking coconut.

Kathleen Tebbe—Preschool
Preston Head Start, Preston, IA

Pam Crane

Families Climb The Coconut Tree

Looking for a family project to shake up enthusiasm for school learning activities? Invite families to help your class climb up a coconut tree. Cut a large coconut-tree shape from white bulletin-board paper. Have children help you paint the tree; then, when the paint is dry, mount it on a wall or bulletin board. Cut out each letter from tagboard. Begin the project by sending home one letter per family along with a note requesting that they decorate the letter as desired. As each letter is returned, add it to the display along with the family's name. If you have fewer than 26 children in your class, continue sending home letters until you have the entire alphabet on display. Family participation like this calls for a chicka-chicka celebration!

Leah Gerard—Three- To Six-Year-Olds,
    Special Needs
Worthington Hills Elementary
Worthington, OH

"Palm" Tree

Hands down—this coconut tree is a lot of fun to paint! To make one, a child colors a tree trunk on a colorful sheet of construction paper. He then writes the letters of his name on the paper. Next he dips a hand in a shallow pan of green paint, then presses it onto the sheet to resemble coconut-tree fronds. When the paint is dry, he glues on paper coconuts. Whose name is on the way up a coconut tree?

Karen Reed—Three-Year-Olds
Wonder Kids Early Learning Center, Warwick, RI

Will There Be Enough Room?

Your children may race to get up this coconut tree as fast as the letters race to get up the tree in the story. If you have a loft in your classroom, transform it into an alphabetical paradise with these simple suggestions. Cut large coconut-tree fronds out of different shades of green craft foam. Using one sheet of craft foam per letter, cut out the alphabet. Tape the fronds and letters on the loft. If desired, place a selection of additional alphabet-themed books in the area.

Sharon Otto—Preschool, Gallup CDC, Lincoln, NE

Caps, Hats, Socks, And Mittens:
A Book About The Four Seasons

Written by Louise Borden
Illustrated by Lillian Hoban
Published by Scholastic Inc.

From sleds to eggs to bugs to pumpkins, celebrate the seasons from a child's point of view. *Fall* into this book with your students; then *spring* forward with these follow-up activities. *Caps, Hats, Socks, And Mittens* is available in paperback, on audiocassette, or as a big book from Scholastic Inc.: 1-800-724-6527.

ideas by Barbara Meyers

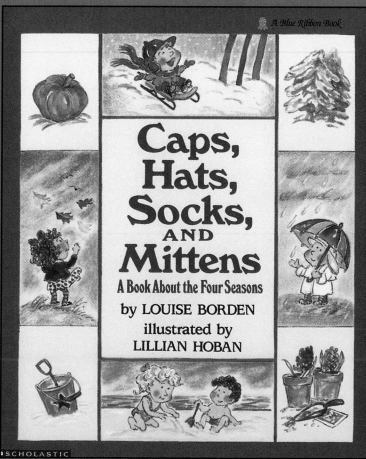

A Blue Ribbon Book

Caps, Hats, Socks, AND Mittens
A Book About the Four Seasons
by LOUISE BORDEN
illustrated by LILLIAN HOBAN

SCHOLASTIC

Illustration by Lillian Hoban from CAPS, HATS, SOCKS, AND MITTENS by Louise W. Borden. Illustrations copyright ©1989 by Lillian Hoban. Used by permission of Scholastic, Inc.

My Favorite Time Of Year

Before reading this book, ask each child to bring from home an item that he wears or uses during his favorite time of the year. Invite him to show his object to the group; then have them guess the corresponding season. After everyone has had a turn, read *Caps, Hats, Socks, And Mittens* aloud. Compare the items in the book to those in the children's collection. Are there any duplicates? If desired, extend this activity by graphing the objects under seasonal headings to find out which season most of the children prefer. Winter, spring, summer, or fall…which season do you like best of all?

Seasonal Senses

Review the senses with your little ones as you look back through this book's charming illustrations. Label each of five pieces of chart paper with a different sense. Instruct a student volunteer to turn to a page in the book and point out an illustrated object. Discuss which senses could be used to experience that object; then list the object on the corresponding sheets. For example, if a child chooses a nut, it could be listed on the "See," "Taste," and "Touch" lists (and others if the child really thinks creatively). What a great way to "summer-ize" the seasons!

Read More About Them

Here's a list of literature that's superbly seasonal!

A Bear For All Seasons
Written by Diane Marcial Fuchs
Published by Henry Holt and Company, Inc.

How Does The Wind Walk?
Written by Nancy White Carlstrom
Published by Macmillan Publishing
   Company

The Berenstain Bears' Four Seasons
Written by Stan & Jan Berenstain
Published by Random House, Inc.

Tell Me A Season
Written by Mary McKenna Siddals
Published by Clarion Books

Winter

W is for *winter,* a cold time of year.
I is for *ice-skating* far and near.
N is for *nighttime,* all snowy and bright.
T is for *trees* with no leaves in sight.
E is for *ears,* so cold and red.
R is for *ready* to ride on my sled!

(Wrap arms around torso and shiver.)
(Pretend to skate.)
(Lay head on "pillow" hands.)
(Stretch arms up like tree branches.)
(Cup hands around ears.)
(Jump up and down with excitement.)

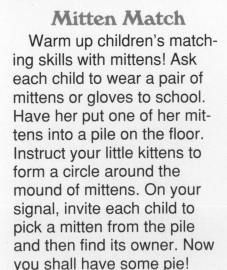

Steven

It's Snowing!

Put a chill in the air with this bell-pepper blizzard. To prepare, mix equal parts of white glue and white tempera paint in a shallow pan. Cut a bell pepper in half as shown; then remove the seeds. Invite each child to use a pepper half to make snowflake prints on a sheet of blue construction paper. Then have him sprinkle his prints with silver or iridescent glitter. After the paint mixture is dry, hang the snowflakes together to create a snowstorm. Brrr, it's cold!

Mitten Match

Warm up children's matching skills with mittens! Ask each child to wear a pair of mittens or gloves to school. Have her put one of her mittens into a pile on the floor. Instruct your little kittens to form a circle around the mound of mittens. On your signal, invite each child to pick a mitten from the pile and then find its owner. Now you shall have some pie!

Spring

S is for *spring*, a wet time of year. (Pretend to hold an umbrella handle.)
P is for *puddles* of mud that appear. (Wiggle hands in a pretend puddle.)
R is for *rain* that falls on the tree. (Ripple fingers down like rain.)
I is for *iris*, the flower for me! (Imitate sniffing a flower.)
N is for *nest*, where eggs can be seen. (Form a nest with hands.)
G is for *grass* that grows tall and green. (Stretch arms high above head.)

"Puddle-licious"!

Ooze your little ones into fine-motor fun with mud! Prepare a puddle for each child by placing a generous scoop of chocolate pudding into a resealable plastic bag. Remove as much of the air from the bag as possible; then seal it. Encourage each youngster to gently flatten her mud puddle on a table and then use her finger to practice letter, numeral, and shape formations. Reward each puddle printer with a spoon. Dig in!

My Flower Garden

Tulips, daffodils, crocuses...spotlight spring by helping your children assemble this nifty bunch of blossoms. To make one flower garden, sponge-paint one-third of a cardboard egg carton brown. Turn the carton over and use an X-acto® knife to slit the top of each egg cup. Color four craft sticks green. To make a flower for each craft-stick stem, glue three tissue-paper circles together at their centers. Glue the flowers to the craft sticks. Glue a pom-pom, sequin, or button to the center of each flower. When the glue is dry, crumple the tissue-paper circles to resemble petals. Glue torn construction-paper leaves to each stem. "Plant" the flowers in the carton's dirt mounds.

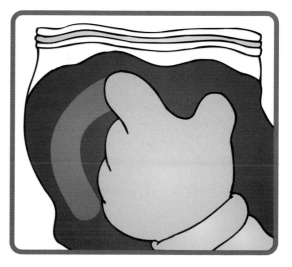

Summer

S is for *summer,* time to sip lemonade.　　(Pretend to drink.)
U is for *umbrella,* giving us shade.　　　　(Curve arms up overhead.)
M is for *many* hot days to go swimming.　　(Make swimming motions with arms.)
M is for *more* baseball games to be winning.　(Imitate swinging a baseball bat.)
E is for *everyone* having lots of fun.　　　　(Pretend to laugh.)
R is for *red* skin warmed by the sun.　　　　(Look up with eyes closed.)

Let's swim!

Toss It Up To Summer

Heat up children's color-recognition skills with a multicolored beach ball. Arrange students in a circle. Give one child the beach ball. Have the rest of the group chant the following rhyme. Instruct the child holding the ball to call out another student's name at the appropriate time in the rhyme; then have him toss the ball to that student. Once the student catches the ball, have her point to and name all of the colors. Continue the summertime toss until everyone has had a turn.

Color Catch
Colors, colors, colors on the beach
　ball.
[Child's name]'s going to catch it and
　name them all!

Build Me A Castle

Grab your shovel and bucket; then use this recipe to entice youngsters to squish and squoosh through the sand to create architectural masterpieces. Provide each child with some sand clay; a craft stick to use as a molding tool; and an assortment of pebbles, seashells, and macaroni to use as embellishments. If desired, have each child construct his castle on a blue plastic plate to represent the sea. Display the completed structures so youngsters can share their sandy sensory experiences with visitors. Ah, summertime at the shore!

Sand Clay
(Makes two cups)
1 cup sand
1/2 cup cornstarch
1 teaspoon alum
3/4 cup hot water

Mix the dry ingredients in a bowl with a spoon. Stir vigorously while adding the hot water. Cook in a pot over medium heat until mixture is thick. Let cool. Molded objects will air-dry in several days.

NOTE: Have the children use the sand clay only under direct supervision. Alum should not be ingested.

Fall

F is for *fall,* time to go back to school.
A is for *air* that's starting to get cool.
L is for *looking* at pumpkins all around.
L is for *leaves* coloring the ground.

(Hold hands in a house shape above head.)
(Shiver.)
(Hold hand above eyes and look from side to side.)
(Ripple fingers down slowly.)

Red, Orange, Yellow, Brown...

Display fall colors all around with this festive artwork. For each child, cut a pumpkin shape from orange crepe paper and four die-cut leaf shapes from coffee filters. Use food coloring to make red-, orange-, yellow-, and brown-colored water in separate bowls. Place the bowls on a newspaper-covered table. To make a pumpkin picture, use straight pins to attach the crepe-paper pumpkin to a piece of white construction paper. Paint over the shape with water to transfer its color. While the water dries, remove the pins. Use clothespins to hold and dip each of the four leaves into a different bowl of colored water. Place the leaves on paper towels to dry. Glue the dried leaves to the bottom of the painted-pumpkin paper.

Laura

Going Nutty

Crack open this center for some nutty fine-motor and math practice. Fill a sensory table with an assortment of nuts, baskets and bowls, and utensils, such as tongs and large spoons. Use this open-ended activity to facilitate counting, matching, sorting, measuring, and any other skills you can go nuts with!

Snowballs

Written & Illustrated by Lois Ehlert
Published by Harcourt Brace & Company

Lois Ehlert's creative collage style and "good stuff in a sack" turn ordinary snowballs into a snow family with a dad, a mom, a boy, a girl, a baby, and even snow pets. After some building and melting, the book concludes with information about snow, pictures of real snowfolk, and a recipe for popcorn balls. Inspire your little ones with this wintry tale and these follow-up activities.

ideas by Lisa Leonardi

Cover of *Snowballs* by Lois Ehlert. ©1995 by Lois Ehlert. Used with permission of Harcourt Brace & Company.

Snowfolk With Style

While you're waiting for a big snow, ask your youngsters and their families to collect "good stuff" for embellishing snowfolk. Ask for items similar to those collected by Lois Ehlert, such as plastic eating utensils, natural items, small toys, fabric scraps, and more. Then, when a good "snowball day" comes along, you'll be ready to roll up some fun making outdoor snowfolk. As your children build snowfolk, take pictures of their progress. Later use the pictures to practice sequencing skills.

No snowball days in your part of the country? Embellish paper snowfolk instead! For each child or pair of children, draw three circles on a length of bulletin-board paper to resemble a snowman. Provide youngsters with those materials in your collection that are lightweight and can be easily glued or taped to the paper. Encourage each child or pair to decorate the snowman as desired.

"Snowdough" Snowballs

With snowballs as the theme, youngsters will flurry to your play-dough center for these hands-on learning experiences. Make a desired amount of the "No-Melt Snow Dough" on page 54; then prepare for the following learning opportunities:

On each of several sheets of construction paper, draw three circles to illustrate small, medium, and large snowballs; then laminate the sheets. Encourage a child to use the dough to make several sizes of snowballs, then place them on a mat.

On sheets of construction paper, draw snowfolk with varying numbers of snowballs. Label each sheet with the corresponding number; then laminate the sheets. Ask a child to prepare a number of dough snowballs, then arrange the appropriate number of snowballs on each sheet.

Snowman Snacks

Invite youngsters to your cooking center to make these tasty treats. To make one, use a craft stick to spread cream cheese onto three miniature butter-popcorn cakes. Arrange the cakes in a row on a napkin. Add pretzel-stick arms and a mouth, eyes and buttons made from chocolate chips. These snowman snacks will melt in your mouth!

Oh, Mr. Sandman

Encourage youngsters to make snowballs at the sand table using damp sand and ice-cream scoopers. Supply twigs, buttons, pebbles, stirring sticks, and other items useful for turning the balls into "sandfolk." Provide sifters for youngsters to use to retrieve the items when the "sandfolk" take a tumble.

All Dressed Up With Nowhere To Snow

Your little ones will enjoy dressing up their own pals as snow pals. Supply a dramatic play center with items that can be used to create "snowpeople," such as a broom, hats, and scarves. Prepare large, laminated paper circles to represent buttons, and provide clothespins for clipping the buttons to clothing. To prepare a carrot nose, laminate a paper carrot; then attach each end of a length of elastic to a side of the carrot. Invite a child to use these items to dress up a partner to resemble a snow boy or girl. Keep your camera handy—these snow pals don't stay around very long!

Sing A Song Of Snowballs

Whether making a collage "snowperson" as described in "Snowfolk With Style" (page 122), a snowman at one of the described centers (pages 123–124), or an outdoor snowman, this song is perfect for singing as you go along.

I Rolled Some Snowballs

(sung to the tune of "I Saw Three Ships")

I rolled some snowballs out of snow,
One winter day, one winter day.
I rolled some snowballs out of snow,
One winter day in the morning.

I rolled a ball big as could be,
One winter day, one winter day.
I rolled a ball big as could be,
One winter day in the morning.

I rolled another—smaller you see,
One winter day, one winter day.
I rolled another—smaller you see,
One winter day in the morning.

I rolled one more; then I had three,
One winter day, one winter day.
I stacked them up quick as could be,
One winter day in the morning.

I saved some "good stuff in a sack,"
One winter day, one winter day.
My snow friend smiled; then I smiled back.
One winter day in the morning.

124

THE VERY HUNGRY CATERPILLAR

Written & Illustrated by Eric Carle
Published by The Putnam Publishing Group

For more than 25 years, the "very hungry caterpillar" has been eating his way into early childhood classrooms. In fact, he's munched his way into a score of countries where Eric Carle's book has been translated into at least 15 languages. The ideas we continue to receive for using this book are a testament to its value for early childhood classrooms. It turns out that the very hungry caterpillar is also the very *helpful* caterpillar! Use his story and the following teacher-tested ideas to reinforce the days of the week, counting, sequencing, and good nutrition.

Puppet Appeal

What could possibly give this story more appeal? How about a reversible caterpillar/butterfly puppet? Hot-glue wiggle eyes and felt stripes to a sock to create the caterpillar. Reverse the sock; then hot-glue wiggle eyes, felt antennae, and decorated felt wings to the inside of the sock. Use the puppet to retell the story as described in the following idea. To change the caterpillar puppet into a butterfly, pull it off one hand, reversing it as you pull. Then slip it onto the opposite hand. It's a beautiful butterfly!

Brenda Hume
Sangaree Elementary School
Summerville, SC

Feed The Caterpillar

Even your most quiet little ones will come out of their cocoons for this activity. In advance make the puppet described in "Puppet Appeal." Then prepare tagboard cutouts representing the type and number of fruits and foods through which the caterpillar ate. Cut a circle through the center of each cutout that is large enough to fit the puppet through. Before retelling the story, give each child one or more cutouts. Then, as you tell the story, invite youngsters to place the cutouts onto the puppet on your arm to represent the caterpillar eating his way through each item. Whew! On Saturday he really will have a stomachache!

Brenda Hume

Creepy Crawlers

With this craft idea, youngsters can make their own puppets for use with your favorite caterpillar songs and fingerplays. Begin by helping each child make three yarn pom-poms. To make one, fold a 3" x 5" index card in half lengthwise; then wrap an eight-foot length of green yarn around the card. Carefully slide the wrapped yarn off the card; then knot a length of yarn around the center of the looped yarn. Cut the loops; then shape the pom-pom. To make the caterpillar, twist part of a bumpy chenille stem around one end of a tongue depressor to represent antennae. Glue wiggle eyes and three pom-poms onto the depressor. Wiggle, wiggle, wiggle away!

Jackie Bartolotta—Pre-K • Cantalician Center For Learning • Amherst, NY

Culinary Caterpillars

That caterpillar had the right idea when he filled up on fruit from Monday through Friday. To prepare a fruit treat for each child, use paper fasteners to connect five small paper cups. At one end of the line of cups, connect a sixth cup upside down. Have each child use markers to add facial features to the upside-down cup in his set. If desired punch a pipe-cleaner through the top of the front cup; then twist it. Provide a supply of fruit so that each child can have one apple piece, two pear pieces, three plum pieces, four strawberry pieces, and five orange pieces. Have each child refer to the book as he counts one apple piece into the first cup, two pear pieces into the second cup, and so forth. Allow youngsters to enjoy their caterpillar snacks while you read aloud another favorite Eric Carle selection.

Patty Jo Glatz—Preschool And Gr. K • Lollipop Tree Preschool • Cora, PA

Caterpillar Cake

Perhaps your little ones prefer the types of treats that the caterpillar enjoyed on Saturday. While they're not as healthful, they sure are fun to nibble on every now and then! Have youngsters help you make this cake as a special treat. In advance bake as many cupcakes as you have children, plus one extra. Using food coloring, tint an amount of icing yellow and tint some coconut green. Prepare one cupcake to be the caterpillar's head by frosting it, then dipping it in coconut. Add chocolate-chip eyes and licorice antennae. Invite each child to frost a cupcake, then dip it in coconut. Have the children arrange the cupcakes so that they form a wiggly caterpillar. Take a picture of your cake; then let the eating begin!

Ruth Stanfill • South Roxana School • South Roxana, IL

A Book For All Ages

Watch a preschooler poke a stubby finger into a hole that the very hungry caterpillar has just eaten through, and you understand why the book appeals to even the youngest of children. Here's a display idea related to the story that also encourages a hands-on approach. Invite each child to fingerpaint a large piece of paper green. When the paint is dry, cut each page into a large circle. Paint a final large circle to resemble the caterpillar's head. Arrange the circles along a wall to create a giant caterpillar. Bet that giant crawler is *really* hungry!

Chris Garchow—Pre-K • St. Paul's Lutheran School
Janesville, WI

Giant Butterfly

How about a giant butterfly to accompany your giant caterpillar display? This class project takes some time, but the result is a beautiful butterfly made with a tissue-paper collage technique similar to the one used by Eric Carle. Cut two halves of a butterfly shape from two pieces of poster board. Tape the two halves together on one side of the shape. Place the butterfly in an art center along with brushes, watered-down glue, and tissue-paper scraps. Invite children to use the brushes and glue to "paint" the scraps onto the shape. When the group feels that the butterfly is complete, display it on a wall near the caterpillar. Magical things are happening!

127

Nursery-Rhyme Units

Hickory, Dickory, Dock!

Only time will tell how popular these activities related to the rhyme "Hickory, Dickory, Dock" will be. We predict that by the time the clock strikes one, you and your little ones will all be having fun!

ideas by Lucia Kemp Henry

Hickory, Dickory, Dock!

Hickory, dickory, dock.
The mouse ran up the clock.
The clock struck one.
The mouse ran down.
Hickory, dickory, dock.

Mouse And Company

Introduce the rhyme; then extend the cast of characters running laps up and down the clock. Modify the rhyme to include the names of different animals. To encourage thinking skills, ask youngsters which animals might move faster or slower up the clock. Also ask them to suggest other types of movements that might be used to scale the clock. "Hickory, dickory, dock. The rabbit hopped up the clock!"

My Own Mouse

To continue your emphasis on positional words, assist each youngster as she makes her own adventure-seeking mouse for use with the following rhyme. To make a mouse, cut a modified oval shape and two circles from felt. Cut two slits in the center of the shape as shown. Punch a hole at the rounded end of the shape; then help the child tie a yarn or ribbon tail through the hole. Direct the child to use generous drops of glue to paste two wiggle eyes and the felt circles to the shape. When the glue is dry, invite the child to slip her finger through the slits and participate in the following action poem.

Where Is The Mouse?

Children:	Where is the mouse?	
Teacher:	Up on top! Up on top the mouse will hop.	*Put mouse on head.*
Children:	Where is the mouse?	
Teacher:	Down inside. Down inside the mouse will hide.	*Cup hand. Put mouse inside.*
Children:	Where is the mouse?	
Teacher:	Over my knee! Over my knee the mouse will flee.	*Move mouse over knee.*
Children:	Where is the mouse?	
Teacher:	Under my hand! Under my hand the mouse just ran.	*Move mouse under hand.*

Scurry Around The Clock

If you and your little ones made the mice described in "My Own Mouse," use them with this hurry-scurry movement activity that reinforces numeral recognition. In advance prepare a large clock face on the floor. Using a plastic hoop as a guide, mark a circle on the floor with colored tape. Next cut the numerals from 1 through 12 out of colorful Con-Tact® covering. Attach them to the floor inside the circle outline to create a clock's face. Invite a child to join you by the clock. Attach a mouse to one of the child's shoes by stringing his shoelace or by guiding his shoe strap through the slits. Count aloud as you strike a block from 1 to 12 times. Encourage the child to scurry clockwise around the clock until the mouse on his shoe has landed on the appropriate numeral. Once familiar with the game, pair students so that one child strikes the block while the other scurries around the clock.

"Tick, tock, says the clock. Tick, tock, one!"

Tick-Tock Counting

Are your little ones getting the hang of "Hickory, Dickory, Dock"? If so, then it's time to practice counting skills. Provide one child in a small group with a tone block or xylophone and a mallet. Provide each of the remaining few children with a pair of rhythm sticks (or tubular wooden blocks). As a group, practice tapping the sticks together twice as you sing "Tick, tock." Next show the child with the block or xylophone how to play it once, twice, and so on. When everyone is ready to play his part, lead the children in the song at the left by tapping a set of sticks together each time you sing, "Tick, tock," and by pausing after each number word as the bell is rung the appropriate number of times.

When The Clock Strikes One, The Family Has Fun

Wind up your activities with this take-home project that lets parents know that when the clock strikes one, it's one-on-one time. To assemble a game bag, have a child color and cut out duplicated copies of the clock, mice, and parent note patterns from pages 132–133. Glue the clock pattern onto a paper lunch bag; then personalize it. Send the game bag home with the parent note and mice tucked inside. "Hickory, dickory, dock. The child puts a mouse in the clock. The clock strikes one. The family has fun! Hickory, dickory, dock!"

Timely Tales

Hickory, Dickory, Dock
Written by Robin Muller
Illustrated by Suzanne Duranceau
Published by Scholastic Inc.

*The Completed
Hickory Dickory Dock*
Written by Jim Aylesworth
Illustrated by Eileen Christelow
Published by
Simon & Schuster, Inc.

13

Patterns

Use with "When The Clock Strikes One, The Family Has Fun" on page 131.

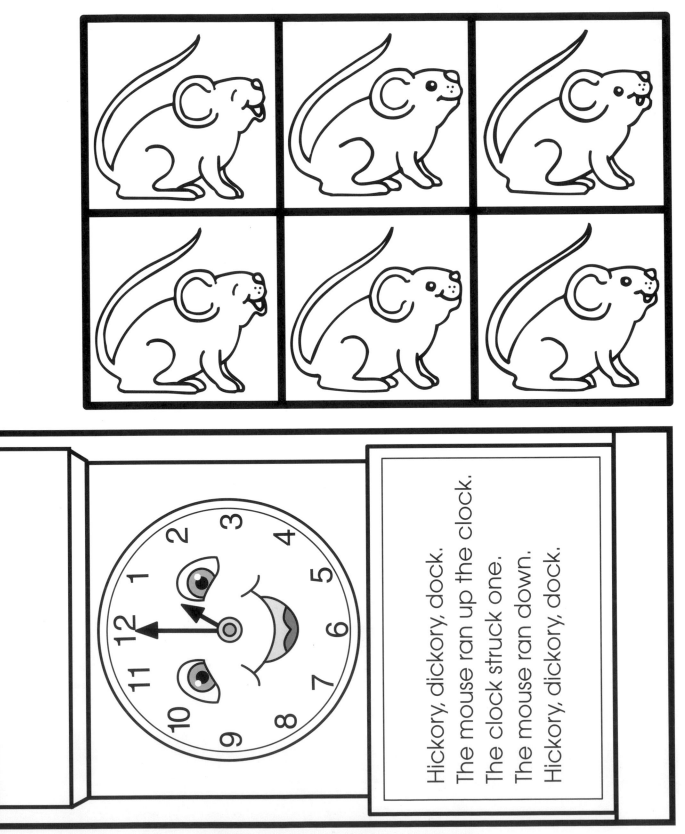

Hickory, dickory, dock.
The mouse ran up the clock.
The clock struck one.
The mouse ran down.
Hickory, dickory, dock.

Parent Note

Use with "When The Clock Strikes One, The Family Has Fun" on page 131.

Dear Parent,

Here's an activity based on the timely rhyme "Hickory, Dickory, Dock." Play this game with your child. By the time the clock strikes one, you'll both be having counting fun!

To play, place the mice on a table along with the open bag. Ask your child to take as many mice as she or he would like from the table. Count the selected mice together; then recite the rhyme, modifying it so that the number words are the same as the number of mice in your child's hand. Have your child drop the mice in the bag. Continue until all of the mice are in the bag; then empty the bag and play again!

Hickory, dickory, dock.
(One) mouse ran up the clock.
The clock struck (one).
The mouse ran down.
Hickory, dickory, dock.

Hickory, dickory, dock.
(Two) mice ran up the clock.
The clock struck (two).
The mice ran down.
Hickory, dickory, dock.

Miss Muffet Goes Modern

Are you familiar with Miss Muffet, her tuffet, and the spider that frightened her away? Use the ideas in this unit to learn about the *new* Miss Muffet and her colorful arachnid friends.

ideas contributed by Lucia Kemp Henry

Little Miss Muffet sat on a tuffet,
Eating her cookies three.
Along came a spider
Who sat down beside her,
And stayed with Miss Muffet for tea!

Out With The Old, In With The New

Recite the familiar rhyme describing Miss Muffet's upsetting encounter. Then recite the updated rhyme above. Ask youngsters to compare and contrast the attitude and circumstances of the two tuffet sitters. Then take a poll. Which Miss Muffet would they rather be?

Miss Muffet's Not The Only One...

According to David Kirk's *Miss Spider's Tea Party* (Scholastic, Inc.), Miss Muffet's not the only one with a fear of spiders. Read aloud this story that stars a friendly spider who invites her insect neighbors to a tea party. Your little ones will be as delighted as the insect guests with Miss Spider's graciousness. Follow up the story by having students make these spider cookies. Then seat youngsters on their tuffets and serve the cookies with some tea.

Spider Cookies

Use a permanent marker to personalize a foil square for each child. Place a 1/4-inch-thick slice of refrigerated cookie dough on each child's square. Direct each child to break four pretzel sticks in half and press eight halves into opposite sides of the slice. Have each child then press two M&M's® brand mini baking bits into his slice to resemble eyes. Place the children's foil squares and cookies on a tray; then bake the cookies according to package directions.

Oh, Miss Muffet; oh, Miss Muffet;
Oh, hello! How do you do?
I'm a small and friendly spider.
May I sit down here with you?

Little spider; little spider,
Oh, hello! How do you do?
You're a small and friendly spider.
Sit **beside** me, please won't you?

Finger Friends

Unlike the original Miss Muffet, your little ones may become fond of spiders when they make these friendly finger puppets. For each child, use a kitchen knife to press a finger-sized hole into a two-inch Styrofoam® ball. Have each child use tempera paint to paint the ball the color of his choice. When the paint is dry, have him press eight pipe-cleaner legs into the ball and glue on wiggle eyes. Press a small piece of masking tape labeled with the child's initials onto the bottom of the spider. Invite youngsters to use their puppets while singing the above song to the tune of "Clementine." Repeat the song, substituting *beside* with *above, below,* and *behind.*

Glue

below

More Finger Fun

The finger fun continues with this booklet project. Duplicate a tuffet pattern (page 138) onto the top and bottom half of each of two sheets of paper. Program each half with a position word *(beside, on, above,* or *below).* Duplicate a class supply of the programmed pages; then cut them in half. Give each child a set of pages stapled together between a cover, if desired. To complete his booklet, a child presses a fingerprint onto the page so that the print's position corresponds to the word on that page. He then uses a marker to add legs and features to each spider.

Miss M's Spider Game

Here's a game that the modern Miss Muffet would proudly endorse. To prepare a game for two players, duplicate a pair of spider patterns and a pair of tuffet patterns (page 138) onto four colors of construction paper. Cut out the patterns. Prepare a spinner displaying the four colors. To begin play, each child is given one of each color of spider and tuffet to arrange in rows in front of him. In turn each child spins the spinner, then places that color of spider on or removes it from its matching tuffet. Play continues until a player's four spiders are seated on matching tuffets.

Miss Muffet's Math Manipulatives

Not only does the modern Miss Muffet invite spiders to stay for tea; she also invites them to participate in math fun. If you think your little ones would enjoy math Miss Muffet's way, duplicate multiple sets of the spider patterns (page 138) onto various colors of construction paper. Cut out the patterns. Draw several large webs on poster board, adding glittery touches to the webs if desired. Working with a small group, use the spiders and webs for all sorts of classification and counting fun.

Get Caught Learning!

Invite parents to get caught having fun with their children when you send home these learning games. For each child, duplicate copies of the spider patterns on page 138 onto several colors of paper; then cut them out. Have each child color a copy of the Miss Muffet pattern and parent note (page 137). Glue the pattern onto a paper lunch bag; then personalize the bag. Send the bag home with the parent note and spiders tucked inside.

Dear Parent,

No need to fear when these spiders are near! They're here for all sorts of math fun! Recite the traditional Miss Muffet rhyme with your child. Then recite the updated rhyme about the modern Miss Muffet. For fun, sort Miss Muffet's arachnid friends by color. Or make patterns using two colors of spiders. Miss Muffet and her spiders hope you get caught in a web of learning fun!

Little Miss Muffet sat on a tuffet,
Eating her curds and whey.
Along came a spider
Who sat down beside her,
And frightened Miss Muffet away!

Little Miss Muffet sat on a tuffet,
Eating her cookies three.
Along came a spider
Who sat down beside her,
And stayed with Miss Muffet for tea!

Little Miss Muffet

Patterns

Use with "More Finger Fun" on page 135, and "Miss M's Spider Game," "Miss Muffet's Math Manipulatives," and "Get Caught Learning!" on page 136.

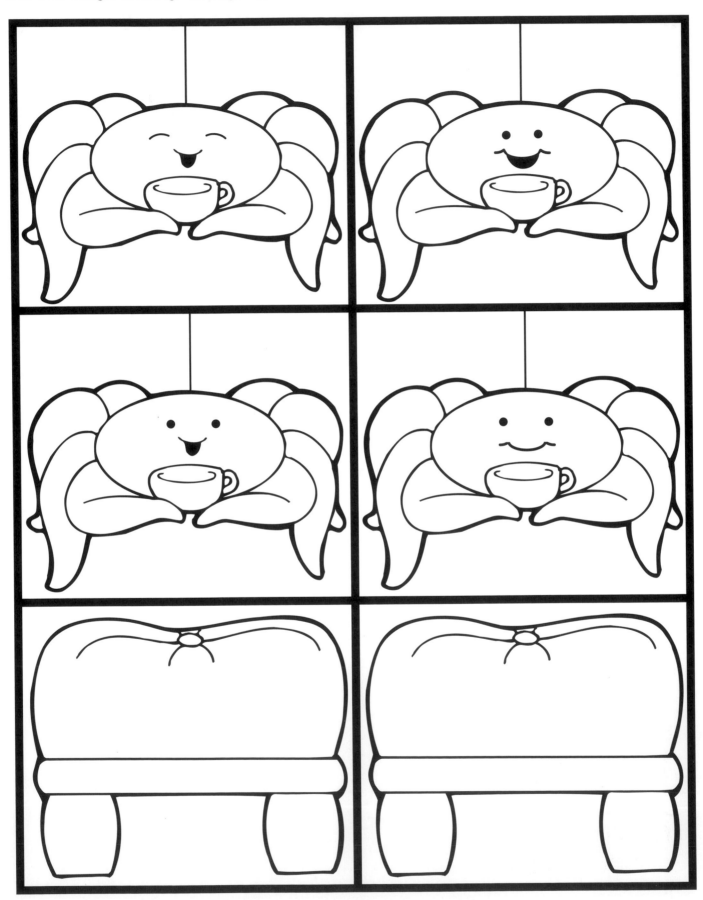

Jack Be Nimble, Jill Be Quick

It's time to update the classic nursery rhyme about jumping Jack and his candlestick. These activities for Jacks *and* Jills will fill your classroom with active learners!

Jack Be Nimble—And Jill Jump, Too!

To prepare candle flannelboard pieces, duplicate the patterns on page 143 onto various colors of construction paper. Laminate. Cut out the candles; then back them with felt. Introduce the original rhyme. Then invite youngsters to help you modify the rhyme as you place different colors, numbers, and sizes of candles on your flannelboard (see the candle below). Then place the pieces and the board in a center for children to enjoy independently.

Jack jump over the candlestick.

Jill be nimble. Jill be quick.
Jill jump over the candlestick.

Jack be nimble. Jack be quick.
Jack jump over **two** candlesticks.

Jill be nimble. Jill be quick.
Jill jump over the **red** candlestick.

Jack be nimble. Jack be quick.
Jack jump over the **tall** candlestick.

Jumping Jacks And Jills

Get youngsters' legs, feet, arms, and hands moving with this bouncy song. Your children will jolly well enjoy jumping along!

The Jumping Song
(sung to the tune of "B-I-N-G-O")

Let's jump up and down right now,
'Cause jumping's lots of fun, oh!
Jump! Jump! Jump! Jump! Jump!
Jump! Jump! Jump! Jump! Jump!
Jump! Jump! Jump! Jump! Jump!
Oh, jumping's lots of fun, oh!

Let's jump with our arms out
    wide…
Let's jump with our arms up
    high…
Let's jump with our hands on
    heads….
Let's jump with our hands on
    hips…

—Lucia Kemp Henry

139

This Little Light Of Mine

Youngsters will jump at the chance to make these candle look-alikes. To make one, use tempera paint to paint a cardboard tube. When the paint is dry, decorate the tube using additional paint or seasonal stickers. Personalize the candle. Gently crumple a ten-inch square of yellow or orange tissue paper; then tape the paper inside the tube to resemble a flame. If desired, spray the tissue-paper flame with adhesive glitter, or dribble glue over the flame and sprinkle on glitter. Arrange the candles in a window, or use them with the following activities.

Jump For Joy!

Keep your little jitterbugs jumping, jiggling, and generally wiggling with this movement activity. Seat youngsters in an open area; then ask them to brainstorm additional ways that Jack could move over or around the candlestick, such as *march, run,* or *slide.* Write each movement word on a separate index card. Also write each child's name on an index card. Place the sets of cards in separate containers. Provide each child with his candle (see "This Little Light Of Mine"). From the two containers, select a movement card and a name card. (If desired, display the selected cards in a pocket chart.) Then ask the child whose name was chosen to place his candle on the floor for the group to admire. Encourage him to move over or around the candle in the suggested manner as the group chants the rhyme, substituting the child's name and the movement. Return the movement card to the container. Play until each child has been featured in the activity.

Rodney

march

Leaps And Bounds

Your little ones will be as nimble as Jack when they participate in this simple but fun musical activity. Randomly arrange the children's candles (see "This Little Light Of Mine") on the floor in an open area of your room, making sure there is plenty of room for jumping over the candles. Direct the children to dance freely about the room—jumping over candles in their paths—as you play a lively instrumental selection.

Once the children have warmed up, try this variation that emphasizes listening skills as well as spatial awareness. Ask each child to stand beside his own candle. Designate a group to pick up their candles and dance and jump about the room as the music plays. For example, ask the Jacks (boys) only or the Jills (girls) only to move. Or request that those children with a specific color of candle dance. Everyone is sure to have some hot movement fun!

My Own Candlestick

Your little Jacks and Jills will delight in making their own candles. Half-fill a coffee can with cold water. Place about one pound of household paraffin wax and some crayon pieces in a second, identically sized coffee can. Half-fill a pot of water; then bring it to a boil. Place the can of wax in the water. Stir the wax as it melts. When the wax has melted, place the can along with the can of water onto a work surface that has been protected with newspaper. For each child, cut a length of heavy cotton string so that it is slightly longer than the height of the can. Tie the string to one of the rounded corners of a clothes hanger. Direct the child to hold the opposite end of the clothes hanger as he repeatedly dips his string alternately into the wax, then into the cold water. When the candle is the desired width, flatten the bottom of the warm candle by pressing it onto the tabletop. Cut the candle off the string, leaving enough string for a wick. If desired, provide each child with a ball of clay or Crayola® Model Magic®. Direct him to shape the clay into a candleholder. Encourage youngsters to present their candles and holders as gifts to loved ones.

Luminous Learning

These take-home projects will shed some light on the ease with which parents can help youngsters learn at home. For each child, duplicate a copy of the parent note (page 142) onto yellow paper. Duplicate a set of candles and the nursery-rhyme pattern (pages 142 and 143) onto white construction paper. Cut out the note and patterns. Direct each child to color the nursery-rhyme pattern, then glue it to a personalized paper bag. Direct her to color each of her candles a different color. Place the candles in her bag; then fold down the top of the bag. Tape the parent note to the top of the bag; then tape the bag closed. Have each child take her bag home for some family fun.

Bright Learning Ideas!

- Ask your child to arrange the candles from shortest to tallest or from tallest to shortest.

- Ask your child to place a specific color of candle or number of candles on the floor. Modify the rhyme as he/she jumps over the candle(s).

(Child's name) be nimble. (Child's name) be quick.
(Child's name) jump over the (color) candlestick!

(Child's name) be nimble. (Child's name) be quick.
(Child's name) jump over (number) candlestick(s)!

Jack be nimble.
Jack be quick.
Jack jump over
The candlestick!

More Bright Ideas

For lots of hands-on ideas using candles, see "The Magic Of Manipulatives" on pages 256–257.

Mary, Mary, How Does Your Garden Grow?

Come into the garden to see how Mary's rows of lovely flowers grow! Use the ideas in this unit with your little ones and you're sure to sow some seeds of learning.

by Lucia Kemp Henry

Mary, Mary, Quite Contrary

Mary, Mary, quite contrary,
How does your garden grow?
With silver bells and cockleshells,
And pretty maids all in a row.

Fabulous Faux Flowers

The next best thing to Mary's own garden blossoms are the flowers that your little ones make to accompany the following rhyme. To make a flower puppet, glue a Styrofoam®-ball half onto a paper bag; then add a paper stem, leaves, and flower petals. Glue wiggle eyes onto the Styrofoam® ball. Reinforce the size concepts presented in this poem by displaying the tall, medium-sized, and short flowers from the centerfold. Then invite each child to slip his puppet over his hand and to participate in the following action poem. Keep Mary's figure nearby so she can keep an eye on her flowers, no matter what their size.

Flowers All In A Row

Children: Mary, Mary, tell us, Mary! How does your garden grow?
Teacher: I bought a lot of pretty flowers and planted each kind in a row.
Children with puppets line up in a row.

Children: Mary, Mary, tell us, Mary! How does your garden grow?
Teacher: I planted all the **big, tall** flowers in a nice, straight row.
Children hold puppets up high.

Children: Mary, Mary, tell us, Mary! How does your garden grow?
Teacher: I planted all the **medium-sized** flowers in a nice, straight row.
Children hold puppets at chest level.

Children: Mary, Mary, tell us, Mary! How does your garden grow?
Teacher: I planted all the **small, short** flowers in a nice, straight row.
Children hold puppets at knee level.

My Own Candlestick

Your little Jacks and Jills will delight in making their own candles. Half-fill a coffee can with cold water. Place about one pound of household paraffin wax and some crayon pieces in a second, identically sized coffee can. Half-fill a pot of water; then bring it to a boil. Place the can of wax in the water. Stir the wax as it melts. When the wax has melted, place the can along with the can of water onto a work surface that has been protected with newspaper. For each child, cut a length of heavy cotton string so that it is slightly longer than the height of the can. Tie the string to one of the rounded corners of a clothes hanger. Direct the child to hold the opposite end of the clothes hanger as he repeatedly dips his string alternately into the wax, then into the cold water. When the candle is the desired width, flatten the bottom of the warm candle by pressing it onto the tabletop. Cut the candle off the string, leaving enough string for a wick.

If desired, provide each child with a ball of clay or Crayola® Model Magic®. Direct him to shape the clay into a candleholder. Encourage youngsters to present their candles and holders as gifts to loved ones.

Luminous Learning

These take-home projects will shed some light on the ease with which parents can help youngsters learn at home. For each child, duplicate a copy of the parent note (page 142) onto yellow paper. Duplicate a set of candles and the nursery-rhyme pattern (pages 142 and 143) onto white construction paper. Cut out the note and patterns. Direct each child to color the nursery-rhyme pattern, then glue it to a personalized paper bag. Direct her to color each of her candles a different color. Place the candles in her bag; then fold down the top of the bag. Tape the parent note to the top of the bag; then tape the bag closed. Have each child take her bag home for some family fun.

Bright Learning Ideas!

- Ask your child to arrange the candles from shortest to tallest or from tallest to shortest.

- Ask your child to place a specific color of candle or number of candles on the floor. Modify the rhyme as he/she jumps over the candle(s).

(Child's name) be nimble. (Child's name) be quick.
(Child's name) jump over the (color) candlestick!

(Child's name) be nimble. (Child's name) be quick.
(Child's name) jump over (number) candlestick(s)!

Jack be nimble.
Jack be quick.
Jack jump over
The candlestick!

More Bright Ideas

For lots of hands-on ideas using candles, see "The Magic Of Manipulatives" on pages 256–257.

Parent Note

Use with "Luminous Learning" on page 141.

Bright Learning Ideas!

- Ask your child to arrange the candles from shortest to tallest or from tallest to shortest.

- Ask your child to place a specific color of candle or number of candles on the floor. Modify the rhyme as he/she jumps over the candle(s).

(Child's name) be nimble. (Child's name) be quick.
(Child's name) jump over the (color) candlestick!

(Child's name) be nimble. (Child's name) be quick.
(Child's name) jump over (number) candlestick(s)!

Nursery-Rhyme Pattern

Use with "Luminous Learning" on page 141.

Mary, Mary, How Does Your Garden Grow?

Come into the garden to see how Mary's rows of lovely flowers grow! Use the ideas in this unit with your little ones and you're sure to sow some seeds of learning.

by Lucia Kemp Henry

Mary, Mary, Quite Contrary

Mary, Mary, quite contrary,
How does your garden grow?
With silver bells and cockleshells,
And pretty maids all in a row.

Fabulous Faux Flowers

The next best thing to Mary's own garden blossoms are the flowers that your little ones make to accompany the following rhyme. To make a flower puppet, glue a Styrofoam®-ball half onto a paper bag; then add a paper stem, leaves, and flower petals. Glue wiggle eyes onto the Styrofoam® ball. Reinforce the size concepts presented in this poem by displaying the tall, medium-sized, and short flowers from the centerfold. Then invite each child to slip his puppet over his hand and to participate in the following action poem. Keep Mary's figure nearby so she can keep an eye on her flowers, no matter what their size.

Flowers All In A Row

Children: Mary, Mary, tell us, Mary! How does your garden grow?
Teacher: I bought a lot of pretty flowers and planted each kind in a row.
Children with puppets line up in a row.

Children: Mary, Mary, tell us, Mary! How does your garden grow?
Teacher: I planted all the **big, tall** flowers in a nice, straight row.
Children hold puppets up high.

Children: Mary, Mary, tell us, Mary! How does your garden grow?
Teacher: I planted all the **medium-sized** flowers in a nice, straight row.
Children hold puppets at chest level.

Children: Mary, Mary, tell us, Mary! How does your garden grow?
Teacher: I planted all the **small, short** flowers in a nice, straight row.
Children hold puppets at knee level.

Sand-Table Flower Garden

Challenge youngsters to plant flowers of all heights and sizes right in your sand table. Enhance your sand center with small plastic shovels, empty yogurt containers, and a basket of inexpensive, fake flowers in three different heights. (Trim the stems of the flowers, if necessary.) As your little gardeners plant pots and rows of flowers, demonstrate how to compare the sizes of the flowers using words such as *big, tall, tallest, short, shorter, shortest,* and so forth.

Flower Garden

How did your youngsters' sand-table garden grow? Did it bloom with colorful faux blossoms? Follow up their dramatic play by reading aloud *Flower Garden* by Eve Bunting (Harcourt Brace & Company). As you read, point out the steps the girl takes in creating her garden, from putting the "garden in a shopping cart" to putting the "garden in a window box." After reading, take your youngsters on a visit to a garden center to see and smell all the flowers they'll find there. If a trip is not possible, purchase a bunch of inexpensive flowers from a florist. Give your budding flower specialists plenty of time to observe the blossoms with their eyes and noses; then invite floral descriptions blooming with special scents and wonderful colors.

Colorful Flowers Game

Prepare this simple game for partners that looks like the container of colorful flowers that the girl in *Flower Garden* prepared for her mother. To prepare the game, obtain a large, six-section, plastic seedling container from a nursery; six 2 1/2-inch Styrofoam® eggs; five artificial flowers (red, blue, yellow, purple, and orange); and a green leaf stem. Paint each Styrofoam® egg one of the six colors. When the paint is dry, hot-glue each egg—wide end up—into a section of the container. Use a pencil to poke a hole into each egg. Cut a construction-paper square in each of the six colors. To play, each partner in turn draws a square, says the color, and then puts the matching flower or leaf stem into the corresponding section of the container. Wow! What pretty flowers you planted together!

Sing A Colorful Song

Continue the emphasis on colorful flowers and how they grow by teaching your little ones this song. Distribute one red, orange, yellow, blue, or purple artificial flower to each child in the group. Encourage the children to move their flowers as suggested. Sing the final two lines of the song slowly, encouraging each youngster to hold up her flower as its color is mentioned.

Sing A Song Of Flowers
(sung to the tune of "Sing A Song Of Sixpence")

Sing a song of flowers, flowers all around.　　*Wave flower.*

Flowers that are growing, growing in the ground.　　*Hold flower near ground.*

Flowers of each color make a pretty view.　　*Hold flower in front of eyes.*

Red and orange and yellow,　　*Hold flower above head.*

And blue and purple, too!

Plant A Garden Of Home Learning

Prepare this flower-themed activity to send home with each child for a special home delivery of learning fun. To assemble a game bag for each child, have a child color a copy of the patterns on page 148. Cut out the patterns; then glue Mary onto a colorful paper bag. Personalize the bag. Tuck the flower patterns and parent note inside the bag. If desired, fold the top of the bag down once; then punch two holes side by side through the thicknesses. Insert an artificial flower's stem through the holes, securing it with tape, if necessary. Mary's rhymes and flowers are sure to help your youngsters' home learning experiences grow!

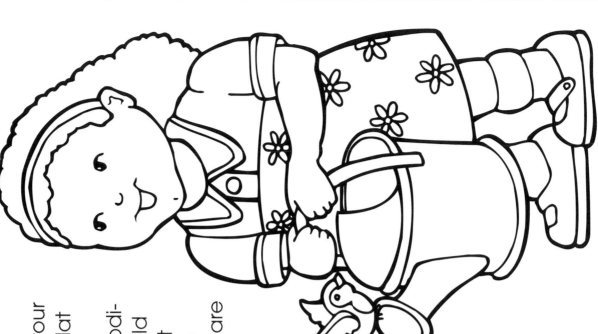

Dear Parent,

Mary and her rows of flowers are sure to help you and your child grow a garden of learning fun! To play, lay the bag flat on a table along with the flowers. Review the traditional rhyme as shown on the bag. Then recite a verse of the modified rhyme below, inserting your child's name. Ask your child to find the three flowers that match the description in that verse, and to arrange the flowers in a row. Continue in the same manner for each verse until all three sizes of flowers are "planted" in nice, straight rows.

(Child's name), (Child's name), tell me, (Child's name),
How does your garden grow?
My very special garden grows
With **tall** flowers in a row.

(Child's name), (Child's name), tell me, (Child's name),
How does your garden grow?
My very special garden grows
With **short** flowers in a row.

(Child's name), (Child's name), tell me, (Child's name),
How does your garden grow?
My very special garden grows
With **medium** flowers in a row.

Patterns

Use with "Plant A Garden Of Home Learning" on page 146.

Mary, Mary, quite contrary,
How does your garden grow?
With silver bells and cockleshells,
And pretty maids all in a row.

One, Two, Three, Four, Five; I Caught A Fish Alive!

Have you been casting about for fresh learning opportunities for your little ones? If so, use this traditional rhyme and a new version of it to keep your youngsters hooked on counting.

by Lucia Kemp Henry

One, two, three, four, five;
I caught a fish alive.
Six, seven, eight, nine, ten;
I let it go again.
Why did you let it go?
Because it bit my finger so.
Which finger did it bite?
The little finger on the right.

A Fishy Favorite

Develop your little ones' counting skills with this traditional rhyme. As you recite the rhyme, put flannel numerals on your board. Then throw back that fishy rhyme, and reel in some one-to-one correspondence practice. As you recite the new rhyme (at the right), place the correct number of fish-shaped flannel pieces (pattern on page 154) onto your board. Then take them off as you count down.

One, two, three, four, five;
I caught some fish alive.
Six, seven, eight, nine, ten;
I caught some fish again.
Why should you let them go?
Because they like to swim, you know.
I'll let them swim away,
So I can fish another day.
Ten, nine, eight, seven, six, five, four,
three, two, one!

A School Of Swimmers

Count on these fish puppets to put a spatial spin on number discovery. For each child, duplicate two copies of the patterns on page 152 onto construction paper. To make one puppet, color the tails and draw a smile on each of the two body patterns. Glue a wiggle eye on each fish-body pattern. Sponge-paint both body patterns; then sprinkle on glitter. When the paint and glue are dry, cut out the patterns. Glue a set of patterns to each side of a Mrs. Grossman's™ mini sticker bag. When the glue is dry, glue the front ends of both fish together, clipping them together until the glue is dry.

When each child has made a fish puppet, have the children put their hands in their puppets. Ask ten children to raise or wiggle their puppets in turn as you count aloud and recite the rhymes on page 149. For even more fabulous fish fun, ask each child to sit on the floor, remove a shoe, and put his puppet on his foot. Encourage youngsters to lift their legs and wiggle those fish through the air.

I Caught A Fish!

By now your little ones are probably ready to test the waters and hook some fish on their own! Make a fishing pole and fish so youngsters can angle for fish at your water table and reel in a mess of motor experiences at the same time. To make a school of fish, trace the small fish pattern on page 154 onto colorful craft foam the desired number of times. Cut out the fish. (Keep the scraps for the *Fish Eyes* activity on page 151.) Use dimensional fabric paint to add smiles and to glue jewel eyes onto the fish. Trim strips of magnetic tape; then attach the pieces to the fishes' tails. Make a fishing pole by tying a length of yarn around a wooden dowel. Secure the yarn with tape. Tie the opposite end of the yarn around a magnet. Once the fish are floating in your water table, encourage each child to take a turn at reeling them in. Let's count the catch! One, two, three,…

Go Fish

To make the fishing at your water table more of a challenge, prepare counting mats. Duplicate 55 of the fish cards on page 153 onto construction paper; then cut them out. Label each of ten sheets of construction paper with a different numeral from one to ten. Glue the corresponding number of fish cards to each sheet. Laminate the sheets. Store them in a bucket near the water table. Encourage a child to select a mat. Have her put each fish she catches on the mat until the number of foam fish is the same as the number of fish on the mat. Remind her to put the fish back so she can fish again!

Fishing For Home Learning

Invite parents to reel in some one-on-one time with their children with this take-home counting and numeral-identification game. For each child, duplicate a copy of the game patterns and parent note on pages 153–154. Have each child color his pages; then cut them out. Also have him color a small paper plate blue. To assemble a game for each child, fold the poem pattern along the bold line; then cut on the broken lines. Tape the bottom portion of the pattern to the bottom of the plate, curving the pattern as necessary so that it stands up. Put a second plate below the first; then staple the plates together to secure the pattern. Tuck the parent note, fish cards, and numeral cards into a resealable plastic bag; then send the materials home. Parents and children alike will get hooked on learning fun.

Fish Eyes:
A Book You Can Count On

The school of colorful fish in this book by Lois Ehlert (Harcourt Brace & Company) is sure to open your youngsters' eyes to the fun of counting. In fact, when they cast their eyes on this fishy number line, it will be hard to keep them away from playing with numbers. To make the number line, use the large fish pattern on page 154 to prepare ten construction-paper fish. Tape three 5" x 28" strips of poster board together end-to-end; then glue on the fish cutouts. Number the fish. To make the manipulative fish eyes, cut ten one-inch circles and ten half-inch circles from colorful craft foam. Glue a smaller circle to each larger circle; then attach the loop side of a piece of self-adhesive Velcro® to the back of each set of circles. Attach the hook side of a piece of self-adhesive Velcro® to each fish. To use the number line, a child places an eye on each fish as she counts in order from one to ten.

Patterns
Use with "A School Of Swimmers" on page 150.

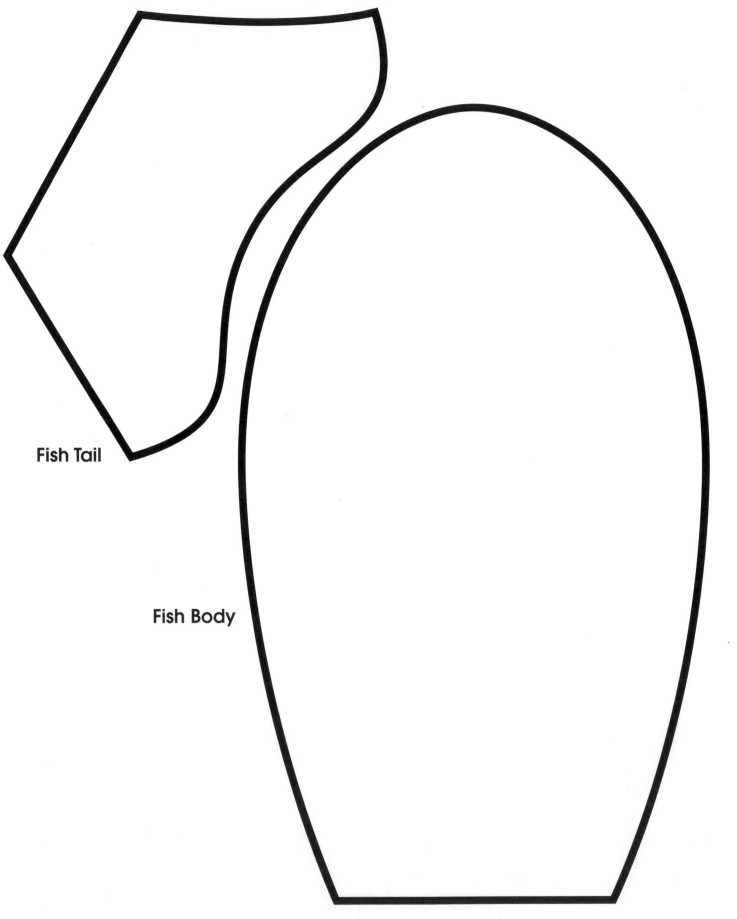

Fish Tail

Fish Body

poem pattern

One, two, three, four, five;
I caught a
fish alive!

©The Education Center, Inc. • *THE MAILBOX* • *Preschool* • June/July 1998

Fish Cards

Use also with "Go Fish"
on page 150.

numeral cards

4

5

1

2

3

Dear Parent,

One, two, three, four, five! With this fishy game, counting comes alive! Begin by asking your child to help you chant the traditional rhyme below. Then put the fish cards, numeral cards, and fishing game on a table.

- Ask your child to pick a numeral, then count that number of fish into the pond.
- Put a number of fish in the pond. Then have him/her count the fish and find the corresponding numeral.

Have fun helping your little one get hooked on counting!

One, two, three, four, five;
I caught a fish alive.
Six, seven, eight, nine, ten;
I let it go again.
Why did you let it go?
Because it bit my finger so.
Which finger did it bite?
The little finger on the right.

©The Education Center, Inc. • *THE MAILBOX*® • *Preschool* • June/July 1998

Large Fish Pattern

Use with *Fish Eyes: A Book You Can Count On* on page 151.

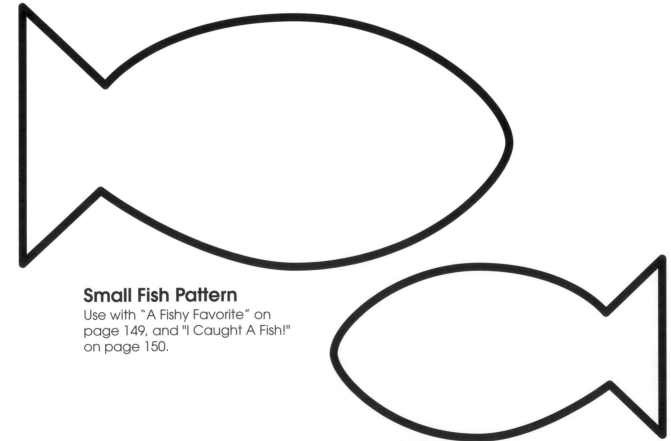

Small Fish Pattern

Use with "A Fishy Favorite" on page 149, and "I Caught A Fish!" on page 150.

©The Education Center, Inc. • *THE MAILBOX*® • *Preschool* • June/July 1998

Diddle, Diddle, Dumpling

What happens when a very sleepy boy gets ready for bed? You're provided with a chance to review opposites, practice matching skills, and discuss bedtime routines. Diddle, diddle, dumpling—thank you, John!

by Lucia Kemp Henry

One Shoe Off And One Shoe On

Diddle, diddle, dumpling;
   my son John
Went to bed with his trousers on;
One shoe off and one shoe on.
Diddle, diddle, dumpling;
   my son John.

Prior to introducing the rhyme, duplicate the pattern on page 158. Color the pattern; then cut it out. Display the picture. Ask students to describe what is off, what is on, what *should* be on, and what *should* be off.

Sing the following song to tell this ready-for-bed boy good night!

Good Night, John
(sung to the tune of "Are You Sleeping?")

Time for sleeping; time for sleeping.
Good night, John. Good night, John.
Do you have your shoes off?
Do you have pajamas on?
Good night, John! Good night, John!

155

Off Or On?

This movement activity will get your youngest students off to a great start in understanding the opposite pair *off* and *on*. In advance, gather pairs of adult-sized clothing items, such as a pair of large shoes, garden gloves, loose socks, and boots. Give each different pair of items to a child in the group to put on. Direct these children to stand up. Lead the remainder of the group in chanting the following rhyme, modifying it until each standing child has been directed to take off one of his items. Repeat the activity until each child has demonstrated the concepts *off* and *on.*

Diddle, diddle, [Child's name]; dee-dee-don.
One thing's off and one thing's on.
One [shoe] off and one [shoe] on.
Diddle, diddle, [Child's name]; dee-dee-don.

Footwear Pairs

Pairing things up and putting them on continue in this activity that focuses on footwear. Prepare a center by filling a shoe rack with a selection of footwear, such as beach thongs, shoes with buckles, slip-on loafers, sneakers with Velcro® fasteners, and tennis shoes with laces. Also provide a stack of shoeboxes to serve as sorting containers. To use this center, have a pair of youngsters match the shoes and then put each pair in a box. Ask the students to sort the shoes according to style or fastener. When the shoes have been sorted, suggest that the children try them on. After all of your youngsters have tried this center on for size, take a survey to find out which footwear pair your youngsters found the easiest to fasten.

Searching For Socks

After you prepare a center for shoes, prepare one for socks, too. Ask each child to bring a pair of socks to school. Write each child's name on two small pieces of masking tape; then attach the tape to each of the child's socks. Place the socks in a laundry basket. Write each child's name on a separate clothespin. Hang a length of clothesline in the center; then arrange the clothespins on the line. To use the center, a child finds the matching socks in the laundry basket. He then hangs the pair on the line using the clothespin labeled with the corresponding child's name.

It's Bedtime, Already?

When a young child such as John gets ready for bed, he encounters lots of things that go together. To help your little ones master their bedtime routines, enlarge and reproduce the picture cards on page 158. Color the pictures. Laminate them, if desired, before adding felt to their backs. Randomly arrange the cards on your flannelboard; then challenge a group of children to match the picture cards that go together. When the cards are paired, ask each child to tell you how she would use these items and the order in which she would use them when preparing for bed. Ready for bed?

Bedtime Routine

Here's a book and activity that will put your preschoolers right in the middle of the bedtime muddle without the real-life mess. Read *Piggy Washes Up* by Carol Thompson (Candlewick Press) for a hilarious presentation of those perplexing bedtime chores. Follow Piggy through his bedtime routine; then ask your little ones to compare their routines to that of this purposeful pig. Finally ask youngsters to reenact the bedtime tasks in the sequence that Piggy followed.

Time For Bed, Sleepyhead

As the nursery rhyme has shown, getting ready for bed can sometimes be a challenge for our preschool friends. This take-home game provides parents with an opportunity to pair up with their children in an activity that helps make bedtime a familiar routine. Duplicate and cut out a class supply of the parent letter, picture cards, and envelope pattern (on pages 158–159). Direct each child to color a set of the envelope pattern and cards. Glue each child's envelope pattern to a personalized envelope; then tuck the cards and parent letter inside the envelope. Learning and family fun make quite a match!

Patterns

Use with "It's Bedtime, Already?" and "Time For Bed, Sleepyhead" on page 157.

washcloth

soap

toothpaste

toothbrush

comb

brush

pajama pants

pajama top

blanket

pillow

Diddle, diddle, dumpling;
my son John
Went to bed with his trousers on;
One shoe off and one shoe on.
Diddle, diddle, dumpling;
my son John.

Use also with "One Shoe Off And One Shoe On" on page 155.

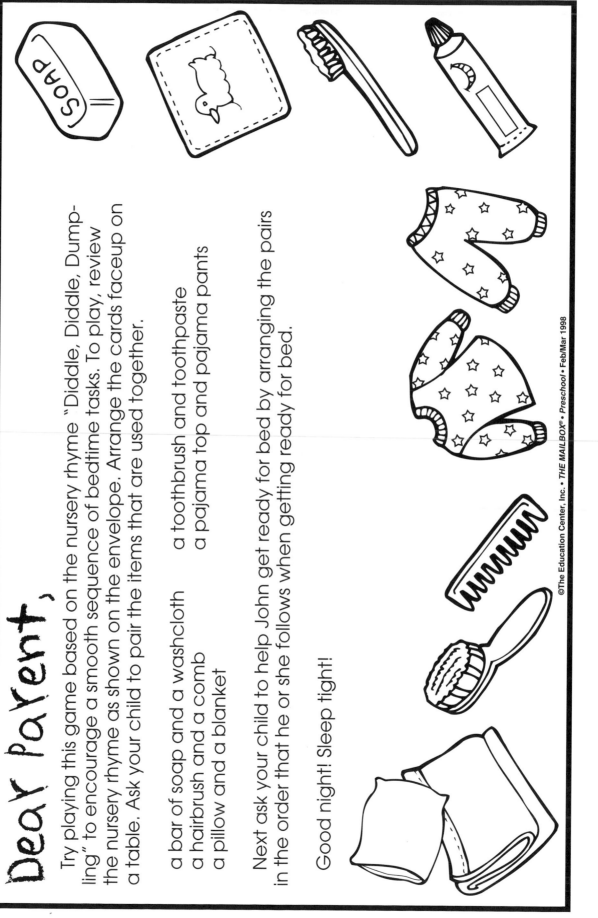

Dear Parent,

Try playing this game based on the nursery rhyme "Diddle, Diddle, Dumpling" to encourage a smooth sequence of bedtime tasks. To play, review the nursery rhyme as shown on the envelope. Arrange the cards faceup on a table. Ask your child to pair the items that are used together.

a bar of soap and a washcloth   a toothbrush and toothpaste
a hairbrush and a comb   a pajama top and pajama pants
a pillow and a blanket

Next ask your child to help John get ready for bed by arranging the pairs in the order that he or she follows when getting ready for bed.

Good night! Sleep tight!

©The Education Center, Inc. • *THE MAILBOX®* • Preschool • Feb/Mar 1998

ONCE UPON A STORY...

Once Upon A Story...

1, 2, 3 To The Zoo

Hop on board Eric Carle's animal train (The Putnam & Grosset Group) for a trip to the counting zoo. Youngsters are sure to enjoy naming the variety of pictured animals and counting the members in each group. After sharing this book, encourage students to chug on over to the block center to create a zoo setting or a counting train of their own. Make sure there are plenty of stuffed and plastic animal toys to fill the zoo cages or train cars. Challenge older preschoolers to build ten cages, with each cage holding a different number of animal toys from one to ten. All aboard!

Kim Richman
The Learning Zone
Des Moines, IA

Shoes

Read aloud this whimsical, rhyming narrative by Elizabeth Winthrop (HarperCollins Children's Books); then encourage students to take a look at their own shoes. Help youngsters group themselves by classifying their shoes into types—such as shoes with buckles, shoes with Velcro® straps, and shoes with laces. For more shoe fun, try this matching game. Seat your little ones in a circle. Have each child remove one shoe and place it in the middle of the circle. Invite a volunteer to choose a shoe (not his own) from the pile and set it in front of the child who is wearing the matching shoe. Continue until each child has a turn to pick from the pile. If the shoe matches, wear it!

Angie Williams—Three- And Four-Year-Olds
The Community Childcare Center
Plainfield, IN

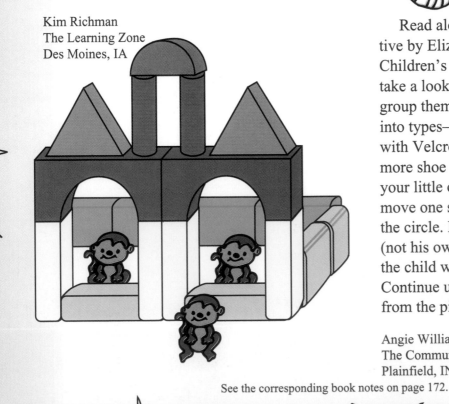

See the corresponding book notes on page 172.

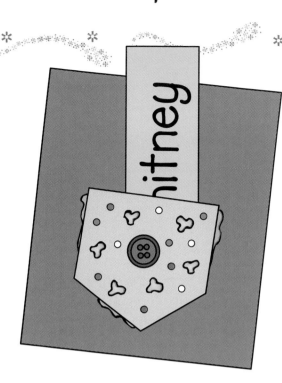

The Lady With The Alligator Purse

After hearing this delightful, nonsense rhyme by Nadine Bernard Westcott (Little, Brown and Company), youngsters will be chompin' at the bits to get inside this gator display for more reading fun. To make the alligator, have children paint a large appliance box green. When the paint is dry, cut windows from the two side panels. Then cut off one end of the box to represent the gator's mouth. To make teeth tape a white, plastic trash bag to the top inside of the box at the opening; then trim the bag to fit the opening and cut slits as shown. Add tagboard eyes above the teeth and a few small pillows or a blanket inside. Put a basket of alligator-themed books near the gator's mouth. Invite students to choose a book, then "feed" the gator. Delicious!

Patricia Moeser—Preschool
U. W. Preschool Laboratory Site #1
Madison, WI

A Pocket For Corduroy

From kangaroos to Corduroy, everyone needs a pocket! After reading aloud this classic tale by Don Freeman (Viking Children's Books), invite your preschoolers to practice their penmanship and pocket-making skills. To make a pocket, have each child trace a pocket pattern onto construction paper and cut it out. Then assist him in gluing the sides and bottom of the pocket onto another sheet of construction paper. Encourage him to embellish his pocket with markers, sequins, buttons, or other craft items. While the glue is drying, have the child label a strip of construction paper with his name. Later have him slip the strip into the pocket. If desired, display the potpourri of pockets with this verse: "Peek inside our pockets. They all are not the same. Peek inside our pockets. Look! We printed our names!"

Sharon L. Winter—Pre-K
Our Lady Of Hope/St. Luke School
Baltimore, MD

See the corresponding book notes on page 172.

163

Once Upon A Story...

Thomas' Snowsuit

Any child who has ever had to wear something he didn't like will love *Thomas' Snowsuit* by Robert Munsch (Firefly Books Ltd.). This hilarious story of a boy who refuses to wear his new snowsuit will have your little ones rolling with laughter. Before sharing the story, gather various sizes of winter snowsuits. Read the story aloud; then display the snowsuits. Ask your children to comment on the variety of sizes. Ask which suit would best fit a baby, a child, a teenager, or an adult. Seriate the snowsuits from smallest to largest. In a center area, place a copy of the book and the snowsuits for children to try on. Thomas said, "NNNNNO!" to his snowsuit, but your children will say, "YYYYYES!" to this fun activity!

If You Give A Moose A Muffin

Everyone knows that if you give a moose a muffin, he'll want some jam to go with it. Chances are that if you read your students *If You Give A Moose A Muffin* by Laura Joffe Numeroff (HarperCollins Children's Books), they'll want some muffins to go with it! Invite each student to make a muffin-box moose to share with his family. To make a moose, trace one side of a box of muffin mix onto construction paper. Cut out the shape; then glue it onto the box. Glue a brown pom-pom nose, wiggle eyes, paper ear shapes, and paper antler shapes to the box. Draw a smile on the moose. Encourage students to prepare the muffins with their families. Don't forget the jam!

Joan Tietz—Pre-K
St. James Lutheran
Lafayette, IN

See the corresponding book notes on page 173.

Polar Bear, Polar Bear, What Do You Hear?

Read aloud *Polar Bear, Polar Bear, What Do You Hear?* by Bill Martin Jr. (Henry Holt And Company, Inc.); then play the following listening game with your students. Ask a child to sit in the center of a group circle; then blindfold her. Invite a student from the group to stand next to the blindfolded child, then whisper the sentence, "[Child's name], [Child's name], who do you hear?" Instruct the blindfolded child to guess the identity of the student, then recite the sentence, "I hear [Child's name], whispering in my ear." Direct the child to remove her blindfold to see if she made a correct guess; then have her return to the group. The second child then takes her place. Continue until each child has had a chance to sit in the center of the circle.

The Button Box

Buttons here; buttons there; buttons, buttons everywhere! Your students will see how one child finds delight in his grandmother's button box when you share *The Button Box* by Margarette S. Reid (Puffin Unicorn Books). If you have a collection of buttons, invite each child to select a favorite. Then have him visit your easel to paint a picture of a piece of clothing. When the paint is dry, have him cut out his picture, then glue on the button. Display the pictures on a clothesline strung in your classroom.

See the corresponding book notes on page 173.

Once Upon A Story...

Will You Be My Valentine?

The children in Steven Kroll's *Will You Be My Valentine?* (Holiday House, Inc.) enjoyed exchanging secret valentines. Chances are that your little sweeties will enjoy this take-home activity, as well! To prepare in the same manner as the teacher in the story, write each child's name on a slip of paper and put the names into a hat. Share the book; then invite each child to close his eyes and select a name. Along with the personalized slip of paper, send home a construction-paper heart shape and a note explaining the project. Request that each child decorate his heart shape as a valentine for the child whose name he selected from the hat. On the designated day, invite each child to display his project, then present it to his secret valentine. It's no secret—you're sure to have a great time!

Connie S. Bryant—Preschool
Emerald Isle Recreation Center
Emerald Isle, NC

The Cat In The Hat

Celebrate the birthday of Dr. Seuss on March 2 by reading aloud his most famous title, *The Cat In The Hat* (Random House Books For Young Readers). As a story extension, make a Cat-style hat for each child to paint and wear. To make one, turn a grocery bag inside out. Roll the opening of the bag down to make the brim of the hat. Encourage the child to paint his bag with stripes or in the creative manner of his choice. When the paint is dry, place the bag on the child's head. Then, to make the hat fit his head, tie a piece of yarn around the bag over the child's forehead. Who's the cool cat in the hat?

Jessica Lorimor—Preschool
Morningside College Child Care Center
Sioux City, IA

See the corresponding book notes on page 174.

Jamie O'Rourke And The Big Potato: An Irish Folktale

The saints preserve us! When Jamie O'Rourke plants a magic seed, his whole village gets more potato than they can stand to eat. Jamie, however, ends up with the deal of a lifetime! Before sharing this story by Tomie dePaola (G.P. Putnam's Sons) with your older preschoolers, play a game of Pass The Potato. Seat your children in a circle; then instruct them to pass a large potato until you say a designated magic word, such as *leprechaun, Ireland,* or *pratie.* Following the game, read the story aloud. Each time you say, "Potato," direct the child holding the potato to pass it to the child next to him in the circle. If you substitute the word *pratie* with *potato,* your youngsters will pass the potato 25 times! Now that's a fun way to develop listening skills!

Rhonda Dunham—Four- And Five-Year-Olds
Beachwood Nursery School
Beachwood, NJ

Hide And Snake

Slither visual-discrimination practice and creativity into this literature activity related to *Hide And Snake* by Keith Baker (Harcourt Brace & Company). Invite one or two children at a time to join you in searching for the sneaky snake in this story. After searching, round the ends of a length of crepe-paper streamer for each child. Encourage each child to use markers to draw a face and designs on her streamer so that it resembles a snake. Ask each child to help you "hide" her snake by twisting and slithering it among items in your classroom. Let's play "hide-and-go-snake"! I see yours; do you see mine?

See the corresponding book notes on page 174.

Once Upon A Story...

In The Tall, Tall Grass

If you're looking for a springtime book with rhythm and rhyme, read aloud *In The Tall, Tall Grass* by Denise Fleming (Henry Holt And Company, Inc.). After your little ones follow the caterpillar's journey through the grass, invite them to make these classy, grassy hats to practice their scissor skills. Provide each child with a strip of green construction paper that is long enough for a headband. If desired mark cutting lines on the strip. Direct each child to fringe his strip, then add a variety of insect stickers. Staple the strip to fit the child's head. These turf toppers turn out really neat!

Beth Walker—Four- And Five-Year-Olds
BCC Child Development Center
Melbourne, FL

The Carrot Seed

Your youngsters' best efforts will result in some tasty snacking at the conclusion of this surprisingly fun follow-up to a reading aloud of *The Carrot Seed* by Ruth Krauss (HarperCollins Children's Books). Prior to reading the story, purchase a class supply of carrots (with leafy tops attached) from a grocery store. "Plant" the carrots in a tub of dirt or in loose soil outside your classroom. Read the story aloud; then invite each child to pull a carrot out of the dirt. Have him scrub the carrot clean. Then invite him to dip his carrot in ranch dressing for nibbling. Or send the carrots home along with the recipe on the book note found on page 18.

Faith M. Tidd—Pre-K
Cohocton Head Start
Cohocton, NY

See the corresponding book notes on page 175.

I See A Song

This follow-up activity to *I See A Song* by Eric Carle (Scholastic Inc.) brings out the magic of music and imagination. Read aloud the book's brief introduction. Then direct youngsters to enjoy the illustrations as you play a classical music selection. Show the pictures again, this time asking for descriptions of the song that the musician saw. Help youngsters describe the way the music and pictures made them feel. Next provide each child with paper and crayons, markers, or paints. As you play the music again, encourage the children to listen to the song and draw or paint freely. I see a song! Do you?

Megan Bonnema—Preschool
Portage, MI

The flies landed on my grandpa's toes!

Old Black Fly

Shoo fly! Shoo fly! Shoo. Encourage your listeners to participate in reading aloud this chaotic tale by Jim Aylesworth (Henry Holt And Company, Inc.) by reciting the repetitive phrases. Have a flyswatter nearby in order to provide a surprise "SWAT!" at the conclusion of the story. To extend the fun, invite each child to take a swat at this art project that's so fun it's worth the mess. For each child draw several black flies on a large sheet of painting paper. Invite a child to dip a flyswatter into a pan of paint, then swat it onto the flies on her paper. Remind the child of the pesky fly's actions; then ask her to describe what the flies on her paper were doing. Record her sentence on a strip of paper to display with the painting when it is dry. Buzz…splat!

Lori Parlier
Hubbard Elementary
Forsyth, GA

Classical Music

See the corresponding book notes on page 175.

Once Upon A Story...

A House For Hermit Crab

Dive right into a reading of Eric Carle's *A House For Hermit Crab* (Simon & Schuster Children's Books). Then follow up by teaching your youngsters "The Hermit Crab Cha-Cha"!

The Hermit Crab Cha-Cha
(sung to the tune of "The Silliest Goat I Ever Saw")

The hermit crab (Cha-cha-cha),
He has no home (Cha-cha-cha).
He has no shell (Cha-cha-cha),
To call his own (Cha-cha-cha).
He moves along the ocean floor,
To find the home he's hoping for.

The hermit crab (Cha-cha-cha),
Soon finds a shell (Cha-cha-cha).
He crawls inside (Cha-cha-cha),
It fits him well (Cha-cha-cha).
He moves along the ocean floor,
Until his home fits him no more!

adapted from an idea by Marsha Feffer—Pre-K
Bentley School, Salem, MA

Strega Nona

After sharing the story *Strega Nona* by Tomie dePaola (Simon & Schuster Books For Young Readers) with your older preschoolers, give them the opportunity to practice some magical math skills of their own. To prepare for this activity, glue each of ten paper plates onto a separate construction-paper placemat. Label each placemat with a different numeral from one to ten. Glue lengths of yellow yarn to each plate to resemble spaghetti. Put the placemats, a bowl of brown pom-poms (meatballs), and a spoon in a center. Invite each child to visit this center to serve up some spaghetti with the correct number of meatballs on each plate. "Bubble, bubble, pasta pot." We like *Strega Nona* a lot!

Carri Pawlyshyn and Jeannine Peluso—Pre-K
Boston College Children's Center
Chestnut Hill, MA

See the corresponding book notes on page 176.

It looked like an octopus, but it was melted ice cream!
Julian

Baby Beluga

Dive right into the fun of a baby whale's day with Raffi's *Baby Beluga* (Crown Books For Young Readers). If desired, play the song ("Baby Beluga," Kimbo Educational) as you display the pages of the accompanying book. Afterward have your youngsters describe the events in the whale's day. Then provide each child with a blue crepe-paper streamer to hold. As you replay the song, invite students to move their streamers with the rhythm of the music, watching the wavelike motion of the streamers as they move.

It Looked Like Spilt Milk

Take advantage of youngsters' high-flying imaginations by reading aloud *It Looked Like Spilt Milk* by Charles G. Shaw (HarperCollins Children's Books). After a discussion about clouds, continue to develop creative-thinking skills by asking your students to imagine what melted ice cream could look like. Then send them off to your art center to create this delicious display.

Pour several colors of tempera paints into separate bowls. Stir a small amount of sand into each bowl until the paint is the consistency of melted ice cream. Have a student drop a spoonful of paint onto a paper plate to create a design. When the paint is dry, glue one side of an ice-cream cone to the plate. Write the child's dictated completion to the sentence "It looked like [object], but it was melted ice-cream." Display the captions and the ice-cream creations on a bulletin board.

Theresa Knapp
Webster, NY

See the corresponding book notes on page 176.

Book Notes

After reading each of the books mentioned below and on pages 162 and 163, send home copies of the corresponding note.

All Aboard!
Today we practiced counting as our teacher read

1, 2, 3 To The Zoo
by Eric Carle.

Let's count again at home! Place household objects in groups of one to ten. Then listen as I count them!

©1997 The Education Center, Inc.

Shoe-be-doo-be-doo, today's story was about shoes!

Shoes
by Elizabeth Winthrop

Let's hunt through our closets to see if we can find shoes with buckles, laces, straps, zippers, and even no fasteners at all!

©1997 The Education Center, Inc.

Today we read
A Pocket For Corduroy
by Don Freeman.

According to Corduroy, everyone needs a pocket! Help me find clothes that have pockets to wear today.

©1997 The Education Center, Inc.

Have you heard about Miss Lucy and Tiny Tim? Ask me to sing you the story of

The Lady With The Alligator Purse
by Nadine Bernard Westcott.

It's so funny! Let's talk about some other things that make us laugh.

Hee Hee

©1997 The Education Center, Inc.

Book Notes

After reading each of the books mentioned below and on pages 164 and 165, send home copies of the corresponding note.

Today we heard a funny story called
Thomas' Snowsuit.

Thomas was asked to put on his snowsuit but he said, "NNNNNO!"

Let's go to the library to find more books by Robert Munsch.
Say, "YYESS!"

Ask me to tell you the story
If You Give A Moose A Muffin
by Laura Joffe Numeroff.

Then let's make some delicious muffins.

Do you hear what I hear?

Today I heard the story
Polar Bear, Polar Bear, What Do You Hear?
by Bill Martin Jr.

Ask me to tell you some sounds I hear at home, outside, and in the car.

Our story today was

The Button Box
by Margarette S. Reid.

Let's look in our closets to see how many different kinds of buttons we can find.

Book Notes

After reading each of the books mentioned below and on pages 166 and 167, send home copies of the corresponding note.

I know that February 14 is Valentine's Day!

Today we read *Will You Be My Valentine?* by Steven Kroll.

Ask me to be your valentine, and I'll give you a big hug!

Today we read *The Cat In The Hat* by Dr. Seuss.

Let's play a word game. Each time I say "Cat," you say a rhyming word.

Ready? Cat!

bat
chat
fat
flat
hat
mat
pat
rat
splat

Ask me to tell you where I found the snake in

Hide And Snake

by Keith Baker.

This book is hiding at the library. Let's go find it!

Jamie O'Rourke And The Big Potato

by Tomie dePaola is a funny story!

A leprechaun gave Jamie a magic seed that grew a giant potato! We can grow a potato plant, too.

Wash a potato. Put some toothpicks in the potato, then put it in a jar of water.

Book Notes

After reading each of the books mentioned below and on pages 168 and 169, send home copies of the corresponding note.

A caterpillar crunches his way through the grass in the book

In The Tall, Tall Grass
by Denise Fleming.

Let's sit together in the grass. Wonder if we'll see any critters....

©1998 The Education Center, Inc.

The Carrot Seed
by Ruth Krauss
is a story about a boy and a giant carrot.

Look! Here's a carrot I pulled out of the dirt. I cleaned it, too!

Let's make carrot salad:

1. Grate the carrot.
2. Add some mayonnaise and raisins.
3. Stir.

©1998 The Education Center, Inc.

Today we listened to music and looked at the book

I See A Song
by Eric Carle.

Would you like to see a song? Let's listen to music and color or paint. Use your imagination!

©1998 The Education Center, Inc.

Shoo fly!

Old Black Fly
by Jim Aylesworth is a crazy story about a pesky fly.

SWAT!

Ask me what happened to the fly!

©1998 The Education Center, Inc.

Book Notes

After reading each of the books mentioned below and on pages 170 and 171, send home copies of the corresponding note.

Today we read about a magical pasta pot in

Strega Nona

by
Tomie dePaola.

Let's make pasta and chant "Bubble, bubble, pasta pot."

We sang "The Hermit Crab Cha-Cha" after reading

A House For Hermit Crab

by Eric Carle.

I'll sing it for you— just ask!

cha cha
cha cha
cha cha

Did you know that clouds can look like many things?

Ask me about a story called

It Looked Like Spilt Milk

by Charles G. Shaw.

Let's go outside to look at the clouds. What do they look like to you?

Ask me to sing you the story of

Baby Beluga

by Raffi.

Want to go to the library to find more Raffi books we can sing?

IT'S CIRCLE TIME!

IT'S CIRCLE TIME!

Buddy Bear

Help young children practice their communication skills with Buddy Bear. Place a bear puppet in a handled bag. Attach a parent note to the bag explaining Buddy Bear's visit and requesting that he be returned to school after one night's stay. Send Buddy home with a different child each day. Each morning start sharing time with the song below. Encourage the child who took Buddy home to use the puppet to tell about his visit. Continue Buddy's visits during the fall months. Then as winter approaches, help youngsters prepare a cave for Buddy's hibernation. "Wake" Buddy up on the first day of spring for more adventures with your little ones.

(sung to the tune of "Frère Jacques")
Who has Buddy,
Who has Buddy,
Buddy Bear?
Buddy Bear?
What have you been doing,
What have you been doing,
Buddy Bear?
Buddy Bear?

Esther Hartmann—Pre-K
Trinity Lutheran
Cape Girardeau, MO

Sammy Smoke Detector

Use Sammy Smoke Detector to capture your little ones' attentions when explaining fire safety. In advance, attach paper facial features to the plastic cover of a smoke detector. During a circle time, introduce Sammy. Explain that Sammy's job is to sound a loud signal if he smells smoke from a fire. Push the tester button on the detector so that youngsters may hear Sammy's signal. Discuss your fire-escape plan with the children; then practice leaving the building. With Sammy around, your little ones will feel safe and sound.

Gayle Selsback—Director/Teacher
Playhouse Nursery School
Maple Grove, MN

Holiday Countdown

Heighten anticipation of upcoming holidays with holiday countdown chains. Make a paper chain (one link for each day until the featured holiday) from construction paper. Attach the chain to a seasonal cutout and display it in the classroom. Each day during circle time, have a different child cut a link from the chain. When the last link is cut, it's holiday time!

Doris Weeaks—Four-Year-Olds
Walnut Ridge Baptist Church
Mansfield, TX

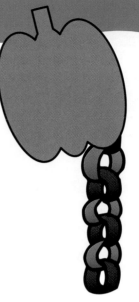

Jack-O-Shapes

Carve up some jack-o'-lantern fun with this circle-time game. Prior to a group time, hide jack-o'-lantern cutouts around the classroom; then lead youngsters in singing the following song as they set out to find the cutouts. When each child locates a cutout, have him return with it to the circle area. Then invite each youngster to describe where he found his smiling pumpkin cutout.

(sung to the tune of "Itsy-Bitsy Spider")
Funny jack-o'-lantern,
Where are you hiding?
Are you over here?
Or are you under there?
I will keep on looking, until I find you.
Funny jack-o'-lantern,
There you are!

D. Lyn Stevens—Preschool, A. M. Chaffee, Oxford, MA

Who's That Ghost?

Your little spooks will love this ghostly guessing game. Seat youngsters in a circle. Choose a volunteer to stand away from the circle and close his eyes. Invite another volunteer to be the ghost. Place a sheet with eye openings over the ghost's head; then have him stand in the center of the circle. Instruct the first child to return to the circle and try to guess "whoooooooooo's" under the sheet!

179

IT'S CIRCLE TIME!

A Pleasant, Present Surprise

Surprise your little ones with this holiday guessing game. To prepare, turn a large box upside down; then wrap the sides and top with holiday paper. Top the box with a large bow. During a group time, ask a volunteer to close his eyes. Then ask a second volunteer to hide under the gift-wrapped box. Ask the first child to open his eyes, then look at the remaining children in the group. Provide him with plenty of chances to guess the child who is under the box, giving him clues if necessary. When the identity of the child under the box is guessed, have that child return to the group and close his eyes. Continue play as a new volunteer hides under the box. Aren't holiday surprises fun?

Pat Smith—Four-Year-Olds
Bells Elementary
Bells, TX

Creative Communication

Believe it or not, pudding can help your youngsters learn to communicate! To prepare for this delicious group activity, pour one or two boxes of pudding and the required amount of milk into a clean coffee can. Secure the lid on the can with a strip of duct tape. Seat the class in a circle on the floor. Pose a question, such as "What is your name?", or ask a theme-related question, such as "What do you like to do in the snow?" Roll the can to a child; then ask that child to answer the question. Next direct the child to roll the can to another member of the group. Continue until each child has answered the question. Then open the can and serve the pudding in small paper cups. Next question, please!

Mary Lauffenburger—Preschool
Warren Forest Company Head Start
Warren, PA

Wee Wisdom

This class book is sure to provide parents with many smiles and laughs of delight. Bind a supply of blank pages between construction-paper covers. Title the book "The World According To Us"; then decorate the cover. On the first page of the book, list the names of your young philosophers. Then, during group times, pose a question to your class. Write the question on a page in the book; then record each child's response. When the book is complete, send it home with a different child each night. It won't be long before parents request volume two of this charming book.

Christine Hartlieb—Four-Year-Olds
Junior Junction Childcare Center at St. Elizabeth's Hospital
Utica, NY

It's Better To Give

Youngsters will experience the joy of giving with this simple activity. To prepare, cut out a supply of pictures from a toy catalog. Glue each picture onto a square of wrapping paper. Place the pictures in a gift-wrapped box. During a group time, ask a child to select a gift from the box, decide the member of the class who would enjoy that gift, and then give that child the present. Continue until each child has given and received a gift.

Faith M. Tidd—Pre-K
Cohocton Head Start
Cohocton, NY

Christmas Cheer

Parents will enjoy this unique gift idea that records your class's Christmas cheer! Begin by audiotaping a holiday greeting to parents; then name each child in the class. During group times record your class singing their favorite holiday songs. When the tape is complete, duplicate a copy for each parent. Gift wrap the tapes; then send one home with each child. It's beginning to *sound* a lot like Christmas!

Kim Richman—Preschool
The Learning Zone
Des Moines, IA

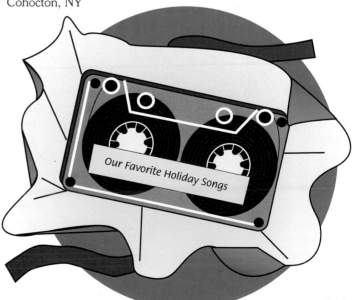

The Sharing Song

Sharing comes straight from the heart as youngsters play this circle-time game. Seat children in a circle. Give a construction-paper heart cutout to each of three students. Have these three children walk around the outside of the circle while everyone sings the following song. At the end of the song, have each child give his heart to someone seated in the circle and exchange places with that child. Repeat the activity until everyone has had a chance to share. How sweet!

(sung to the tune of "London Bridge")

I am learning how to share, how to share, how to share.
I am learning how to share. This heart's for you.

Debbie Brown—Four- And Five-Year-Olds
Corson Park Daycare
Millville, NJ

Circle-Time Drive-In

Invite children to drive up to circle time and learn the feature presentation of personal space with this idea. Collect a class supply of duplicating-paper boxes. Cut the bottom out of each box. Have each child use paint, construction paper, scissors, and glue to make her box into a vehicle. Prior to circle time, give children a chance to "drive" around the room; then ask them to park at the circle. Have students remain in their vehicles during circle time to reinforce the idea of personal space. Soon the vehicles won't be necessary at circle time and can be used for outside play. Vroom, vroom!

Lynn Colbert—Preschool
Astor Center For Child Development
Bronx, NY

A Valentine Big Book

Put your collection of valentines to good use in this valentine big book. To make the book's pages, cut six sheets of poster board in half. Label each of ten of the pages with a different number phrase from the song below. Glue the corresponding number of valentines to each page. Make a cover titled "Ten Little Valentines." Stack the pages between the cover and a blank page; then bind the pages together at the bottom. To use, simply flip each page down as you sing the song. Store this big book in the reading center for solo or duet readings.

Ten Little Valentines
(sung to the tune of "Ten Little Indians")

1 little, 2 little, 3 little valentines.
4 little, 5 little, 6 little valentines.
7 little, 8 little, 9 little valentines.
10 little valentines for me!

Dayle Timmons—Special Education Pre-K
Alimancani Elementary School
Jacksonville, FL

Name It!

Here's a terrific circle-time activity that reinforces color, shape, *and* name recognition. To prepare for the activity, cut out a class supply of geometric shapes from colored construction paper; then label each shape with a different child's name. When you're left with a few minutes to fill, hold up a shape and ask, "Whose shape is this?" Encourage the group to spell and say the child's name, then name the color and type of shape. What a rousing review!

M. Frances Guerin—Preschool
Hilltop Learning Center
Tewksbury, MA

Let's Play With Clay

Mold fine-motor skills with this hands-on rhyme. Give each child in a small group an amount of play dough; then lead the group in the following action rhyme. At the end of the rhyme, demonstrate how to shape the dough into a ball, a snake, and a pancake. Say the rhyme again, this time inserting a child's name in the last line. Encourage the named child to lead the group in making a play-dough shape. Repeat until each child has had a turn to be the leader.

Hello, little ball of clay.
Would you like to play today?
I'll pat you.
I'll squeeze you.
I'll roll you with my hand.
Wait 'til you see what [I have] planned!

Ann Flagg—Pre-K
Clarion, PA

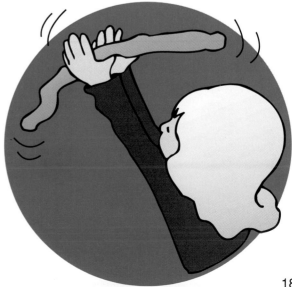

183

IT'S CIRCLE TIME!

On The Hunt

On the hunt for unique ways to improve name recognition? Here's an idea that doubles as a parent communication technique as well. Prior to a storytime, die-cut a class supply of shapes that relate to the story you will be reading. Program each shape with a different child's name on one side and the title and author of the book on the other side. "Hide" the shapes around the room by taping them—name side up—onto walls and furniture. After reading the story, send the children out to find their personalized shapes. Send the shapes home to let parents know the title of the day's story.

adapted from an idea by Jennifer M. Koch—Pre-K
Morningside College Child Care Center
Sioux City, IA

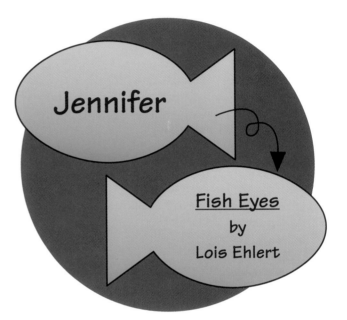

Can You Count The Stars?

You can count on your students being starstruck over this flannelboard counting activity. Cut out a number of felt stars. During group time, have your little ones help you recite the following rhyme; then invite them to count aloud with you as you place a number of stars on your flannelboard. Or turn your board away from the group; then place a number of stars on the board before you recite the rhyme. After saying the rhyme, surprise youngsters with the number of stars and have them count aloud with you. Can you count the stars? Let's try!

One star, two stars, three stars, four;
I think there are many more
Shining stars up in the sky.
Can you count them? Let's all try!

Heidi Barket—Preschool
Eastside Christian Preschool
Pottsville, PA

Match Your Socks Off

Sock some matching fun to your youngsters with this class game. In advance, collect enough pairs of socks so that each child in your group will have one sock. If possible, gather socks of various colors and designs. If some pairs of the socks are similar, use fabric paints to paint matching designs on pairs of socks. To play, have the children stand in a circle with their hands behind their backs. Walk around the circle and hand each child a sock. Play some music; then challenge the children to find their partners before the music stops by looking for socks that match. When the music stops, congratulate those children who have found their matches. Collect the socks; then redistribute them for another round of play. It's learning fun that will knock their socks off!

Lisa Leonardi
Norfolk, MA

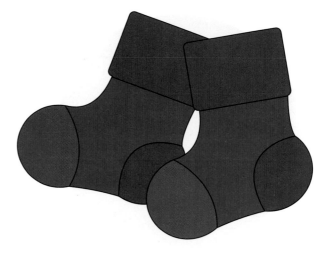

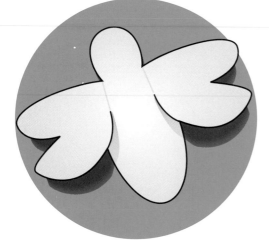

Catching Fireflies

A favorite sign of summer is a night sky full of fireflies! Prepare this activity as a follow-up to reading aloud *Ten Flashing Fireflies* by Philemon Sturges (North-South Books Inc.). To prepare, cut out several tagboard firefly shapes per child. Color the shapes with a yellow glow-in-the-dark crayon or paint them with glow-in-the-dark fingernail polish. Bend the fireflies' wings upward; then attach the fireflies to your walls using Sticky-Tac. Give each child a clear plastic jar. Dim the lights. Encourage each child to "catch" a designated number of fireflies to put in her jar. Ooh, look at them glow!

Dana Smith—Noncategorical Preschool
Donaldsonville Elementary
Donaldsonville, LA

What A Treasure!

This group-time activity is a priceless way to remind each of your children that she is unique and valuable. Decorate a lidded box to resemble a treasure chest. Place a mirror in the box; then replace the lid. Explain to your children that as they take turns looking into the box, they will see your treasure. Then give each child an opportunity to look into the box and view her reflection in the mirror. This activity gives a loving message that is appropriate at the beginning of the year, at the end of the year, or anytime in between when you'd like to boost self-esteem.

Dianna Bruckner—Two-Year-Olds
Winter Park Day Nursery
Winter Park, FL

Head, Shoulders, Knees, & Toes

Did Someone Say Pasta?

Youngsters are sure to have oodles of noodle fun with this large-motor activity that makes a perfect follow-up to a reading aloud of *Strega Nona* by Tomie dePaola (Simon & Schuster Children's Books). To prepare a giant rigatoni tunnel, obtain a queen-sized, fitted bedsheet. Fold the sheet together lengthwise so that the printed sides are together; then sew the long sides of the sheet together. Reverse the sheet; then insert plastic hoops into both of the rounded ends to create a tunnel. Ask adult volunteers to hold the hoops at the ends so that the tunnel is extended. Invite youngsters one at a time to crawl in, through, and out of the rigatoni tunnel. Now that's a pasta-perfect activity!

Linda J. Haffner—Preschool
St. James Lutheran Preschool, Cleveland, OH

Dot-To-Dot

Little ones can hop dot-to-dot with this sequential motor-skill game. Cut 6-inch dots from different colors of Con-Tact® covering. Secure the circles to the floor in the pattern of five dots on a die. When you need an instant activity, challenge a child to hop on the dots according to a directed oral sequence of colors. For example, you might say, "Hop on a blue dot, a red dot, then a yellow dot" or "Hop on a yellow dot three times, then a green dot three times." Modify your directions to match individual students' needs and abilities. Or offer to let a child give you directions.
Happy hopping!

Joyce Montag—Preschool
Slippery Rock Park
Slippery Rock, PA

Going Around In Circles

Moving in a circle as a group is a part of many favorite songs and games, but with preschoolers it can look easier than it really is! To help your youngest groups gain this ability, begin with lines of children that travel around the room like a train, following the leader, or like elephants holding tails and trunks. Use this poem to help guide children into moving together in a circle.

Standing in a nice straight line,
I'll hold your hand, and you hold mine.
One hand in front, and the other in back.
We'll make a line and stay on track.

Now...
We're in a circle, not a line!
I'll hold your hand, and you hold mine.
One hand in front, and the other in back.
The line goes around and stays on track.

Dr. Grace Morris
Southwest Texas State University
San Marcos, TX

188

Reach Up H-I-G-H, Reach Down L-O-W

Youngsters understand high and low sounds best when moving! So get ready to move your body and the sound of your voice up and down to match this action rhyme. For more fun, encourage children to stretch up as you play a xylophone so that the tones move up; then encourage children to move their bodies downward as you play the bells so that the tones move down.

Reach up high,
Reach down low,
Round and round and round we go.
Climb up high, up to the top.
Way back down we fall, kerplop!

Use a high voice.
Use a low voice.

Gradually use a higher voice.
Gradually use a lower voice.

Dr. Grace Morris
Southwest Texas State University
San Marcos, TX

Bip, Bop, Boop, Bap!

Games that involve passing will be a snap when you use easy-to-grip yarn balls. To make a yarn ball, cut a four-inch square from cardboard. Wrap a length of yarn (about 6 1/2 yards long) around the square 100 times. Carefully slide the wrapped yarn off the cardboard; then tie and knot a length of yarn around the center of the looped yarn. Cut the loops; then shape the ball.

Use a yarn ball to play this game that reinforces steady beat. Have youngsters sit in a circle with their legs crossed, so that each child's knees are touching the knees of the children on either side of him. As you chant the following rhyme slowly, move the yarn ball around the circle by directing each child—when the ball lands in his lap—to pick it up and drop it in the lap of the child to his left.

Bip, bop, boop, bap!
Put the ball right in a lap.
Passing yarn balls is a snap.
Bip, bop, boop, bap!

Dr. Grace Morris

Scrambling For Eggs

Put a little bounce in your bunnies' steps with this egg hunt! In advance, program a class supply of small slips of paper with movement directions such as "Hop like a rabbit" and "Fly like a butterfly." Insert each slip into a separate plastic egg; then hide the eggs in your room. To begin, direct each child to find one egg and then return to your group area. In turn, have each child crack open his egg. Whisper the written direction into his ear; then encourage him to announce the direction to the class and lead the group in the actions. At the end of the game, have each child replace the paper in his egg, then hide his egg in a new location to prepare for your next egg hunt.

Hop like a rabbit.

Moving Metamorphosis

The chance to dramatize the changes that occur as a caterpillar turns into a butterfly will leave each of your little ones aflutter. To prepare, tuck two scarves inside a sleeping bag that has been placed on the floor. Arrange large flower cutouts on the floor in an open area of your room. Invite a child to imagine she is a caterpillar and to crawl on the floor pretending to munch on leaves. Guide the child to crawl into the loosely closed sleeping-bag cocoon. When the child is ready, encourage her to hold a scarf in each hand, crawl out of the cocoon, and float among the flowers. My, isn't she beautiful?

Charlet Keller—Preschool, ICC Preschool, Violet Hill, AR

Alphabet Action

Here's a great way to teach letter recognition to children who love to move! In advance prepare a class supply of identical action mats. To make a mat, glue a different set of letters to each side of a large sheet of construction paper. Laminate the paper. To play, arrange the mats on the floor so that the same set of letters is visible on all the mats; then direct each child to stand next to a mat. Announce a direction such as "Tap your toe on the letter *T*" or "Hop on the letter *H*." As a variation, program mats with different colors of geometric shapes or numerals.

Miriam Blumenkrantz—Four-Year-Olds
Yeshiva Shaarei Tzion
Highland Park, NJ

Bubble Bath

Splish, splash! Everyone will want to take a bath with this song and movement idea that helps your little ones identify body parts. Fill a large box with biodegradable packing pieces to represent a bathtub full of bubbles. Invite a volunteer to hop in the tub and name a body part. Have him lead the group in singing the following song as they pretend to wash. Scrub-a-dub-dub! Who's next in the tub?

Bath Tune
(sung to the tune of "Mulberry Bush")

This is the way I wash my [body part],
Wash my [body part], wash my [body part].
This is the way I wash my [body part],
When I take a bath.

Amy Aloi—Head Start
Berkshire Elementary
Forestville, MD

This is the way I wash my toes...

Jump The Brook

The fun of this large-muscle activity will make your little ones jump for joy, and the chance to review basic concepts such as size, color, and number sets will make *you* jump for joy! Cut a supply of fish cutouts, reinforcing the concepts of your choice by varying the sizes or colors of the fish. Ask youngsters to help you decorate the fish. Position two mats on the floor so that there is enough space between them for one fish. Describe the size or color of a fish as you place it between the mats; then invite each child, in turn, to jump the brook. Continue adding one fish at a time, moving the mats farther apart until the children can no longer jump the brook without the fish "nibbling" the jumpers' feet. Splash!

Janet Graves—Preschool
Columbus State Child Development Center
Columbus, OH

Songs & Such

SONGS & SUCH

Autumn Is Here

Have each child tape die-cut leaves to a length of yarn or clear fishing line. Then invite him to whirl and swirl his leaves while singing this autumn song.

(sung to the tune of "Have You Ever Seen A Lassie?")

The leaves are really changing,
And changing, and changing.
The leaves are really changing,
For autumn is here.

See red leaves and brown leaves,
And green leaves and gold leaves.
The leaves are really changing,
For autumn is here!

Linda Rice Ludlow—Preschool, Bethesda Christian School
Brownsburg, IN

Halloween Pretending

Each time you sing this song, invite a student to pretend to be the character of her choice. Pretending is fun!

(sung to the tune of "Clementine")

Halloween is such a fun time.
It's not scary, not for me.
I pretend I'm someone different.
It's as fun as fun can be.

Mary Sutula, Orlando, FL

Mr. Scarecrow

(sung to the tune of "Twinkle, Twinkle, Little Star")

Mr. Scarecrow standing tall,   (Hold hand above head and look up.)
You just don't scare me at all.   (Shake head "no.")
Stuffed with straw from head to toe. (Touch head; then touch toes.)
Quite a funny guy to know.   (Hold tummy and chuckle.)
Mr. Scarecrow standing tall,   (Hold hand above head and look up.)
You just don't scare me at all!   (Shake head "no.")

Betty Silkunas
Lansdale, PA

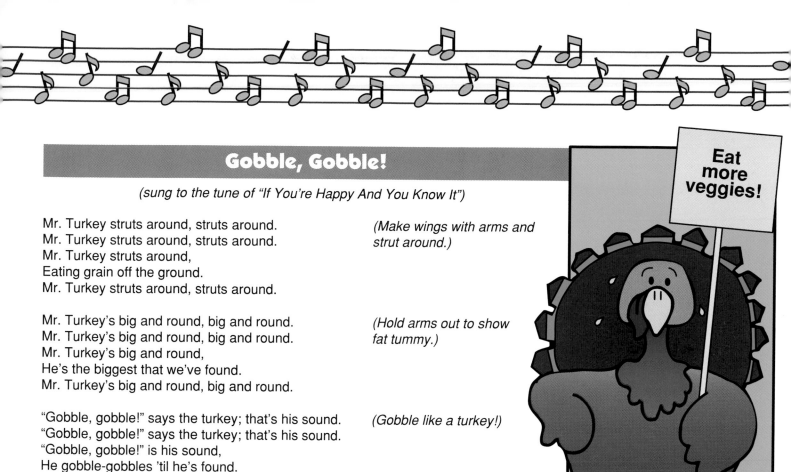

Gobble, Gobble!

(sung to the tune of "If You're Happy And You Know It")

Mr. Turkey struts around, struts around.
Mr. Turkey struts around, struts around.
Mr. Turkey struts around,
Eating grain off the ground.
Mr. Turkey struts around, struts around.

(Make wings with arms and strut around.)

Mr. Turkey's big and round, big and round.
Mr. Turkey's big and round, big and round.
Mr. Turkey's big and round,
He's the biggest that we've found.
Mr. Turkey's big and round, big and round.

(Hold arms out to show fat tummy.)

"Gobble, gobble!" says the turkey; that's his sound.
"Gobble, gobble!" says the turkey; that's his sound.
"Gobble, gobble!" is his sound,
He gobble-gobbles 'til he's found.
"Gobble, gobble!" says the turkey; that's his sound.

(Gobble like a turkey!)

Now Thanksgiving Day is here, day is here.
Now Thanksgiving Day is here, day is here.
Now Thanksgiving Day is here,
Mr. Turkey needs to fear.
Now Thanksgiving Day is here, day is here.

(Make a scared face with a hand on each cheek.)

A Healthful Feast

Children from various cultural backgrounds will enjoy naming favorite foods in order to cook up new verses for this tasty song. Continue until each child has had a turn and all tummies are full!

(sung to the tune of "Paw Paw Patch")

Chorus:
Let's start cooking Thanksgiving dinner.
Let's start cooking Thanksgiving dinner.
Let's start cooking Thanksgiving dinner.
My, oh my, what a healthful feast!

Cook the [turkey]; put it on the table.
Cook the [turkey]; put it on the table.
Cook the [turkey]; put it on the table.
My, oh my, what a healthful feast!

Christmastime

Have students ring jingle bells as you sing about the meaning of the holiday season.

(sung to the tune of "Do You Know The Muffin Man?")

I am glad it's Christmastime,
Christmastime, Christmastime.
I am glad it's Christmastime,
A special time of year.

It's time to give and time to share,
Time to love and show you care.
For friends and family everywhere,
A special time of year!

Mary Sutula
Orlando, FL

Moving Into A New Year

Gather your youngsters into a group circle; then get ready to stomp, hop, wiggle, and jump into the New Year!

(sung to the tune of "We Wish You A Merry Christmas")

We wish you a happy New Year,
We wish you a happy New Year,
We wish you a happy New Year,
Full of fun and good cheer!

Oh, come do a little stomping,
Oh, come do a little stomping,
Oh, come do a little stomping,
This happy New Year!

Oh, come do a little hopping....

Oh, come do a little wiggling....

Oh, come do a little jumping....

Dayle Timmons—Special Education Pre-K
Alimancani Elementary School
Jacksonville, FL

"Snowkey" Pokey

Have your little snowfolk form a circle; then get ready for a flurry of movement fun! To modify the verse, ask students to name additional pieces of winter attire. Keep warm!

(sung to the tune of "The Hokey Pokey")

You put your [mittens] in, you put your [mittens] out,
You put your [mittens] in, and you shake them all about.
You do The "Snowkey" Pokey and you turn yourself around.
That's what it's all about.
"Snowkey" Pokey!

Gayle Selsback—Preschool, Playhouse Nursery School
Maple Grove, MN

Sprinkle, Sprinkle, Little Snow

Provide each student with two white crepe-paper streamers to twirl and swirl as she sings about snow.

(sung to the tune of "Twinkle, Twinkle, Little Star")

Sprinkle, sprinkle, little snow;
Falling down on us below;
Small and white and powdery,
Such a joy for all to see.
Sprinkle, sprinkle, little snow;
Falling down on us below.

Linda Ludlow—Preschool
Bethesda Christian School
Brownsburg, IN

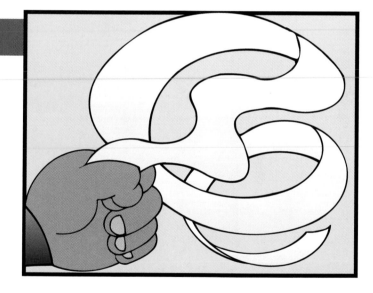

I Like Winter!

(sung to the tune of "London Bridge")

Wintertime is frosty cold,
Frosty cold, frosty cold.
Wintertime is frosty cold.
I like winter!

Wintertime is stormy bold….

Wintertime is snowy white….

Wintertime is chilly bright….

Lucia Kemp Henry

SONGS & SUCH

I'll Send You A Letter

If you're looking for a way to practice name recognition, this first-class game really delivers! Personalize an envelope for every child. If desired, tuck a small treat—such as a valentine or stickers—inside each envelope. Also locate a real or dramatic-play mailbox near your group area. To begin, hand an envelope to a child in the group. Instruct her to put the envelope in the mailbox as the group sings the first and second verses of the following song. Appoint a volunteer postal worker to remove the envelope from the box, and to deliver it to the appropriate child as the group sings the third verse. Continue until each child has delivered and received a letter.

(sung to the tune of "For He's A Jolly Good Fellow")

I'll send you a letter.
I'll send you a letter.
I'll send you a letter.
This letter is to [Child's name].

I'll put it in the mailbox.
I'll put it in the mailbox.
I'll put it in the mailbox.
This letter is to [Child's name].

I'll bring you a letter.
I'll bring you a letter.
I'll bring you a letter.
This letter is to [Child's name].

adapted from a song by D. Lyn Stevens—Preschool
A.M. Chaffee School
Oxford, MA

It's Shadow Time!

(sung to the tune of "The Itsy-Bitsy Spider")

The furry, little groundhog
Goes in his hole to sleep;
Through the cold winter's
Snow and ice so deep.

In February,
He stretches to and fro.
Does the furry, little groundhog
Get scared by his shadow?

Shamrock Rhythms

This rhythm activity helps youngsters feel the beat and reinforces prereading skills. Cut out five paper shamrock shapes; then cut one of the shamrocks in half vertically. Working with one or two children at a time, arrange four whole shamrocks in a row on the floor. As you tap each shamrock, say, "Green." Continue tapping the four shamrocks and saying green to establish the rhythm. Next replace one of the shamrocks with two shamrock halves. Say, "Green," as you tap each shamrock (whole beat), and say the syllables in *shamrock* as you touch each shamrock half (half beats). See the illustrations for some suggested rhythm patterns. Invite the children to help you create rhythm patterns for reciting together. The luck of the Irish is sure to make this music game fun for all!

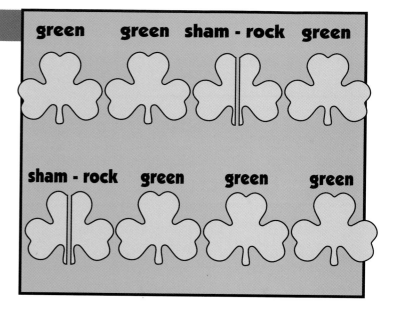

Little Puppy Dog

Incorporate this song into your pet unit. Your energetic youngsters will enjoy "wagging their tails" as they sing along.

(sung to the tune of "A Ram Sam Sam")

A puppy dog, a puppy dog;
Wag your tail,
Little puppy dog.

A puppy dog, a puppy dog;
Bark, bark, bark,
Little puppy dog.

Chase balls and chew sticks;
Wag your little tail and bark for me.
Dig holes and scratch fleas;
I love you, and you love me!

A puppy dog, a puppy dog;
Wag your tail,
Little puppy dog.

A puppy dog, a puppy dog;
Bark, bark, bark,
Little puppy dog.

Carrie Lacher

SONGS & SUCH

In The Zoo

(sung to the tune of "The Farmer In The Dell")

The monkeys in the zoo,
The monkeys in the zoo,
They bend their knees and swing from trees,
The monkeys in the zoo.

The zebras in the zoo,
The zebras in the zoo,
They look so right in black and white,
The zebras in the zoo.

The seals in the zoo,
The seals in the zoo,
They swim and splash the whole day through,
The seals in the zoo.

The lions in the zoo,
The lions in the zoo,
They lift their heads and give a roar,
The lions in the zoo.

The children at the zoo,
The children at the zoo,
They have such fun till the day is done,
The children at the zoo.

Elizabeth McDonald—Preschool, School Readiness Center
Naperville, IL

Camping Trip

Have any of your little ones ever been camping? Have them
tell about their adventures. Better yet, invite a parent to bring
camping supplies—such as a sleeping bag, backpack, and
flashlight—to your class. Include each item discussed below.

(sung to the tune of "Brush Your Teeth" as sung by Raffi)

We're going on a camping trip, and what will we bring?
We're going on a camping trip, and what will we bring?
We'll bring a [tent]. (Clap, clap, clap, clap, clap, clap, clap,
   clap, clap.)
We'll bring a [tent]. (Clap, clap, clap, clap, clap, clap, clap,
   clap, clap.)

Dianna Bruckner—Two-Year-Olds, Winter Park Day Nursery
Winter Park, FL

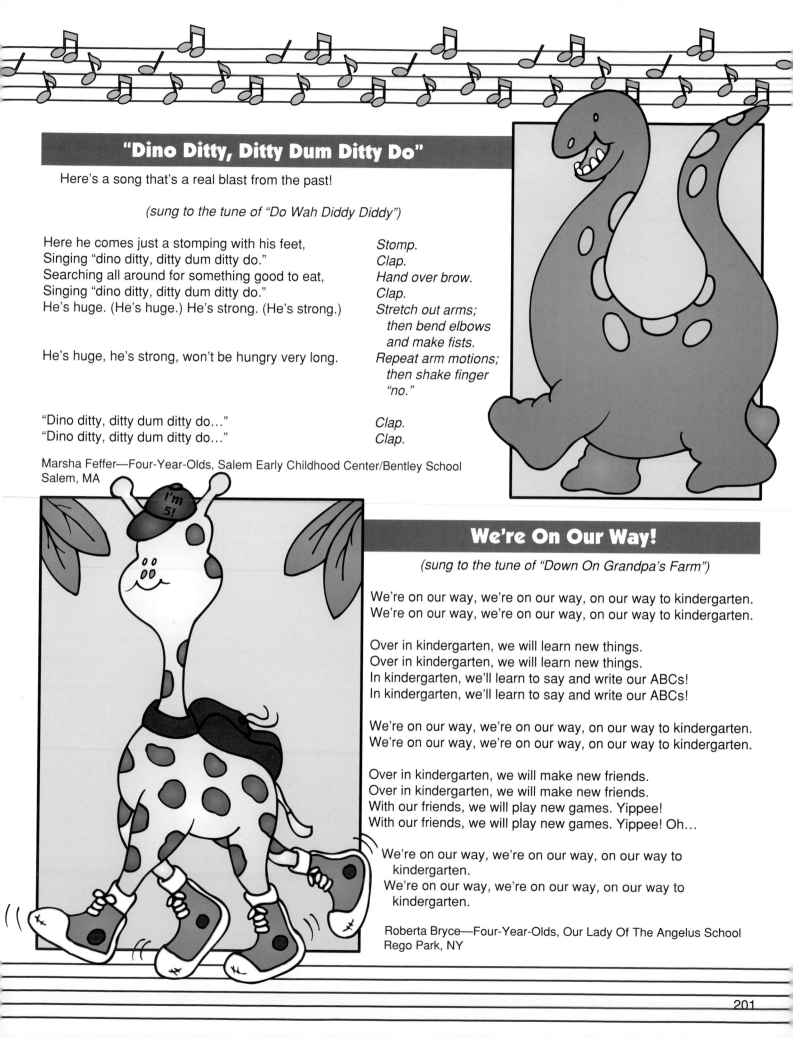

"Dino Ditty, Ditty Dum Ditty Do"

Here's a song that's a real blast from the past!

(sung to the tune of "Do Wah Diddy Diddy")

Here he comes just a stomping with his feet,   Stomp.
Singing "dino ditty, ditty dum ditty do."   Clap.
Searching all around for something good to eat,   Hand over brow.
Singing "dino ditty, ditty dum ditty do."   Clap.
He's huge. (He's huge.) He's strong. (He's strong.)   Stretch out arms;
                                                                    then bend elbows
                                                                    and make fists.
He's huge, he's strong, won't be hungry very long.   Repeat arm motions;
                                                                    then shake finger
                                                                    "no."

"Dino ditty, ditty dum ditty do…"   Clap.
"Dino ditty, ditty dum ditty do…"   Clap.

Marsha Feffer—Four-Year-Olds, Salem Early Childhood Center/Bentley School
Salem, MA

We're On Our Way!

(sung to the tune of "Down On Grandpa's Farm")

We're on our way, we're on our way, on our way to kindergarten.
We're on our way, we're on our way, on our way to kindergarten.

Over in kindergarten, we will learn new things.
Over in kindergarten, we will learn new things.
In kindergarten, we'll learn to say and write our ABCs!
In kindergarten, we'll learn to say and write our ABCs!

We're on our way, we're on our way, on our way to kindergarten.
We're on our way, we're on our way, on our way to kindergarten.

Over in kindergarten, we will make new friends.
Over in kindergarten, we will make new friends.
With our friends, we will play new games. Yippee!
With our friends, we will play new games. Yippee! Oh…

We're on our way, we're on our way, on our way to
    kindergarten.
We're on our way, we're on our way, on our way to
    kindergarten.

Roberta Bryce—Four-Year-Olds, Our Lady Of The Angelus School
Rego Park, NY

Fingerplays, Poems, & Rhymes

Stop And Go

Teach your youngsters a little traffic safety using this catchy verse.

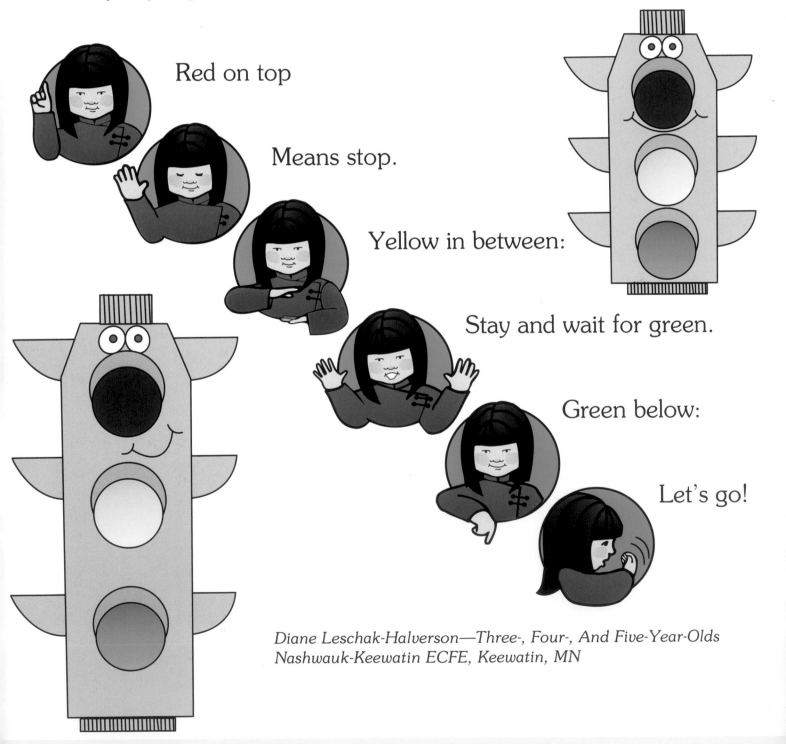

Red on top

Means stop.

Yellow in between:

Stay and wait for green.

Green below:

Let's go!

Diane Leschak-Halverson—Three-, Four-, And Five-Year-Olds
Nashwauk-Keewatin ECFE, Keewatin, MN

Poems, & Rhymes

An Apple Surprise

 Way up high in the apple tree,

 A little brown worm smiled at me.

 I winked my eye,

And what do you suppose?

 A shiny, red apple dropped on my nose!

—dayle timmons

Oh, No! A Fire!

Oh, no! There's a fire!

Bring hoses, ladders, axes, too.

Firefighters to the rescue!

Wear boots, hats,

safety masks;

Spray the water, what a task!

Saving people night and day,

Thanks, firefighters! Hip, hip, hooray!

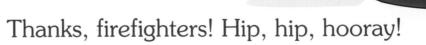

—*Carrie Lacher, Friday Harbor, WA*

Poems, & Rhymes

Mr. Squirrel

Who's that scampering up the tree,

Carrying acorns...1, 2, 3?

It's Mr. Squirrel with a tail so furry.

He's ready for winter, so don't you worry!

—Betty Silkunas, Lansdale, PA

Call Rudolph!

Eight little reindeer pulling Santa's sled;

One fell down and bumped his head.

The elves called Santa and Santa said,

"Can seven little reindeer pull my sled?"

Seven little reindeer…
Six little reindeer…
Five little reindeer…
Four little reindeer…
Three little reindeer…
Two little reindeer…

One little reindeer pulling Santa's sled;
He fell down and bumped his head.
The elves called Santa and Santa said,
"Call Rudolph!"

—dayle timmons

Kwanzaa Candles

Use this poem as a fingerplay or to introduce a real *kinara* (candleholder) and the *mishumaa saba* (seven candles) used during Kwanzaa.

Seven little candles all in a line,
Waiting to be lighted at Kwanzaa time.
Come let's count them—one, two, three,
Four, five, six, seven candles I see!

—Christina Yuhouse—Preschool, New Horizons School, Latrobe, PA

Fingerplays,

Made With Love

This valentine chant and game will fill your circle time with love! Have each child color a personalized heart shape. Seat youngsters in a circle; then direct them to pass one of the hearts around the circle as they chant. When the chant is over, ask the child holding the heart to say something sweet about the child whose name is on that heart. Aw, shucks!

If you're feeling really sweet,

Make a heart that's nice and neat.

Add some kisses and a hug;

A valentine is made with love!

—Carrie Lacher

Poems, & Rhymes

Baby Alligator

A baby alligator was green and small;

He hadn't any sharp teeth, none at all.

He snapped at a beetle, and he snapped at a fly.

But he didn't catch a thing, so he started to cry.

The baby alligator grew big and long.

Soon his teeth were sharp and strong.

Now he snaps at the beetle, and he snaps at the fly;

He's a happy alligator, and we know why!

—Carrie Lacher

We're Going On A Bug Hunt!

Creep and crawl your way into language and movement fun with this popular chant that has been given a "buggy" twist. Take your class outside on a sunny day; then have them repeat each line of the chant and move with you. Next provide youngsters with empty, plastic spice bottles for catching critters on a real bug hunt.

idea by Linda Cupit—Pre-K, Crowville High School, Crowville, LA
poem by Carla Goethe—Pre-K, P.P.A.T. Child Care, Davenport, IA

We're going on a bug hunt!
We're going to catch some big ones.
What a sunny day!
Are you ready? OK!

Oh, my! A bee!
A black and yellow bee,
Flying **over** the flowers.
Buzz…

We're going on a bug hunt!
We're going to catch some big ones.
What a sunny day!
Are you ready? OK!

Oh, my! An ant!
A tiny, black ant,
Crawling **through** the grass.
Shh…

Poems, & Rhymes

We're going on a bug hunt!
We're going to catch some big ones.
What a sunny day!
Are you ready? OK!

Oh, my! A grasshopper!
A big, green grasshopper,
Hopping **around** the tree.
Boing, boing…

We're going on a bug hunt!
We're going to catch some big ones.
What a sunny day!
Are you ready? OK!

Oh, my! A spider!
A big, black spider,
Creeping **on** the tree.
Creep, creep…

We're going on a bug hunt!
We're going to catch some big ones.
What a sunny day!
Are you ready? OK!

Oh, my! A butterfly!
A pretty, orange butterfly,
Floating **in** the sky.
Whoosh, whoosh…

213

CRAFTS FOR LITTLE HANDS

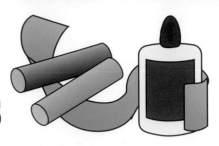

Crafts For Little Hands

Some Mighty Fine Swine

Your little ones will be hog-wild about these precious piggy projects! To make one, sponge-paint one side of two large paper plates and one small paper plate pink. When the paint is dry, poke a brad through the center of the smaller plate; then loosely attach this plate to one of the larger plates. Cut out and glue construction-paper ears, eyes, and a snout to the smaller plate. Staple the rims of the large plates together so that the unpainted sides face each other. Stuff the body of the pig with crumpled tissue paper. As a final touch, cut a tail from a pink construction-paper circle as shown; then glue the tail to the back of the pig. "Sue-ey"!

Lisa Scaglione—Four- And Five-Year-Olds
Children's Village Preschool
Sherrill's Ford, NC

Good "Moos"

Have you "herd" the good news? Making these "moos" strengthens fine-motor skills! Trace a cow pattern onto a sheet of white construction paper. Tear brown or black construction-paper spots; then glue the spots onto the cow. Add a button or wiggle eye. When the glue is dry, cut out the cow shape. Send these cows out to pasture by mounting them on a green background.

Amy Kapsis—Three- And Four-Year-Olds With Special Needs
Marathon Childhood Center
Middle Village, NY

Zany Zebras

Add zest to your craft time with these zebra projects. Cut a zebra shape from white construction paper. Place the zebra flat in a box's lid or plastic container. Place a paddleball in a spoon. Dip the ball into any color of paint; then drop the ball in the lid or container. Tilt the lid or container back and forth so that the ball rolls painted lines onto the zebra. Fringe a length of paper that matches the color of the paint. When the paint on the zebra is dry, glue the paper to the back of the zebra to resemble its mane.

Beverly Sandberg, Peace Lutheran Preschool, Palm Bay, FL

216

Smile Like A Crocodile!

Wrap up a reptile unit with these snappy swamp lovers. To make one, place a plastic strawberry basket in the center of a sheet of green tissue paper; then wrap the paper upwards, tucking the ends in the basket. Glue two green pom-poms to the top of the basket; then glue wiggle eyes to the pom-poms. Cut apart the top and bottom sections of a cardboard egg carton. Cut off the flap from the bottom half of the carton. Paint both sections green. When the paint is dry, insert the sections into the basket as shown. Display the smiling crocodiles on a paper pond. Snap!

Abi Reiffman—Two-, Three-, And Four-Year-Olds
Yavneh Hebrew Academy
Los Angeles, CA

Turtle Time

These turtles will suit your little ones to a T. Sponge-paint a paper-plate half the colors of your choice. From green construction paper, cut a turtle head, a tail, and two legs. Glue the paper pieces to the back of the painted plate. Add a wiggle eye to the turtle's head to complete the project. Top off your turtle time by reading aloud any of the tales about Franklin the turtle by Paulette Bourgeois (all Franklin titles published by Scholastic Inc.).

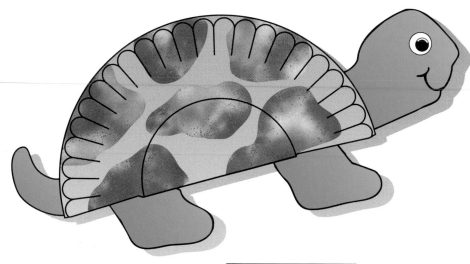

rabbit

Animal Outline Art

Keep this art project handy for anytime. Prepare stencils by tracing animal shapes onto tagboard pieces. Cut out the shapes. (Or use a die-cutter to cut shapes out of tagboard.) Label the stencils, if desired, so that students can copy the animals' names. A student may trace a stencil several times on one sheet of construction paper, and then color or paint the designs. Encourage youngsters to overlap the animal designs to yield interesting results.

rabbit

Crafts For Little Hands

Fall Foliage

You'll rake up piles of creative ways to display these leaves. Collect a supply of large paper grocery bags; then cut out the bottom and down one side of each bag. Thoroughly wet the papers and crumple them. Spread the papers flat to dry. Cut leaf shapes out of the papers; then sponge-paint the leaves a variety of fall colors. When the paint is dry, arrange the leaves as a border around a display. Or mount a supply on a wall to resemble a large wreath. To make an individual wreath, glue a construction-paper wreath shape onto an identically shaped cardboard shape. Glue an arrangement of the leaves atop the wreath. Autumn is all around!

Mary Marcucci—Preschool
Home Childcare
Chandler, AZ

Time To Harvest The Pumpkins

Youngsters are sure to enjoy harvesting this patch of pumpkins. Squirt orange tempera paint to which a few drops of dishwashing detergent has been added, into a thoroughly cleaned milk jug. Replace the lid. Shake the jug until it is coated with paint. After removing the top to allow the paint to dry, spray-paint the top green. If desired, add personality to the pumpkin by gluing on paper shapes. Display the patch of pumpkins in an open area among large paper leaves and crepe-paper vines.

Gina Blair—Preschool/Title I
Morning Sun Elementary
Morning Sun, IA

Fingerpainted Frights

These jack-o'-lanterns are frightfully fun for little fingers to paint. To make one, paint a large piece of paper with a mixture of yellow and orange fingerpaint. When the paint is dry, cut the paper into a pumpkin shape. To make the eyes, the nose, and a grin, press a hand into black paint, then onto the pumpkin as desired. Top the pumpkin with a paper stem. Aren't these the most handsome grins you've seen?

Vickie Zalk—Three-Year-Olds
Hope Creative Preschool, Winter Haven, FL

Pumpkin Tambourine

Celebrate the harvest by shaking a pumpkin tambourine! To make one, paint the backs of two paper plates orange. When the paint is dry, secure the rims of the plates together with several paper clips; then use a hole puncher to punch an even number of holes through the rims. Remove the paper clips. Through every pair of holes, thread a length of green yarn through both plates. Thread a jingle bell onto the yarn; then tie the yarn in a bow. Shake, shake, shake that tambourine!

Let's Talk Turkey

If these turkeys could talk, don't you wonder what they'd say? Glue a wooden ice-cream spoon onto the center of a brown paper circle. Then glue colorful construction-paper feathers to the edge of the brown circle. Finish the turkey by gluing wiggle eyes, a paper beak, and a wattle to the spoon. Gobble, gobble! Eat more vegetables, please!

Charlene Vonnahme—Preschool
Carroll Area Child Care Center
Carroll, IA

I Spy Pumpkin Pie

I spy pumpkin pie—and smell pie, too! These crafty pumpkin pies smell just like the real thing. Fill a paper bowl with torn, orange tissue-paper pieces. Spray the pieces with cinnamon-scented air freshener. While the pieces are damp, sprinkle on pumpkin-pie spice. Trace the top of an empty bowl onto a piece of orange paper; then cut out the circle. Punch holes through the circle; then glue the circle onto the rim of the "pumpkin-filled" bowl. Present these air fresheners as gifts, and spicy thank-yous are sure to follow.

adapted from an idea by Charlet Keller—Preschool
ICC Preschool, Violet Hill, AR

Crafts For Little Hands

What An Angel!

Parents are sure to treasure these hand-made angels. Begin by painting white hand-prints onto blue construction paper; then set the prints aside to dry. Cut a circle from the appropriate color of skin-toned construction paper. Glue the circle to a white construction-paper triangle. Use markers to draw a face on the circle; then glue on pieces of yarn or tinsel to represent hair. Embellish the angel's robe with materials such as lace, glitter, pearls, sequins, or ribbon flowers. Cut around the shapes of the dry handprints; then glue them to the back of the angel to represent wings. As a finishing touch, twist a pipe cleaner to resemble a halo; then tape it to the back of the angel's head. Heavenly!

Deborah Olsen—Four-Year-Olds
The School Of Grace
Raleigh, NC

Sleep In Heavenly Peace

When sleeping on these pillows, your little ones will have the sweetest of dreams. Provide a prewashed, white pillowcase for each student, or ask each child to bring one. Before painting a pillowcase, insert a personalized sheet of paper that is the length and width of the pillowcase. Using fabric paint, generously paint a child's hand yellow or gold. Have him press his hand onto the pillowcase to form an angel's wings. After the child's hand has been washed and dried, paint it once more with a different color of his choice. Have him press his hand on the pillowcase again to form the angel's body. Using the appropriate colors, paint a head, hair, a halo, eyes, and a mouth. Add a message, the child's name, and the date. Add additional designs to the pillowcase if desired. Follow the manufacturer's instructions to permanently set the paints if necessary.

Sleep In Heavenly Peace

Melissa 1997

Janice Hughes and Jean Bower—Four- And Five-Year-Olds
Messiah Lutheran Nursery School
Williamsport, PA

Dreidel Delight

These dreidels are so unusual, making them will leave your youngsters spinning with delight. Prepare a dreidel template similar to the shape shown. Use a white candle to trace the shape onto white construction paper. Then paint over the shape with watered-down blue tempera paint. While the paint is wet, sprinkle on gold or blue glitter. When the paint is dry, shake off the excess glitter.

Linda Blassingame
JUST 4 & 5 Developmental Laboratory
Mobile, AL

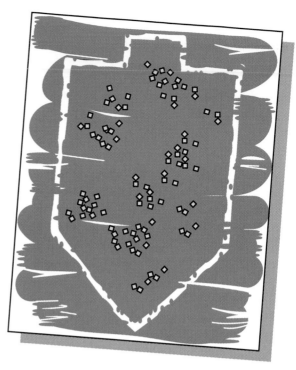

We Love Christmas!

Fill your room with candy canes this Christmas. To make one of these sweet hearts, use red paint, crayons, or tissue-paper squares to decorate two construction-paper candy-cane shapes. When the canes are complete, glue the tips together to create a heart. Now that's a candy-cane Christmas!

Beth Lemke—Pre-K
Heights Head Start
Coon Rapids, MN

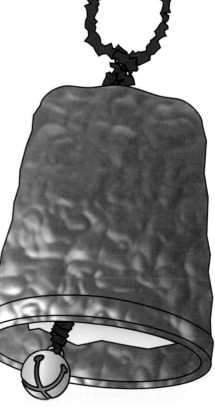

I Heard The Bells

Don't wait for Christmas Day to hear the bells ring. Make these bells in your classroom today! To make a bell, cover an empty yogurt container with aluminum foil. Insert the end of a pipe cleaner through the loop in the top of a jingle bell; then twist the pipe cleaner to fasten it securely to the bell. Poke a hole in the bottom of the container; then slide the pipe cleaner through the hole. Twist the end of the pipe cleaner into a loop. Ring the bells during a group time; then hang them on a tree. "Jinga-linga-ling!"

Deborah Lensing—Three-Year-Olds
Twin River Childcare Center
White River Junction, VT

221

Dressed For The Weather

Youngsters can head out into the snow with style when wearing these snazzy shirts. To design one, prewash a black or dark blue sweatshirt. Using white fabric paint, paint the bottom of a child's foot; then have him press his footprint onto the front of the shirt. Using squeezable white fabric paint that dries shiny, outline the footprint and create a border of snow as shown. When this paint is dry, invite the child to complete the shirt by using various colors of squeezable paint to add features to the snowman and snowflakes to the background. This snowman is really stylin'!

Jody Johnson—Preschool
Little Lamb Preschool
Madison, SD

The Invisible Snowman

Young children are fascinated by the results of this fun winter project. From construction paper, cut a hat, eyes, a nose, pieces of coal, and a scarf or shapes for creating a scarf. Arrange the pieces on the adhesive side of a large square of clear Con-Tact® covering to resemble a snowman. Gently press an identically sized piece of Con-Tact® atop the first piece. Cut around the arranged pieces, shaping the area between the hat and the scarf to resemble the snowman's head. Hang the projects with monofilament line from your ceiling or tape them to a window. These snowpeople are sure to be oh, so popular. And the best part is that they never melt!

Kathy Burrows—18-Month-Olds to Six-Year-Olds
Country Meadows Child Care
Bridgeville, PA

Cool Dude

This winter guy requires some assistance to make, but the result is really cool! Cut a strip of quilt batting to match the circumference and height of a plastic container such as those used to package powdered drink mix. Brush the sides of the container with craft glue; then press the strip onto the container. Glue wiggle eyes, a yarn mouth, and a felt carrot nose to the batting. Tie a strip of fabric or length of ribbon around the snowman. To make a top hat for the snowman, tape the ends of a strip of construction paper together to create a tube; then tape the tube onto a paper circle. Or top this snow dude off with a miniature straw hat (available at craft stores).

Susan Hammett and Marilyn Blair—Pre-K
Cedar Springs Preschool
Knoxville, TN

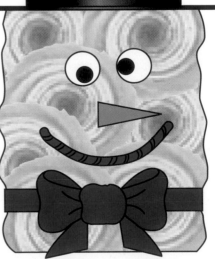

Crafts For Little Hands

Valentine Clifford®

This version of The Big Red Dog® is sure to melt a lot of hearts. Cut out a large, red heart; a large, narrow pink heart; two small, white hearts; and a black heart. To make Clifford®, turn the red heart upside down to represent his face. Cut the pink heart in half; then attach one half to each side of the red heart to represent ears. Finally glue on the white heart eyes and the black heart nose. Clifford®, we "wuff" you!

Chris Kargol—Early Childhood Exceptional Education
Manitoba Elementary School
Milwaukee, WI

Got Valentines?

Get ready for your valentine exchange with these handled heart holders. To make a holder, remove the label from a clean, empty milk jug. Use a permanent red marker to draw a large heart on the front of the jug. Use scissors to cut down the jug's sides and around the top of the heart, leaving the handle intact as shown. Personalize the back panel of the jug. Decorate the holder by gluing red, pink, and white tissue-paper pieces on the heart shape. If desired, punch holes around the cut edges and lace the holder with colored yarn.

Linda Kirk—Preschool
Rainbow Child Care Center, Bakersfield, CA

Be Mine!

Speed up youngsters' pulses as they use fine-motor skills to construct this heartfelt display. To make one heart project, trace a heart pattern onto a piece of white construction paper; then turn the paper facedown. Dip scraps of fabric into a mixture that is half water and half glue, and arrange the scraps on the back of the paper so that they overlap. When the glue is dry, cut out the traced heart shape. Glue the heart to a red or pink sheet of construction paper so that the fabric collage is showing. Arrange the hearts together on a wall. Happy Valentine's Day!

adapted from an idea by Tina Summers—Pre-K
I.C. Preschool
North Little Rock, AR

Shamrocks Galore And More!

Excite your little leprechauns with this open-ended art activity. Brush green and white paint onto a large sheet of black construction paper. Press a few shamrock cutouts into the wet paint. If desired, also add glitter and metallic confetti. When the paint is dry, mount the artwork on a larger sheet of green paper. Adapt this idea to fit other special occasions as well!

Fran Tortorici—Three-Year-Olds
Castleton Hill Moravian Preschool
Staten Island, NY

Magic Paint

The surprise at the end of this art project is that you've created a rainbow of color! Paint liquid starch onto a piece of art paper. Dip a damp paintbrush into powdered paint; then dab it onto the wet paper. The starch will change the powder into a thick paint. Repeat the process with other colors of powdered tempera to make a colorful design.

Colorful Kites

Welcome spring with these sun-catching kites. To make one, trace and cut out a kite shape from construction paper. Then cut the middle from the kite, leaving a frame. Attach the kite frame to the adhesive side of a piece of Con-Tact® covering; then trim around the frame to remove the excess. Place the kite on a table with the adhesive side facing up. Fill its middle with an assortment of small tissue-paper squares. Complete the project by adding a yarn tail. Tape the kites to your classroom windows for a great stained-glass look. Get ready; here comes a breeze!

Amy Jenkins—Preschool
Children's Country Day School
Mendota Heights, MN

Crafts For Little Hands

Outrageous Octopus

This craft idea for little hands makes an outrageous creature with oodles of arms. To make one octopus, open a brown paper lunch bag; then insert a forearm into the bag. Paint the outside of the bag purple. When the paint is dry, crumple a sheet of newspaper; then insert it into the bag. Use a rubber band to seal the bag just above the paper. Turn the bag upside down; then cut the portion below the rubber band into eight sections. Separate and twist each of the sections. Complete the tentacled creature by gluing on wiggle eyes. One, two, three, four, five, six, seven, eight! That octopus looks really great!

Jennifer Liptak—Three-Year-Olds
Building Blocks Of Learning
Denville, NJ

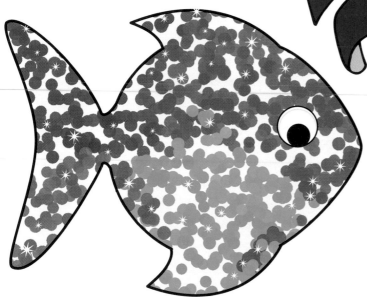

Something's Fishy

The groovy technique used to paint these fish makes them look real enough to catch! Prepare a painting mitt for each different color of paint by folding a rectangular piece of bubble wrap in half, then stapling the sides. Put a mitt on one hand; then dip it into a shallow pan of paint. Press the mitt onto a large piece of white paper. Using a different mitt for each color of paint, paint the paper until it is covered. While the paint is wet, sprinkle on glitter. Cut a fish shape out of the paper when the paint is dry. Don't let this idea get away!

Pat Johnson—Three-Year-Olds
Church Of The Redeemer Preschool
Columbus, OH

Creeping, Crawling Crabs

Red will be the color of the day when youngsters make these crafty crustaceans. To make one, fold a paper plate in half. Unfold the plate; then glue two sections of an egg carton onto one half of the outside of the plate as shown. When the glue is dry, paint the plate and the egg-carton sections red. When the paint is dry, refold the plate. Glue four red construction-paper strips to each side of the plate and glue wiggle eyes to the egg-carton sections. Which way to the beach?

Lesley J. Armstrong—Preschool
Sunrise Valley
Lawrence, KS

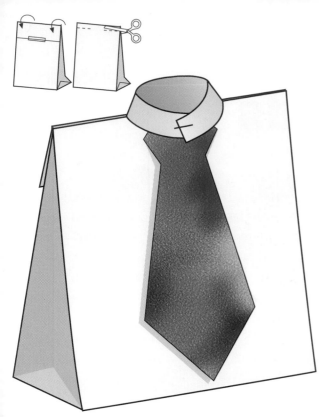

Father's Day Gift Bag

Dad will love this one-of-a-kind designer shirt and tie! Place a Father's Day treat inside a white or colorful paper lunch bag. To transform the bag into a shirt and tie, fold down the top three inches. Tape the folded section to the bag. One inch below the fold, cut two inches toward the center of the bag on both sides. Bring the two top pieces toward the front of the bag to resemble the collar of a man's shirt. Staple the pieces together. To design a tie for Dad's shirt, use watercolors to paint a 6" x 3" piece of white construction paper. When the paint is dry, cut the paper to resemble a tie as shown. Glue the tie to the bag under the collar. Made especially for you, Dad—by me!

Dayle Timmons—Special Education Pre-K
Alimacani Elementary School
Jacksonville Beach, FL

Picture-Perfect Fit

Dads and Moms will absolutely love this gift idea to pieces. Remove the glass from a frame; then trace the outside and opening of the frame onto cardboard. Set the frame aside. Use an X-acto® knife to cut out the cardboard frame. Use tempera paint to paint the new frame and the desired number of puzzle pieces. When the paint is dry, glue the pieces to the frame. Print a message onto a tagboard strip; then glue it to the frame. Tape a photograph to the back of the frame. If desired, add magnetic tape to the back of the frame as well.

Donna Jennings—Special Education
    Preschool
United Cerebral Palsy Of New York City
Staten Island, NY

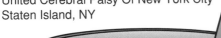

Hold Everything!

Proud parents are sure to display these personalized pencil holders at work or at home. And as a bonus, each one is easy and inexpensive to make! Cut a light-colored piece of construction paper to match the height and diameter of a plastic container. (Powdered-drink containers work well.) Use crayons to decorate the paper. If desired, use craft glue to attach a school photo to the paper. Laminate the paper; then wrap it around the container and secure it with clear tape. Your little ones will present these gifts with love.

Kathy Doeing—Pre-K
St. Paul Preschool
Painesville, OH

BUSY HANDS

BUSY HANDS

Creative Learning Experiences For Little Hands

SQUEEZIN' AND SQUOOSHIN'

ideas by Karen Jones, Community School Of The Arts, Charlotte, NC

SQUOOSHY, SQUIRMY, AND OH SO SENSATIONAL!

For a truly sensory-rich experience, fill a large bucket, water table, or tub with water. Then add enough corn-starch to make the water the consistency of a sauce (between 8 to 12 boxes). For added fun stir in some food coloring and a few drops of mint extract. Add large cooking spoons, shovels, scoops, or plastic putty knives. Is it wet or dry? It's *both!*

SQUIRTING WITH A TWIST

Here's a challenging takeoff on a squirting standard. Provide children with turkey basters instead of eye-droppers. Fill a few buckets with colored water, and place them in a plastic pool or tub. Provide plenty of squirting room. For added zest stir glitter into the colored water. Youngsters will be amazed to find that as they collaborate when squirting the water, new colors are created.

SQUEEZE A LITTLE, SQUOOSH A LITTLE...POP!

Kids love plastic bubble wrap, so set up this center that invites them to squeeze to their hearts' content. Fill a water table or tub with bubble wrap that has been cut into various sizes. Add water and a small amount of dish-washing detergent to the tub. Watch the fun begin!

SUDSY SPONGES

The more hands the merrier when it comes to this sudsy activity! Fill large, easy-to-squeeze sponges with tearless baby shampoo. Add just enough water to moisten the sponges and to get the bubbles started. Place the sponges in a water table or in a plastic pool on the floor. (Keep hand towels and a bucket of water nearby for easy and quick cleanup.) When visiting this center, your little ones will know just what to do...squeeze!

SQUEEZABLE SQUOOSHY BAGS

Prepare some of these squeezable bags so little ones can explore color and texture without even getting wet. Fill various sizes of resealable plastic bags with clear dishwashing detergent and a squirt of liquid tempera paint. For a variation leave the detergent clear, and add glitter, plastic confetti, or beads instead of paint to the soap. Carefully seal each bag; then hot-glue the seal closed. For extra security against spills, place each filled bag in an identically sized bag and seal the top. These fun bags provide great lessons about cause and effect—more squeezing causes more fun!

BALLOONS—GOOD, BETTER, BEST!

Balloons take on new possibilities when you fill them with flour. To speed filling the balloons, cut an empty, plastic soda bottle in half to create a funnel. Stretch the opening of a balloon (12-inch helium balloons work best) around the bottle's neck; then pour enough flour into the funnel to fill the balloon. Remove the balloon from the bottle, and tie its end. Encourage children to squeeze, sort, and count the balloons. For added fun encourage youngsters to toss the balloons into boxes and baskets.

NO-COOK SQUOOSHY DOUGH

This fun dough feels like play dough, but dries harder than clay. The more you make, the better, because it even freezes well, too! Combine two cups of flour with one cup of salt; then stir in a cup of water that has been tinted with food coloring. Knead the dough. Encourage children to simply squeeze the dough, or to sculpt it by adding items such as ice-cream sticks, coffee stirrers, shells, beads, and more. Allow sculptures to dry two to three days. Store any unused dough in air-tight containers. (If necessary, knead flour into the stored dough to return it to its original consistency.)

SQUEEZING RAINBOWS

Launch the year with a colorful class mural. Fill each of several plastic envelope-moistener bottles (found at office-supplies stores) with liquid tempera paint and a few squirts of dishwashing detergent. Cover an area of the floor or a table with a plastic tablecloth; then line sheets of poster board on the protective covering. Ask youngsters to put on painting smocks or rain ponchos. Rainbows of color will soon appear as the children squeeze and roll the paint onto the poster board.

BUSY HANDS

Creative Learning Experiences For Little Hands

STACK 'EM UP!

These hands-on activities offer a ton of fun while the creative process grows...and grows...and grows!

by Karen Jones, Community School Of The Arts, Charlotte, NC

HOURS OF TOWERS

Carefully cut thick Styrofoam® packaging into blocks. Place the blocks in a center along with colorful plastic toothpicks and large sequins. When imaginative youngsters use their fine-motor skills to work with these materials, skyscrapers, cities, and spaceships will be built before your eyes!

UNDER CONSTRUCTION

Involve youngsters in creating permanent additions to your block area. Collect cardboard containers and cans in various sizes. Invite youngsters to paint the containers with a mixture of two parts liquid tempera and one part glue. When the paint is dry, these building materials can take lots of handling and are easy to wipe clean. Let's build...one yellow, three red, one on top, one below...

IF I HAD A HAMMER

Use this suggestion to create a safe and quiet center suitable for any classroom construction site. Place hammers, nuts, bolts, and screws in a center. Instead of wood, include large Styrofoam® chunks in the center. To extend the possibilities, add colorful yarn to the site. Hammer in the morning. Hammer in the evening. Hammer all through the day!

"STICKABLE," STACKABLE SHAPES

Geometric shapes cut from colorful felt will take on new possibilities when you attach the hook sides of Velcro® pieces to them. Place a flannelboard on the floor; then invite a child to build on his learning by sticking and stacking the shapes.

230

LAYERS OF LIGHT

Get ready to watch your classroom bounce with color! Place a piece of colored cellophane in each of several embroidery hoops. Plug in an overhead projector (away from any potentially wet areas). Allow children to stack, restack, and unstack the hoops on the projector's base to explore patterns, shapes, and colors. How about that! Math, science, and language—all in a day's play!

COLORFUL SKYSCRAPERS

Set up a site for the construction of colorful skyscrapers and other sculptures stacked with color. Cut pieces of cardboard into various sizes and shapes. Stock the area with mat-board scraps collected from a frame store. Be sure to supply youngsters with plenty of "cement" (paste) and plastic-knife spreaders for creating their sky-high sculptures.

IN, OVER, AND UNDER

What can busy hands do with Styrofoam® plates and pipe cleaners? They can create wonderful works of art! Gather stacks of Styrofoam® plates, pipe cleaners, and plastic beads. Then encourage free-form sewing as youngsters poke the pipe cleaners in, over, and under the plates.

CLEARLY COLORFUL

Colors come to life when youngsters use watered-down glue to paint colorful tissue-paper shapes onto clear plastic wrap or laminating film. Mount these creative collages on a window. Little ones will be surprised to discover new colors hiding in the layers.

BUSY HANDS

Creative Learning Experiences For Little Hands

SHIMMER AND SHINE!

by Karen Jones, Community School Of The Arts, Charlotte, NC

WHIMSICAL WATERCOLORS

Transform a wet watercolor painting in a twinkling of the eye by sprinkling it with a mixture of salt and glitter. For best results when using watercolor paints, provide youngsters with bowls of water that won't tip easily, quality white construction paper, and watercolors in compact trays.

GLITTER CRAYONS GALORE

To create glitter crayons, place foil muffin liners in a muffin pan. Invite children to drop same-colored pieces of old crayons in each liner, then sprinkle their favorite colors of glitter atop the pieces. Place the pan in an oven set at a low temperature. Remove the pan when the wax has melted. While the wax is still warm, remove the liner papers. When the crayons have cooled, let the drawing begin!

THEY'RE CALLING FOR SNOW!

Mix about two parts white liquid tempera paint with one part glue until you have a sticky, but fluid, mixture. Provide a child with a length of quality aluminum foil on a tray. Invite the child to use brushes, small paint rollers, toy cars, and rubber spatulas as tools for painting the mixture onto the foil. When the child has finished, sprinkle opalescent glitter on the snow scene. When each child has completed a project, arrange the creations together for a dazzling display.

ANGELS WANTED: STARS NEED SHINING

To prepare this center, remove the paint trough from your easel. Put a small amount of water, liquid dish detergent, and a touch of glitter in a large, plastic container (such as a wallpapering trough). Locate the container below the easel. Then, instead of paper, put a length of quality aluminum foil on the front of your easel. When one of your little angels visits this center, provide him with a foam dish mop and a squeegee. Encourage him to paint the soap mixture onto the foil. Then, when he is satisfied with the shine, have him squeegee the suds toward the plastic container.

These ideas use materials recycled from the holidays. *Now* the fun really begins!

SPARKLING STRINGS AND THINGS

Add sparkle to your water table by adding colorful strands of beaded Christmas-tree garland. Remove some beads from the strands, and provide tongs and strainers. Encourage youngsters to sort the individual beads by color and size.

SHINY BUBBLES

Add some gold or silver tempera paint to your favorite bubble mixture. Then protect a section of the floor in an open area of your room with newspaper. Place a length of bulletin-board paper atop the newspaper. Invite youngsters to blow the bubble mixture onto the paper and watch it pop. For a variation, pour a small amount of the bubble mixture into a shallow tray. Encourage youngsters to dip holiday cookie cutters into the mixture, then use the cutters as bubble wands. Blow and pop!

SNOW DOUGH

Add sparkle to your favorite play-dough recipe by omitting food coloring and kneading in pearly flakes of opalescent "snow" (look for this product after the holidays at "melted" prices). This snow dough is almost as fun as the real thing!

PUZZLES WITH PIZZAZZ

This class project provides days of wonder. In an art center, place sheets of poster board, scissors, bowls of glue, brushes, and a variety of leftover holiday materials, such as wrapping paper, tinsel, shiny ribbons, and more. Encourage children visiting the center to decorate the poster board with the materials. When each collage is complete, cut it into several pieces to make a one-of-a-kind floor puzzle.

BUSY HANDS

Creative Learning Experiences For Little Hands

SWIRL AND TWIRL

by Karen Jones, Community School Of The Arts, Charlotte, NC

Put a spin on fun with these hands-on ideas that will keep 'em busy and leave 'em dizzy!

ON YOUR MARK, GET SET, ROLL!

Ping-Pong® balls take on a new twist when decorated with stripes and simple designs. Use permanent markers or paint pens to decorate a supply of balls. Encourage children to roll the balls down slides, through tubes, and down ramps in the block center. Or have them swirl the balls in a water table. The fun keeps on rollin', rollin', rollin'!

DESIGNER TOPS

Transform a small Styrofoam® plate into a spinning top by attaching a piece of tape to its center, then inserting a small golf pencil through the tape and the plate. (Small golf pencils are available at office-supply stores.) Remove the pencil; then decorate the plate with stickers, Con-Tact®-covering scraps, and pieces of colorful tape. Give it a spin!

SWIRLING AWAY THE DAY

Here's a unique twist to fingerpainting: cup painting. Slightly thin an amount of liquid tempera paint with dishwashing detergent. Plop enough of the mixture onto a shallow tray to eventually cover the tray. Place two plastic cups upside down on the tray. Encourage a child to use both hands to glide the cups over the tray. To save a child's design, remove the cups; then gently pat a piece of paper on the tray. Lift the paper to discover the design that has been transferred as a print.

WATER-BOTTLE MANIA

Invite youngsters to use stickers, colored tape, and Con-Tact® paper scraps to decorate the outsides of plastic, water-filled bottles. Put the bottles on the floor, give them a whirl, and watch them swirl!

Fun That Will Make Your Head Spin

Add a whirl of excitement to your water table with painted bowls. Use paint pens or permanent markers to draw spiraled designs onto the insides of several plastic bowls. Challenge youngsters to use chopsticks to steer and spin the bowls in the water.

Dizzy Miss Lizzy

Have you ever wondered what to do with an outdated record player? If so, take a turn with this favorite idea. Press a paper plate onto a record player's turntable. Grab a marker (or two!), select a speed, and draw on the plate as it spins. Your youngsters' delight at this project is sure to sound like music to your ears.

Round In Circles

Use this idea to turn a corner of your room into a creative-learning lab. Hang a funnel from your ceiling so that it is several inches above the ground. Place a dark-colored vinyl tablecloth or Con-Tact® paper directly underneath the funnel. Locate a tub of sand and several laundry-detergent scoops in the center. Encourage visitors to this area to pour sand into the funnel and gently start it swinging. As the funnel circles, youngsters can observe the sand designs on the floor. Have students sweep up the sand and return it to the tub before beginning again.

Barber-Pole Roll

Attach the loop side of a strip of self-adhesive Velcro® in a spiraling design onto a rolling pin. Encourage a child to roll the pin in a shallow tray of paint, then onto bulletin-board paper. For added fun, prepare more than one rolling pin as described; then invite pairs of children to create spiral designs together, each using different colors of paint.

235

BUSY HANDS

Creative Learning Experiences For Little Hands

SLIP AND SLIDE!

ideas contributed by Karen Jones, Community School Of The Arts, Charlotte, NC

SCRUB-A-DUB-DUB

For good, clean fun, invite children to paint with shaving cream directly onto your painting easel—no paper needed! Simply add non-menthol shaving cream and a small amount of water to a bucket. Toss in a soft nylon shower "scrunchie" in place of a brush. Add a squeegee so that youngsters can erase their work and begin again.

BUBBLES ON BUBBLES

For a sensory surprise, tape a large sheet of bubble wrap onto a tabletop. Squirt just enough dish detergent and water onto the wrap to create a slippery surface. Little hands will slip and slide for hours!

COLORFUL PUDDLES

Fill an ice-cube tray with water; then add a drop of food coloring to each section. When the cubes are frozen, store them by color in bowls in the freezer. Invite a child to hold a cube with a pair of tongs and rub it over a tabletop. Encourage him to watch several colors of cubes melt as they slide. Then have him wipe up the puddles with a white paper towel. Ooh, aah. Wipe up some color magic!

SIMPLY ADD SOAP

It sounds simple—but it's so much fun! Plop a couple of bars of soap into your water table. And if you'd like to find a use for those decorative soaps that are gathering dust in your own bathroom, add those, too! To provide a different type of sensory experience, provide rubber kitchen gloves for little ones to wear while playing at this center.

SLIPPERY SUDS

Create your own fingerpaint in a jiffy! Just mix one part liquid tempera paint with one part clear dishwashing liquid. Squirt the paint onto cookie sheets, foil-covered tabletops, plastic sheeting, or vinyl tablecloths. Try fingerpainting with the mixture on windows, too! If a child wishes to save a painted design, gently press a piece of paper onto the painted surface; then peel it off.

PUDDING PAINT

On a roll with slippery experiences? Don't forget this kid favorite—painting with pudding. For added interest slip a simple pattern outline or coloring picture under waxed paper. Then drop a dollop of pudding onto the paper. Remember, very clean hands are required for this painting treat!

237

THE SECOND TIME AROUND

THE SECOND TIME AROUND
Recycling In The Preschool Classroom

Preschool Printers

Use Styrofoam® trays to inspire creative art prints! Cut off the edges of a Styrofoam® tray. Use a sharp pencil to etch—or have a child etch—a design into the tray. To make a print, brush paint over the surface of the design; then press the painted surface onto a sheet of paper. Presto! What perfect prints for preschoolers!

Susan Burbridge—Four-Year-Olds
Trinity Weekday School
San Antonio, TX

Keep On Truckin'

Your youngsters will be on the road to creativity with this crafty recycling idea that uses empty facial-tissue boxes. Stock your art center with a supply of empty facial-tissue boxes, precut black paper circles to represent wheels, precut yellow paper circles to represent headlights, construction-paper scraps, scissors, and glue. Invite your young mechanics to create a variety of vehicles using the materials available. Varoom! Varoom!

Jodie Mangum
Munchkin Manor Learning Center
Bend, OR

Packaging Possibilities

When buying items in bulk, be on the lookout for creative uses for packaging trays. For example, some items purchased in six-packs are packaged in divided trays useful for sorting and counting. Paint packages to make fun additions to a block center. Or cut packages into smaller pieces to make terrific tracing patterns for use in art centers. You'll find lots of creative uses for these handy items.

Alice M. Smith—Preschool
Delran, NJ

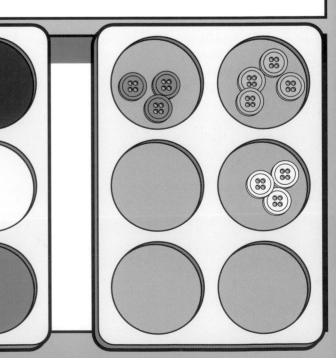

THE SECOND TIME AROUND
Recycling In The Preschool Classroom

Wish Book

Do you ever wish for a way to use the bundles of toy catalogs that arrive in your mail every holiday season? If so try this idea. Provide each child in your class with a catalog and a sheet of construction paper. Invite him to look through his catalog in search of an item he would like to have. Instruct him to cut out the pictured item, then glue it on his sheet of paper. Record his description of the item and his suggested price on the paper. When each child has completed a page, bind the pages together to create a class catalog full of wish-book favorites.

Betty Silkunas, Lansdale, PA

Eric

It's a cool red car. It goes fast. $5 bazillion.

Jeanne

She is a doll. She has a pretty yellow dress. $2.

Catalog I Spy

Baseball Cap $6.00

Vest $15.00

Party Dress $25.00

Don't throw away those mail-order catalogs this holiday season! Instead put them to good use with this variation of the game I Spy. Divide your students into pairs; then provide each pair with a catalog. Direct the pairs to look through their catalogs to find a specific type of object. For example say, "I spy something red." If desired give the students in each pair an opportunity to tell the class about the item they found. For a variation, direct the pairs to search for letters, numerals, or shapes.

Betty Silkunas

Categorize By Size

Youngsters' abilities to compare sizes will really take shape when working on this cooperative display. Visually divide a length of bulletin-board paper into three sections; then label each section "Small," "Medium," and "Large" respectively. Have small groups of students look through catalogs and cut out pictures of items. Help the students consider the actual sizes of the items, then categorize them as small, medium, or large. Direct students to glue their cut-out pictures in the columns.

Betty Silkunas

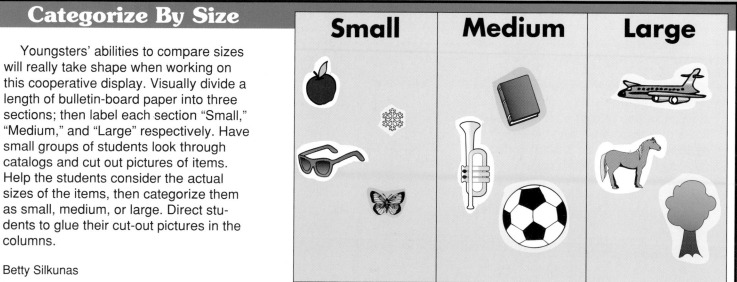

Small	Medium	Large

THE SECOND TIME AROUND
Recycling In The Preschool Classroom

Spool Streamers

Enlist the help of parents in collecting a class supply of empty thread spools; then make these sensational streamers. To make one, thread three different colors of corrugated ribbon through the hole in a spool. Tie the ribbons in two knots—one at each end of the spool—to secure the spool in place. Complete the streamer by brushing clear fingernail polish on the ends of the ribbons to prevent fraying. Students will enjoy using these streamers in movement and music activities, and when they become dingy, just pop them into the washing machine.

Debbie Hugli—Pre-K
Carousel Preschool
Downey, CA

Brown-Bag Big Books

I play in the sun.

Turn discarded paper grocery bags into big books with this handy tip. To prepare two paper-bag pages, lift the folded bottom; then cut as shown. Cut along the folds of both sides. Stack the bag pages printed sides down; then staple them together along one side to create a book. With these handy big books, group writing and journaling activities are in the bag!

Kathy Zimmerman—Preschool
Pleasant Place
Harper, KS

Super Stencils

Discarded vinyl placemats make durable stencils for use at your art table or easel. To make one, trace a simple shape onto a placemat; then use an X-acto® knife to cut out the shape. With this easy idea you can make stencils that relate to all of your seasonal and thematic units. Cleanup is a breeze—simply wash the stencils with soapy water. Super!

Teresa Collins—Preschool
Martinsville Head Start Preschool
Martinsville, IN

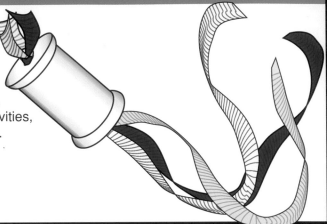

Setting The Stage

Writing Center

The "Write" Time

Right now is the right time to set up a writing center for youngsters' use throughout the year. Stock your center with various types of supplies that can be used for print exploration and writing, such as colored pencils, markers, alphabet stamps, magnet letters and a magnetboard, felt letters and a felt board, and various sizes and colors of paper. Label a supply of cards with words that are meaningful to children—such as food items, household items, and animals—and simple picture clues. Consider also preparing a reference book with a page for each child, displaying her name and photo. For young learners, this open-ended center is "write" on track!

Donna Leonard—Preschool
Head Start
Dyersville, IA

Games Area

Carpet-Square Puzzle

Use carpet squares to make a floor puzzle that is sure to cover problem-solving and visual-discrimination skills. Arrange four carpet squares together on the floor to make a larger square. Paint the outline of a simple shape on the large square, so that part of the shape is on each smaller square. When the paint is dry, place the squares in a games area. Encourage a child or a pair of children to arrange the squares so that the shape is revealed.

Michelle West
Denton City County Day School
Denton, TX

Play-Dough Center

Play-Dough Placemats

If you ask youngsters to use placemats to protect tabletops and to identify personal space when using play dough, then use this idea to add interest to the center. To make a set of play-dough placemats, cut several mats from tagboard. Glue theme-related or seasonal die-cut shapes to each mat; then laminate the mats. Or trace cookie cutters onto paper; then cut out the shapes. Glue these shapes to the mats before laminating them. Make new mats for the center each time you change themes or begin a new season.

Susan Burbridge—Four-Year-Olds
Colonial Hills United Methodist School
San Antonio, TX

Reading Area

Floating Away

To fill your reading area with fun, take advantage of end-of-the-summer sales on inflatable floats. Encourage students who visit the center to float away with reading as they relax on these silly seats.

Lori Barbery—Special Needs Preschool
A Child's Haven, Inc.
Taylors, SC

Sensory Table

Lava Landscape

Your little ones will "lava" this landscape that resembles the dinosaurs' land of long ago. To dye rice to fill your sand table, mix several drops of food coloring with enough rubbing alcohol to soak the amount of rice you would like to dye that color. Soak rice in each different color of alcohol you prepare. Drain the rice; then spread it out to dry. Add the colored rice to an empty sand table or tub along with toy dinosaurs. Watch out! This volcanic center could erupt with excitement.

Nancy Irgens—Preschool
ICC Preschool
Violet Hill, AR

Block Area

"Dino-mite" Building

The fun won't become extinct at your block area when you add these prehistoric props. Collect a supply of egg cartons; then cut the top off each one. Encourage youngsters who visit the block area to arrange the egg cartons atop block caves to resemble stalactites. Prepare foliage for the environment by attaching paper palm-fronds to one end of each of several cardboard tubes. Little ones' imaginations are sure to take them back in time when they're playing at this fun center.

Charlet Keller—Preschool
ICC Preschool
Violet Hill, AR

etting The Stage:

Water Table

Bobbing Jack-O'-Lanterns

Your youngsters will have a ball when strengthening fine-motor skills at this seasonal center. Use a black permanent marker to draw jack-o'-lantern faces on a quantity of orange Ping-Pong® balls; then float the balls in your water table. Place a fishnet (or large spoon) and a jack-o'-lantern bucket nearby. Using one hand, a child manipulates the net to scoop the jack-o'-lanterns, then drops them into the bucket. For a variation, encourage a youngster to use his other hand or to wear a blindfold.

Beth Jones—Junior Kindergarten
Stevensville School
Stevensville, Ontario, Canada

Block Area

Block Buildup

Math skills will really stack up with this constructive idea. Trace blocks of a variety of shapes and sizes onto pieces of construction paper; then program each shape with a different numeral. Cut out the shapes; then laminate them for durability. Tape the cutouts to the floor of your block area. Challenge youngsters to build block towers that correspond to each cutout's shape and numeral. This center is a blockbuster!

Maggie Woldum—Preschool
Head Start Preschool
Bozeman, MT

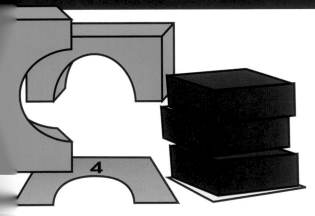

Manipulatives Center

Bushel Of Leaf Fun

Youngsters will rake up lots of sorting and classification practice with this interactive display. Collect leaves from several different types of trees. Laminate each leaf. Mount a fall character on a background. Gather as many miniature plastic baskets as you have types of leaves, plus one extra. Attach one different type of leaf to the front of each basket. Staple the baskets to the board. Store the laminated leaves in the extra basket. To use, a student sorts the leaves into the correct baskets. What a bushel of fun!

Wilma Droegemueller—Preschool
Zion Lutheran School
Mt. Pulaski, IL

Games Center

Profile Puzzles

Shape up visual-discrimination skills with these fun puzzles. Gather collections of small items. Arrange each collection on a piece of poster board; then use a black marker to trace around each item's shape. Laminate if desired. To use a puzzle, a child places each object from a collection on its corresponding outline.

Sharon Washer—Four- And Five-Year-Olds
Bolivar-Richburg Preschool
Bolivar, NY

Sensory Table

Seasonal Sensation

What's orange and black and creeping with spiders? The contents of your sensory table when you fill it with orange and black shredded paper (available at party-supply stores) and a quantity of plastic spiders. Encourage a child to find the spiders, then count them. Your little ones are sure to love this sensory-table surprise!

Susan Burbridge—Four-Year-Olds
Colonial Hills United Methodist School
San Antonio, TX

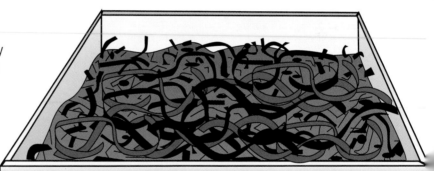

Science Center

Pick-A-Pocket

This idea will spark curiosity and keep your science center neatly organized at the same time. Hang a shoe organizer with clear pockets near your science table. Fill the pockets with materials to investigate such as feathers, seashells, pinecones, rocks, twigs, and leaves. Also place magnifying glasses in several pockets. Now observation and exploration materials are clearly visible, and cleanup is a breeze!

Jodi Sykes—Pre-K
North Grade
Lake Worth, FL

Setting The Stage:

Dramatic Play Area

Behind The "Sea-nes"

Under the sea? Well, not quite. With this dramatic play prop, you'll have to change the words of that popular song to *behind* the sea. To make this exciting sea scene, use clear Con-Tact® covering to secure pictures of ocean life to a clear shower curtain. Then hang the curtain from the ceiling near a dramatic play area or a science center that has a sea-life focus. Add materials such as snorkeling gear and books about ocean life to the area. Get ready for some dramatic ocean-life exploration!

Karen Beary—Preschool
The Children's Center
Kingston, MA

Games Center

"Cowabunga" Cow Bowling

Your little ones will be "udderly" delighted to make and play this bowling game. Collect a supply of empty, clean milk or juice cartons. Seal the lids. Mix a small amount of dishwashing liquid into an amount of white paint. Invite youngsters to paint the cartons white. Then, when the paint is dry, have students paint black spots on the cartons. To bowl, a student arranges the desired number of cartons randomly or in a triangle. (If desired suggest a number of cartons based on the child's abilities.) He then rolls a soft ball toward the cartons in order to knock them down. When he has knocked down all of the cartons, he or his bowling pals "moo." This game will keep 'em "moo-ving"!

Darlene V. Martino—Pre-K, Palmyra Head Start, Palmyra, NY

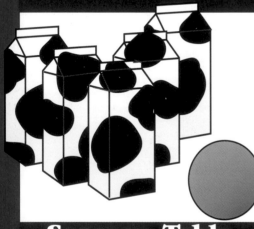

Sensory Table

Beads And Bowls

For a change of pace, fill a sensory table with lots of large beads and a supply of plastic containers and their lids. After students have enjoyed free exploration at the table, challenge them to fill the containers with specific colors or numbers of beads. Consider returning water or sand to the table *before* putting away the beads and containers. Stand back and watch as your little ones have fun and make discoveries, too!

Linda Kutach—Pre-K
Hutto Elementary
Hutto, TX

Sand Table

Like Sand In An Hourglass...

Reuse an empty two-liter plastic soda bottle by turning it into a discovery toy for your sand or rice center. To make one, cut off the top third of a bottle. Invert the top portion of the bottle; then insert it into the bottom portion as shown. Tape the portions together, being sure to cover any rough edges. Encourage students to pour sand or rice into the funnel and watch as it fills the container. If desired cut windows on the side of the bottle for better peeking and faster emptying.

Heather Snider
Oklahoma City, OK

Math Center

All Sorts Of Fun

Use colored tape to divide a round or square table into a sorting area with two, three, or four sections. To encourage students to sort by color, tape a different-colored shape in each section if desired. Keep a variety of manipulatives nearby so that individual students or groups of students can come to the table for plenty of sorting fun.

Kim Hilario—Pre-Kindergarten
Adobe Christian Preschool
Petaluma, CA

Literacy Center

Meet The Press

Our sources tell us that this idea for developing literacy and language will make big news in your classroom. Transform your literacy center into a newsroom and television news set by stocking it with clipboards, blank paper, writing utensils, toy microphones, and old newspapers. To facilitate up-to-the-minute weather reports, add a map to the area. To encourage aspiring reporters and photographers, add toy cameras and broken real cameras to the center.

For extra fun make this paper camera that produces "instant" photos. Fold an 8" x 7" black paper rectangle in half; then glue the sides together. Add paper shapes as shown so that the pocket resembles a camera. Glue newspaper pictures to 3" x 5" index cards; then insert the cards into the pocket. To use the camera, a child pretends to take a picture. He then pulls out a card and describes the newsworthy scene.

Mary Lynn Storrie—Four-Year-Olds, St. James School, Louisville, KY

The Magic Of Manipulatives

The Magic Of Manipulatives

Rubber Stamps

Youngsters will stamp their way into learning when you incorporate these suggestions for using rubber stamps into your classroom learning centers.

ideas by Lori Kent

Stock your art center with a variety of rubber stamps, colorful ink pads, and sheets of art paper. Encourage youngsters to design decorative papers for use as book covers or gift-wrap paper.

Sanitize a rubber stamp that has a simple design. Brush food coloring onto the stamp; then press the stamp onto a slice of cookie dough. When the cookie is baked, the colorful design will remain. Stamping is delicious!

Add a collection of geometric-shaped rubber stamps, ink pads, construction-paper scraps, scissors, and tape to your block area. Assist your little ones in creating signs for their block sculptures.

Stamp several simple patterns onto sentence strips. Challenge a child to copy the pattern of his choice onto a blank sentence strip. Staple the ends of his strip together to make a patterned headband.

Encourage a child to use alphabet stamps to spell his name on a piece of paper. If desired, use the stamps to prepare a name card for each child. Challenge youngsters to spell their friends' names too.

Place a collection of numeral, date, and business stamps, and ink pads in your dramatic play area. Add office supplies, such as an assortment of papers, a calculator, and a collection of interesting pencils and pens. Little ones will be working from nine to five in no time!

Encourage a child to use alphabet stamps to stamp the alphabet onto a length of adding-machine tape. If desired, have him cut the letters apart and resequence them.

Place coin and dollar stamps, ink pads, paper, scissors, and a toy cash register in a plastic tub for a quick math center you can bank on anytime.

Suggest that children use stamps to create imprints in moist sand.

Have each child stamp thematic or seasonal ink stamps onto lengths of adding-machine tape to create streamers. Staple the streamers to one end of a cardboard tube. Encourage a child to move his streamers as he listens to or sings a seasonal song.

Encourage a child to create a scene using storybook or theme-related stamps. Ask the child to dictate a story to you about the picture. Record the story; then compile each child's work into a class book.

Make games using stamps. To make a Concentration-style memory game, stamp each design in a set of at least five stamps onto two index cards.

To make a modified Go Fish game for two players, stamp each design in a set of at least five different stamps onto four cards. To play, each player begins with four cards and then plays the game according to the rules for Go Fish.

Invite children to make their own stickers by stamping rubber stamps onto self-adhesive mailing labels or nametags. Have children use the stickers to create collages or sticker books.

Use rubber stamps to add interest to parent newsletters.

253

The Magic Of Manipulatives

Cardboard Tubes

Gather an assortment of wrapping-paper, toilet-paper, and paper-towel tubes. Then let the good times roll with these totally tubular ideas, dude!

ideas contributed by Joyce Montag and Angie Kutzer

Make a class supply of binoculars by stapling together pairs of toilet-paper tubes. Paint the pairs different solid colors. Encourage a child to use a pair to find objects that match her binoculars's color.

Stand various-sized tubes in the sand at a sand table. Have a child count the number of scoops of sand needed to fill each tube.

Challenge youngsters to work in pairs to arrange a variety of tubes in order from longest to shortest.

Lead youngsters in this name-recognition cheer. Give each child a cardboard-tube megaphone. Use the traditional "Give me a [letter]" cheer to spell a child's name. As the students repeat each letter, write it on chart paper. Have the child whose name was spelled stand as the group answers your question, "What's that spell?" Say it again!

Staple crepe-paper streamers to one end of each of a class supply of tubes. Have children use the tubes to move creatively to instrumental music.

Cut strips into one end of a tube; then bend the strips outward as shown. Instruct a child to dip the cut end into a shallow plate of paint, then press the tube on a sheet of paper several times to print a bouquet of flowers.

Susan Ahlhorn—Preschool
Wee Wuns Preschool • Cypress, TX

Glue a Styrofoam® ball to one end of a tube to resemble a microphone. Put the microphone in a dramatic-play or reading center. Encourage each youngster to take a turn singing a solo or "reading" to a group.

Label each piece in a supply of construction paper with a numeral from one to ten. Instruct each student to choose a piece of paper, dip the end of a cardboard tube into paint, and then print the correct number of circles onto the paper.

Use tubes as rhythm sticks. Give each child a tube and direct him to tap the tube on the floor or tabletop to echo your rhythm pattern.

Give a pair of children an inflated balloon, and give each child in the pair a paper-towel tube. Challenge the pair to bat the balloon back and forth with the tubes without letting it touch the floor.

Stand ten paper-towel tubes in a pyramid shape. Have a child stand a short distance away from the tubes with a ball in hand. Ready, set, bowl!

Tape a row of paper-towel tubes horizontally to the floor, leaving 12 inches of space between each tube. Have each child move from one end of the row to the other by performing a gross-motor skill—such as jumping, hopping, or walking sideways—over the tubes.

255

The Magic Of Manipulatives

Candles

Gather an assortment of candles for use with these manipulative ideas that are sure to get your youngsters' excitement burning bright.
ideas contributed by Joyce Montag and Lori Kent

Invite small groups of students to seriate taper candles by length from shortest to longest.

Place an assortment of candles in a math center for sorting by color, texture, or size.

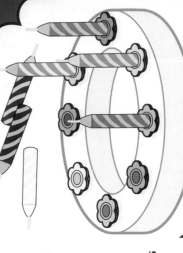

Press different colors of birthday-candle holders into a Styrofoam® ring. Develop one-to-one correspondence skills by asking a child to put one candle in each holder. Or ask him to put a candle in each holder that is its color match.

Float an assortment of colorful tea lights—minus their aluminum holders—in your water table. Encourage youngsters to blow the candles from one end of the table to the other.

Invite a child to use a candle to draw on a sheet of construction paper. Then have him paint over the top of the drawing with thinned tempera paint to reveal the picture.

Encourage students to use numeral-shaped candles to make prints in clay or play dough.

Direct a child to stand near a widemouthed jar, leaning over it. Challenge him to drop a number of birthday candles—one at a time—into the jar. Have him count the number of candles inside and outside the jar.

Place a collection of birthday candles, cake pans, spoons, and spray bottles filled with water near your sand table. Challenge a student to make a sand cake, then arrange the birthday candles in a pattern on his cake.

Program sheets of construction paper with divider lines and dot sets from one to five so that they resemble dominoes. Challenge a child to place a tea light atop each dot on a sheet. Then have him count the total number of candles on each domino. As an added challenge, encourage the child to arrange the sheets in a row so that matching dot sets are end-to-end.

This gross-motor activity is a ringer! Create rings by cutting out the centers of a supply of plastic lids. Set a tall candle in a holder on a table or on the floor. Challenge children to toss the rings onto the candle.

Encourage students to use a variety of candles to make color, size, and shape patterns.

Draw a birthday cake on each of ten sheets of construction paper; then program each cake with a different numeral or dot set from one to ten. Challenge youngsters to place the corresponding number of birthday candles on each cake.

Barry Slate

257

THE MAGIC OF MANIPULATIVES

Magnetic Letters And Numerals

A, B, See how these fresh ideas using magnetic symbols will attract your youngsters' attention. It's as easy as 1, 2, 3!
by Mackie Rhodes

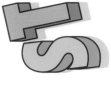

To play [...] game, arrange several pairs of [...] numeral magnets in game for[...] cover each piece with an index [...] invite each player, in turn, to lift two cards [...] ate matching magnets. If he finds a match, [...] keeps the magnets. If he does not find a [...] ch, he replaces the cards.

[...]sequence the letters of [...] a child's name on a magnetic surface; then remove several letters. Challenge the class to identify the missing letters as well as the name that the letters spell.

Combine several letter and numeral sets. Invite a child to find and then put on a magnetic surface all of one specific letter or numeral [...]

Invite youngsters to sort a set of magnets by color, then to name each symbol of a given color.

Evenly distribute a set of alphabet magnets to the students in a small group. Help the group alphabetically sequence its letters onto a magnetic surface; then invite students to recite the alphabet while one member points to each letter.

Randomly put several letters and numerals into a paper cup. Have a child shake the cup, then pour out the symbols. Challenge him to name each symbol that lands faceup.

Encourage students to use a variety of candles to make color, size, and shape patterns.

This gross-motor activity is a ringer! Create rings by cutting out the centers of a supply of plastic lids. Set a tall candle in a holder on a table or on the floor. Challenge children to toss the rings onto the candle.

Draw a birthday cake on each of ten sheets of construction paper; then program each cake with a different numeral or dot set from one to ten. Challenge youngsters to place the corresponding number of birthday candles on each cake.

Barry Slate

Place a collection of birthday candles, cake pans, spoons, and spray bottles filled with water near your sand table. Challenge a student to make a sand cake, then arrange the birthday candles in a pattern on his cake.

Program sheets of construction paper with divider lines and dot sets from one to five so that they resemble dominoes. Challenge a child to place a tea light atop each dot on a sheet. Then have him count the total number of candles on each domino. As an added challenge, encourage the child to arrange the sheets in a row so that matching dot sets are end-to-end.

THE MAGIC OF MANIPULATIVES

Magnetic Letters And Numerals

A, B, See how these fresh ideas using magnetic symbols will attract your youngsters' attention. It's as easy as 1, 2, 3!

by Mackie Rhodes

Evenly distribute a set of alphabet magnets to the students in a small group. Help the group alphabetically sequence its letters onto a magnetic surface; then invite students to recite the alphabet while one member points to each letter.

Randomly put several letters and numerals into a paper cup. Have a child shake the cup, then pour out the symbols. Challenge him to name each symbol that lands faceup.

Invite youngsters to sort a set of magnets by color, then to name each symbol of a given color.

Combine several letter and numeral sets. Invite a child to find and then put on a magnetic surface all of one specific letter or numeral.

To play a Memory game, arrange several pairs of letter and/or numeral magnets in game formation; then cover each piece with an index card. Invite each player, in turn, to lift two cards to locate matching magnets. If he finds a match, he keeps the magnets. If he does not find a match, he replaces the cards.

Sequence the letters of a child's name on a magnetic surface; then remove several letters. Challenge the class to identify the missing letters as well as the name that the letters spell.

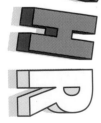

Give each child a numeral magnet. Ask her to gather the corresponding number of objects. As a challenge, ask her to find items that are also the same color as the numeral.

Invite children to make letter impressions in play dough.

Draw a shape on a magnetic board. Encourage a student to outline this shape with letter or numeral magnets; then have him identify each symbol.

Have a child close her eyes, then take a numeral magnet off a magnetic surface. Invite her to choose the corresponding number of classmates. Instruct those students to perform an action, such as stomping their feet or nodding their heads, as many times as the selected numeral.

Place a set of letter magnets in a bag. Have each child, in turn, draw a letter from the bag, then name an animal or action beginning with that letter sound. Invite students to act out the animal or action.

Bury letter magnets in sand; then invite a child to dig up one letter. Ask him to search the room to find an object that begins with that letter's sound or corresponds to that letter's color.

Use magnets as game pieces or as bingo markers.

Instruct a student to build a structure using as many magnets as possible. Then ask the child to identify each symbol, using positional words to indicate its position in the structure.

EXPLORATIONS

Explorations

Luscious Leaves

Cabbage, lettuce, spinach…these leaves are of the tasty variety. Toss up this activity so that your little ones can get a real taste of scientific exploration!

STEP 1

Label a paper-leaf shape as shown to create a graph. In advance of this activity, direct each child to wash his hands. Ask the group, "Do you think you can eat leaves?" Record each child's response on the graph.

yes no
Latasha Sam
Ellen John
Joda Kara
Sue

STEP 2

Emphasize that many types of leaves should not be eaten by people, and remind your little ones that they should not eat anything unfamiliar without first asking an adult. Show the group a head of lettuce and explain that lettuce is one kind of leaf that is eaten often. Give each child a paper towel and invite her to peel off a leaf from the head of lettuce. Ask the children to compare leaves with their neighbors. How do the leaves look alike? How do they look different?

STEP 5

If your little ones are surprised to discover that some of the foods they eat are leaves, have them join you in singing this song.

Oh, I Can Really Eat Some Leaves!
(sung to the tune of "Do You Know The Muffin Man?")

Can I really eat some leaves,
Eat some leaves, eat some leaves?
Can I really eat some leaves,
When I eat my lunch?

Cabbage is a kind of leaf,
Kind of leaf, kind of leaf.
Cabbage is a kind of leaf,
That I can munch at lunch.

Lettuce is a kind of leaf,
Kind of leaf, kind of leaf.
Lettuce is a kind of leaf,
That I can crunch at lunch.

Spinach is a kind of leaf,
Kind of leaf, kind of leaf.
Spinach is a kind of leaf,
That I can eat at lunch.

Oh, I can really eat some leaves,
Eat some leaves, eat some leaves.
Oh, I can really eat some leaves,
When I eat my lunch!

262

Science You Can Do

by Suzanne Moore

To learn that some leaves are edible, you will need:
— two green bulletin-board paper-leaf shapes
— marker
— one paper towel per child
— one head of lettuce, washed
— one head of cabbage, washed
— kitchen knife
— one bunch of smooth-leafed spinach, washed
— magnifying glasses

STEP 3

Next show the group a head of cabbage. Dramatically cut the cabbage in half so your little ones can see how tightly the leaves are nestled. Show the group the bunch of spinach leaves so that youngsters can observe that the leaves grow in clusters. Give one cabbage and one spinach leaf to each child. Ask the children to compare the three types of leaves. Provide magnifying glasses so youngsters can take a closer look at the stems and veins.

STEP 4

Encourage youngsters to taste each of the three different kinds of leaves. Record their comments on the second leaf shape.

The dark green leaf tastes <u>really</u> green!
My cabbage is crunchy.

Did You Know?

- Some types of leaves—such as tomato-plant leaves and potato-plant leaves—are toxic when ingested.
- Leaves make food for a plant.
- A leaf's veins carry food and water in the leaf.
- Many grazing animals and other animals—such as koala bears, giraffes, and elephants—depend on leaves for their food supply.
- Many food products come from leaves. The leaves of the tea plant are used for tea. The oil from peppermint and spearmint leaves is used to flavor gum and candy. Leaves such as bay, sage, and thyme are used to flavor foods.

What Now?

Invite your little ones to help you make this delicious snack using three types of fresh leaves—lettuce, dill, and basil.

Leafy Roll Ups

Scoop eight ounces of soft cream cheese into a large mixing bowl. Add two tablespoons of lemon juice, one-fourth cup of chopped fresh dill, and one-fourth cup of chopped fresh basil to the cheese and mix well with a mixer. To make one treat, spread some of the cheese mixture on a large lettuce leaf. Roll up the leaf, and munch!

Explorations

Soapy Science

Lather up! This dirt-defying activity will help youngsters understand how soap gets us clean.

STEP 1

Direct a small group of youngsters to wash their hands with water only, then dry their hands with paper towels. Have the students look closely at the towels. Ask, "Do you see any dirt on the towels? Do you think your hands are clean?"

STEP 2

Give each child in the group a small jar half-filled with water. Slowly add one tablespoon of vegetable oil to each jar. Have your students observe the interaction of the oil and the water. Ask, "What happened when oil was added to the water? Where is the water? Where is the oil?"

STEP 5

Have students put the jars on the table again and observe the mixture. Ask, "What happened to the water? What happened to the soap? Where is the oil?"

STEP 6

Have the children wash their hands again, this time using soap. After they dry their hands with paper towels, ask them these questions: "Did you see any dirt being washed away when you washed your hands? Why do you think your hands are really clean this time?"

Science You Can Do
by Suzanne Moore

To discover how soap gets us clean, you will need:
— paper towels
— one small, clear jar with a lid per child
— water
— tablespoon
— one tablespoon of vegetable oil per child
— teaspoon
— one teaspoon of liquid dish detergent per child
— soap

STEP 3

Secure the lids on the jars. Then have your students shake their jars for several seconds. Direct the students to put their jars on a table. Again have them observe the oil and water. Ask, "Where is the oil? Where is the water?" Continue watching as the two liquids separate.

STEP 4

Remove the jar lids; then add one teaspoon of detergent to each jar. Direct your students to watch as the detergent forms its own layer. Secure the lids on the jars; then have students shake their jars again.

This Is Why

- Oil is *insoluble*—it will not dissolve in water.
- When a jar of oil and water is shaken, the oil and water temporarily mix. When the jar is still, the oil and water separate again.
- We get dirty because our skin is slightly oily. Dirt sticks to the oil. When our hands are washed with water only, the oil and dirt do not mix with the water. Therefore our hands stay dirty.
- When oil and water mix, an *emulsion* is formed. Oil is broken into tiny droplets suspended in the water. When soap is used during bathing, it surrounds the dirt and oil so they can be washed away.

What Now?

Copy, color, and cut out this badge for each child. Reward students who remember to wash with soap with a membership into your happy hand-washers club!

Happy
Hand Washer

Explorations

Dental Magic

There's magic in a healthy smile. Use this lesson to demonstrate the importance of toothbrushing every day.

STEP 1

In advance hard-boil a class supply of eggs plus one extra. Use a permanent marker to draw a toothy grin on an egg for each child. Also personalize a cup for each child.

STEP 2

During a group time, invite the children to share their dental-health-related experiences, such as visits to a dentist, toothbrushing routines, or a sibling that lost a tooth. Draw a toothy grin on the extra egg. Then explain to the group that eggshells and teeth are made of the same material—calcium.

STEP 5

Suggest that since eggshells are similar to teeth, they can be cleaned in the same manner. Provide each child in the group with an old toothbrush. Working near a sink or tub of water, have the children use the brushes and toothpaste to clean their eggs.

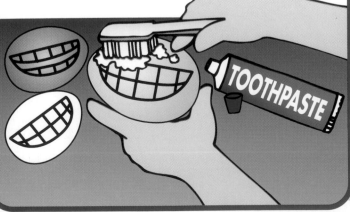

STEP 6

Discuss the results. Remind your little ones that *all* of their teeth should be brushed every day to keep them clean and remove stains. Then sing the following song:

Brush Your Teeth
(sung to the tune of "Clementine")

Brush your front teeth,
Brush your back teeth,
Brush the bottom and the top.
If you brush them each and every day,
Then your smile will never stop.

Science You Can Do
by Suzanne Moore

To learn about keeping teeth clean, you will need:
— one hard-boiled egg per child, plus one extra
— a black permanent marker
— one clear, plastic cup per child
— enough strong tea or caramel-colored soda to fill each child's cup
— paper towels
— spoon
— old toothbrushes
— toothpaste
— a sink or tub of water

STEP 3

Invite small groups of children at a time to join you in a science area. Direct each child to put an egg into his cup. Invite each child to pour tea or soda into his cup so that the egg is covered. (Do not put the extra egg in liquid.) Ask the group to predict what will happen if the eggs soak in the liquid overnight. Set the cups aside.

STEP 4

The next day invite small groups of children to join you again to observe the results of the experiment. Have each child use a spoon to remove his egg from the cup and dry the egg with a paper towel. Observe the changes in the eggshells by comparing them to the extra egg. Lead the group to conclude that the shells were stained by the liquid.

Did You Know?

- How does toothpaste clean the egg-shells and our teeth? Toothpaste contains an abrasive substance—such as finely powdered chalk—and a detergent. Flavors are added to make the taste pleasant, and fluoride is added to help prevent decay.
- Baby teeth are important, too! Dental decay that is not treated in primary teeth can spread to other teeth and even to the permanent teeth below the gum that have not yet emerged.
- Children begin to lose their baby teeth between the ages of five and seven. Permanent teeth are fully developed and will begin to erupt when the child is about six years old.

What Now?

Make old-fashioned toothpaste! Mix three parts baking soda with one part salt. To use, moisten a toothbrush; then coat it with the powder. Try scrubbing a stained egg with this paste. Which works better—the homemade paste or the commercial paste? Which tastes better?

BAKING SODA

SALT

Explorations

The Well-Dressed Nest

If you have a backyard full of birds, follow these directions to offer them a buffet of nest-building materials.

STEP 1

Ask a group of children to help you tear newspaper pages into short strips. Tuck the strips into a mesh berry basket to prevent them from blowing away. Add the lint to the basket.

STEP 2

Ask another group of children to cut six-inch lengths of yarn. Tuck the ends of the yarn into the drainage hole of an upside-down pot.

STEP 5

Return to the location with the newspaper, lint, yarn, and mud. Now you've made a buffet for the birds!

STEP 6

Visit your birds' buffet every day to make observations and to set out more items if needed. Are any materials missing? Can you tell if the mud has been used? On a chart, record any changes that the group notices. Continue your bird-watching through the spring. You might be surprised to see a well-dressed nest made with the items you provided!

Our Observations

- The birds took the white yarn first.

- We see prints in the mud.

Science You Can Do
by Suzanne Moore

To make a buffet of nest-building materials, you will need:

— newspaper
— lint from a clothes dryer
— plastic mesh berry basket
— yarn in pale and bright colors
— scissors
— terra-cotta pot
— dirt and water for making mud
— plastic bowl
— plastic spoon
— plastic plate
— twigs
— chart paper
— marker

STEP 3

Mix dirt and water in a plastic bowl. Pour the mud onto a plastic plate.

STEP 4

As a class, collect small twigs. While collecting twigs, search for a good location for your buffet. When you have found a good spot, lead the group in counting the number of collected twigs; then leave the twigs at the location.

Did You Know?

- Birds build nests as cradles for their eggs. After the eggs hatch, the nests are used as temporary homes for the chicks.
- Nests are built in many types of places—on the ground, in a tree, even between rocks—depending on the species of bird.
- Each type of bird builds its own kind of nest.
- Nests can be built out of a multitude of materials. Besides twigs, birds use animal fur, spiderwebs, feathers, leaves, bark, lichen, snake skins, and shells in building nests.
- Most nests are used to raise only one family of chicks. Some birds, like eagles, reuse their nests every year.

What Now?

If the opportunity to observe the behavior of birds has your little flock all aflutter, share these books. Soon you'll have a class of certified ornithologists!

Our Yard Is Full Of Birds
Written by Anne Rockwell
Illustrated by Lizzy Rockwell
Published by Macmillan
  Publishing Company

Have You Seen Birds?
Written by Joanne Oppenheim
Illustrated by Barbara Reid
Published by Scholastic Inc.

BUILDING CHARACTER

Building
CHARACTER

Ideas For Teaching Virtues In The Preschool Classroom
Courage

ideas contributed by Lisa Cowman

 **New Faces, New Places**

It takes a lot of courage for preschoolers to enter into new and unfamiliar situations. Team up with another teacher to introduce students to the character trait of *courage*. Arrange for your students to be in that teacher's classroom and vice versa during the first few minutes of a school day. Explain to your new group of children that you will be their teacher for a brief time. After a short activity, return students to their correct classrooms. Discuss the experience with your own preschoolers. Was anyone scared? Assure children that it's okay to fear such things as new places and new faces. Then remind them that sometimes *courage* is needed to overcome fears. Praise them for being brave during the teacher and classroom switch.

Was I Scared!

Help children distinguish between times when they need to be brave by themselves and times when they need to go to a grown-up for help. Invite each youngster to share a scary experience with the group. List these experiences; then, after everyone has had a turn to share, read the list aloud. Pause after each entry and ask if the situation calls for courage or for a grown-up's help. For example, if a youngster is scared to sleep by himself, he needs courage to try it alone. On the other hand, if a youngster is scared when a stranger offers a ride, he needs to get a grown-up's help.

After reviewing the list, assist your little ones in making medals of courage to remind them to be brave when it's the best choice. Have each child draw a picture of something he fears on a tagboard circle. Punch a hole near the top of the circle; then thread a length of ribbon through the hole and tie the ends to make a necklace. Encourage youngsters to wear their medals home and to tell parents about courage.

 What's The Plan?

Teach your little ones this action poem to give them a plan for gathering courage during scary encounters.

Jump back, turn around, take a look.	*(Jump back, turn, place hand above eyes.)*
What is that scary thing?	*(Shiver.)*
Jump back, turn around, take a look.	*(Jump back, turn, place hand above eyes.)*
It's so frightening!	*(Shiver.)*
Jump back, turn around, take a look.	*(Jump back, turn, place hand above eyes.)*
Whew, it's just [child's fear]!	*(Wipe brow.)*

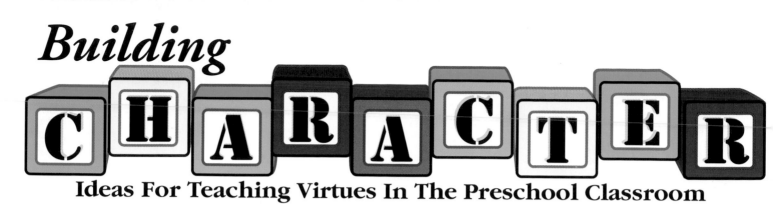

Building CHARACTER

Ideas For Teaching Virtues In The Preschool Classroom
Friendship

by Lori Kent

 ### Friends Do Things Together

Introduce your little ones to the virtue of friendship by reading aloud *Making Friends* by Fred Rogers (The Putnam & Grosset Group). Ask each student to tell something he likes to do with his classroom friends. List all responses on a sheet of chart paper. Have each child decorate a person shape to resemble himself. Display the shapes around the list on a bulletin board. Throughout the day, take pictures of friends playing together. Label each picture with the names of the friends shown; then mount them around the cutouts and chart.

Friends Work Together

Encourage cooperation skills with this group game that will have your youngsters island-hopping to a tropical beat. Prepare by cutting several large circles from bulletin-board paper to represent islands. Position the islands in an open area of your classroom. Invite students to pretend to swim around the islands as you play some tropical music. Stop the music; then have each child stand on an island. Count the number of children on each island. Remove one island and continue play. Each time the music stops, encourage children to work together to fit as many friends on an island as possible, being careful not to allow anyone to fall into the water. Words of encouragement and praise for cooperation skills will have all your little ones on friendly footing!

1. Play on the swing.
2. Play with play dough.
3. Share snack.
4. Read a book.
5. Color.

Friends Share

Follow up your island-hopping adventure with this refreshing activity. Lay the islands used in the previous activity on the floor of your classroom. Divide students into small groups; then have each group sit on an island. Provide each group with a plate with twice as many small snacks as there are people in the group. Have the students work together to divide the snacks evenly. Invite students to eat their snacks as they share a good time together.

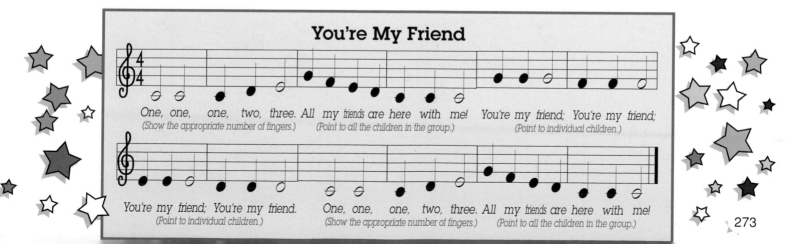

You're My Friend

One, one, one, two, three. All my friends are here with me! You're my friend; You're my friend;
(Show the appropriate number of fingers.) *(Point to all the children in the group.)* *(Point to individual children.)*

You're my friend; You're my friend. One, one, one, two, three. All my friends are here with me!
(Point to individual children.) *(Show the appropriate number of fingers.)* *(Point to all the children in the group.)*

Building CHARACTER

Ideas For Teaching Virtues In The Preschool Classroom
Gentleness

ideas by Ann Flagg and Linda Whitling

Reasons For Gentleness

While your young children are learning to show gentleness in physical ways, help them begin to understand the reasons why it is sometimes important to be gentle, or mild in manner. Ask youngsters to pantomime a situation suggested below; then encourage them to discuss reasons that gentleness is needed in that situation. For example, because a child loves his baby brother and doesn't want to accidentally hurt him, he should hold him gently. Or because a child's friend worked very hard on a block building, he should walk gently around it.

- You're holding a newborn baby. What would you do?
- You're carrying a glass of water for your father. How should you walk?
- Your friend is building a block castle. How should you move around the castle?
- You got a new book for your birthday. How would you turn the pages?
- You're hugging your mother good night. How would you squeeze her?

Gentle Guest

Bring a small animal guest that is easy to hold into your classroom. Then invite willing children to participate in a hands-on lesson in gentleness. If a live animal is not possible, bring a stuffed toy animal and ask the children to pretend that it is real. As the children gently hold or pet the animal, praise them for showing compassion for the animal's feelings, and for being kind and respectful of its needs. What a simple and enjoyable activity—full of opportunities to reinforce virtues.

Praise For Gentleness

Sabu handled the hamster with care.

Manny pushed Ann gently in the swing so she wouldn't get hurt.

Caitlyn gave Colin a hug when he fell to make him feel better.

Rob walked slowly around Barry's block castle.

Jesse carefully poured the punch for snack.

Praise For Gentleness

Your little ones will be eager to give you a hand in fostering a gentle classroom environment when you introduce this mural project. Continue to encourage your class community of children to be gentle. Each time you observe a child behaving gently, have that child dip a palm in paint and press a print on a length of bulletin-board paper. Near the handprint, record the gentle behavior and the reason for the behavior if desired. Continue watching and inviting children to add their handprints until every child is included on the mural. When the mural is complete, display it and celebrate a class of gentle children.

Getting Your Ducklings In A Row

Getting Your Ducklings

Personal Portfolios

Enlist the help of children's families to decorate portfolio boxes for storage of students' work throughout the year. Collect a class supply of empty cereal boxes. Cut the top flaps off the boxes; then cover each box with paper. Personalize each box before sending it home along with a note suggesting that a parent help his child decorate the box. Hang the returned boxes on a clothesline in your room. When you want to save an item for a child's portfolio of work, simply slip the item into his box. What a decorative way to store your little ones' work!

Kim Spankowski—Four-Year-Olds
Kenosha Unified School District Head Start
Kenosha, WI

Chime Time

Smooth out transition-time turmoil with this musical idea. Ring a small wind chime to quietly signal transitions. The results will be music to your ears!

Michelle Espelien—Preschool
St. James Preschool
Burnsville, MN

Box It Up

Store small items—such as bulletin-board letters, stickers, and small manipulatives—in plastic videocassette boxes. Label each box with its contents; then store the boxes on a shelf or in a cupboard. A great idea—any way you stack it.

Amy Drake—Two-Year-Olds
Westview Childcare Ministry
Fort Wayne, IN

buttons

276

In A Row
Tips For Getting Organized

Sticky Solution

Do adhesives pull the paint off your classroom walls? If so, then try this idea. Adhere a piece of clear Con-Tact® covering to a wall where you'd like to display children's work. Then use tape or Sticky-Tac to secure children's work to the covering. What a neat solution to a sticky problem!

Michelle Miget—Four-Year-Olds
Humboldt Elementary
St. Joseph, MO

Banded Boxes

Keeping the lids on individual crayon boxes is a snap with this easy idea. Punch a hole in the center of a crayon box's lid. Slide a paper clip onto a rubber band. From the underside of the lid, thread the rubber band through the hole and pull it until the paper clip is flat against the lid. Secure the paper clip with a wide piece of tape. Place the lid on the box; then wrap the rubber band around the bottom of the box. Now crayons stay securely in their boxes and are easy to store.

Bernadette Hoyer—Pre-K
Howard B. Brunner School
Scotch Plains, NJ

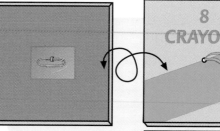

Seat Belt Matchup

Here's a tip that will help your little ones buckle up quickly and safely when riding in your center's van or bus. Affix matching stickers to the corresponding ends of each seat belt; then cover the stickers with clear tape. Each child can quickly identify his seat belt by simply matching the stickers. Getting safely seated is a snap!

Vail McCole—Pre-K
Tigger's Treehouse
Grand Junction, CO

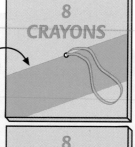

Getting Your Ducklings

Puppets On A String

Need a clever way to store puppets? Here's a space-saving idea you can really hang on to! Hang a plastic chain with clips (available at discount stores) from your classroom ceiling. Clip the puppets available for student use on the part of the chain that is within youngsters' reach. Hang the remaining puppets higher on the chain.

Laura Sacco—Four-Year-Olds
East Woods School
Oyster Bay, NY

Sleepy-Time Wand

Help your little ones relax into a state of sweet dreams with this rest-time wand. To make one cut out two identical star shapes from tagboard. Brush one side of each star with glue; then sprinkle it with glitter. When the glue is dry, glue the stars together glitter sides out, leaving an opening in the bottom. Hot-glue an unsharpened pencil in the opening. During rest time use the wand to sprinkle imaginary pixie dust over the heads of your youngsters. Pleasant dreams!

Kristen Sharpe—Preschool
Kristen's Corner
Mansfield, MA

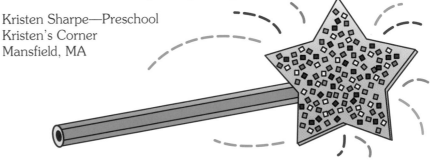

Easy Dismissal

This parent-friendly dismissal routine gives you a chance to say good-bye to each child individually. Write each child's name on a separate index card. Just before dismissal time, place the cards outside your classroom door. When a parent arrives, he slips his child's name card under the door. Quietly help that child gather her things; then deliver her to the parent. Should a parent need to speak to you, suggest that he remain until all of the children have been dismissed.

Joan Banker—Four-Year-Olds
St. Mary's Child Development Center
Garner, NC

In A Row   Tips For Getting Organized

Match Mates

Here's a management tip for seating at snacktimes and circle times that doubles as an opportunity to reinforce visual-discrimination skills. Prepare matching pairs of shapes for various seasons, holidays, and themes. For example, cut pairs of mitten shapes from wallpaper patterns, or similarly decorate pairs of heart cutouts. To use the match mates during a group time, place one shape in a matching pair at a seat or on the floor in your group area. Give the matching shape to a child. Direct each child to find his spot by finding his matching shape.

Susan Burbridge—Four-Year-Olds
Trinity Weekday School
San Antonio, TX

Field-Trip Tip

Here's a tip that will keep your youngsters entertained on bus rides. For each child tie a lacing yarn through one of a lacing shape's holes. As each student boards the bus, hand him a shape. Encourage each child to complete his shape, then exchange it with a friend. No more boring bus rides!

Karen Saner
Burns Elementary School
Burns, KS

All Is Fair

If you have an Easter-egg hunt at your preschool, here is an easy way to make sure each child finds her fair share of the goodies. Have each child paint and decorate an egg carton (or egg-carton half). During the hunt direct each child to fill her carton with eggs. When her carton is full, she may leave the hunt to admire her findings while other children continue to search. Everyone is sure to have her fair share of fun!

Diane Lundgren—Preschool
One Step Ahead Home Preschool
Columbia, MO

Getting Your Ducklings

Helping Hands

Do you ever feel like you need extra hands to help you display students' work? If so this idea will come in handy. Laminate a class supply of construction-paper hand shapes. Personalize a hand shape for each child in your class; then hot-glue a clothespin to the back of each one. Attach each hand to a wall in your classroom by hot-gluing the clothespin to the wall at a child's eye level. (Hot glue may damage wallboard.) When a child has a project to display, have him press on his hand shape to open the clothespin, then insert his work. Look what little hands can do!

Tina Mrozek—Three-Year-Olds
Childrens World Learning Center
Westmont, IL

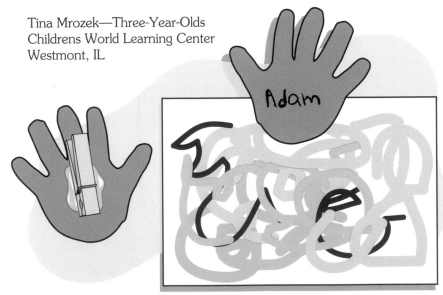

Clean As A Whistle

Here's a tip that will help fingerpaint wash away cleanly and easily. Rub a small amount of petroleum jelly on little hands prior to painting.

Vail McCole—Pre-K, Tiger's Treehouse, Grand Junction, CO

280

Early-Learner's Clock

You'll save lots of time answering those "How long till…" questions with this idea that uses picture cues to help children learn concepts of time. Cut out a paper collar for your clock as shown; then tape it on the wall. Beside each of the clock's numerals, attach a different sticker to the collar. Attach a strip of colored paper to the minute hand. Now when a child asks "How long till…," refer to the colored minute hand and the sticker beside the appropriate clock numeral. For example, you might say, "When the green hand points to the heart."

Carole Smith—Head Start, Mango Elementary
Seffner, FL

In A Row

Tips For Getting Organized

Handy Hang-Ups

Put an end to paint-smock clutter and assist your little ones in being successful "hanger-uppers" with this catchy idea. Affix the hook side of a long strip of Velcro® to a wall near your easel area. Attach the loop side of a piece of Velcro® to the collar of each painting smock. To hang up her smock, a child presses the Velcro® on the collar to the Velcro® strip on the wall. She'll feel independent, and you'll be rewarded with a neat and tidy art area!

Patricia Carpentier
Cedar Grove, WI

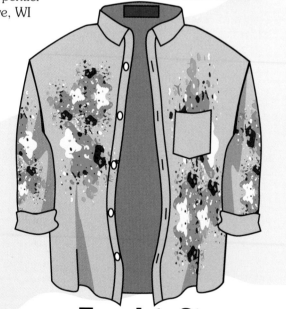

Template Storage

A plastic recipe box with alphabetical dividers is the perfect way to store several sets of letter templates. Simply file the templates alphabetically for easy access. With this method you'll have all your templates in one portable location.

Andrea Smith—Preschool
Day Care Services of Blair County, Leopold Center, Altoona, PA

Musical Names

This version of Musical Chairs will help youngsters recognize their names as well as aid in transitional times. Prepare a name card for each child. Arrange a class supply of chairs in a circle; then place a name card on each chair. Play as you would Musical Chairs, having each child sit on the chair with his name card when the music stops. As you remove a chair each round, have the child whose seat was taken move on to the next activity, such as washing his hands or preparing to go outside. Rearrange the name cards on the chairs before each round. Everyone's a winner in this game!

Gina Mahony—Preschool
Children's Preschool Workshop
Barrington, IL

Building Bridges Between Home And School

Building Bridges
Between Home And School

School: _____

Teacher: _____

Date: _____

A Whole New World!

Your three- or four-year-old may have already experienced the anxiety of being left with a caregiver as you went off to work or out for the evening. As he or she enters preschool, you both may experience the anxiety of separating in a new environment. Here are some tips for making the beginning of preschool a positive experience for all.

• **Talk about the new preschool experience.** Listen carefully, and try to answer questions your child may have about preschool. Encourage an older sibling to share memorable experiences. Look for the books suggested in "The Book Corner" at your library or a bookstore. Use the books as a springboard for discussing the exciting things that he or she may have the opportunity to do at preschool.

• **Share your feelings.** When it is time to separate, allow your child to express any feelings he or she has. Stabilize the situation by sharing your feelings in a reassuring and calm manner.

• **Always say good-bye.** Give closure to your departure, and reinforce trust with your child by letting him or her see you leave.

• **Develop a routine.** Departure routines help reassure a child who is feeling stressed. Involve your child in developing a routine that might include a good-bye song, a special hug, or a "secret" signal.

As with all big steps in life, there may be moments of uncertainty. Keep your hugs and smiles ready, and you'll both do just fine!

The Book Corner

Books About Going To Preschool

Curious Kids Go To Preschool: Another Big Book Of Words
Created by Héloïse Antoine • Illustrated by Ingrid Godon
Published by Peachtree Publishers, Ltd.; 1995

Will I Have A Friend?
It's Jim's first day at school. He plays with clay, has a snack, and takes a nap. Then he meets the friend he's been looking for.
Written by Miriam Cohen • Illustrated by Lillian Hoban
Published by Macmillan Books For Young Readers, 1967

Books Related To Separation Anxiety

Will You Come Back For Me?
Four-year-old Suki is concerned about being left at day care until her mom reassures her in a loving, concrete way.
Written by Ann Tompert • Illustrated by Robin Kramer
Published by Albert Whitman & Company, 1988

Even If I Spill My Milk?
Jamie doesn't want his parents to go to a party, but Mom's gentle reassurance eases her anxious feelings.
Written & Illustrated by Anna Grossnickle Hines
Published by Clarion Books, 1994

To The Teacher: Use this parent communication to strengthen the connection between home and school. Duplicate a copy of pages 285 and 286. At the top of page 285, write your school's name, your name, and the date. Add class-related news to page 286; then trim away these instructions. Duplicate a copy for each child on the front and back sides of a colorful piece of paper.

Together Time

Family-Picture Puzzle

A family is like a puzzle—the pieces can be separated, but when they are all together again, the picture is complete! If separation is sometimes a scary experience for your little one, try this activity.

• Begin by explaining that when your family members separate each day to go to work or school, each member is like a piece of a puzzle. Even though you are apart, you can join back together later in the day.

• Make a family-picture puzzle with your child to illustrate this idea more clearly. Cut a piece of tagboard or construction paper into as many puzzle pieces as there are members of your family. Attach a picture of a different family member to each piece. Give each family member his or her piece; then, as a family, put the pieces back together again.

• On days when your child has anxiety about going to preschool, give him or her the piece or pieces of the puzzle on which you and/or another parent are pictured. Looking at the piece will remind him or her that you will soon all be together again.

Kitchen Capers

Puzzle Cookie

Here's a fun family activity that every member will want to take part in. Follow the directions for making a puzzle cookie. When the pieces of your cookie cool, enjoy them first as a puzzle, then as a treat!

1/2 cup quick-cooking oats
2 teaspoons honey
1/8 teaspoon salt
1/4 teaspoon baking soda

1/2 cup all-purpose flour
1/4 cup wheat germ
1/4 cup margarine, softened
1/4 cup buttermilk

Grind the oats in a blender until firm. Pour the oats into a large bowl; then stir in the salt, soda, flour, wheat germ, and honey. Cut in the margarine. Stir in the buttermilk. Roll the dough on a piece of aluminum foil to 1/4-inch thick. Transfer the foil to a cookie sheet. Cut the dough into as many puzzle pieces as there are members of your family. Separate the pieces slightly. Bake the cookies at 400°F for about 15 minutes. When the pieces cool, encourage each participant to help put the puzzle together; then take it apart again and enjoy it piece by piece!

Read All About It!
Our Class News

The ideas in this newsletter are contributed by Jan Brennan—freelance writer and mother of four.

Building Bridges
Between Home And School

School: _____

Teacher: _____

Date: _____

Childhood Fears

Afraid of your child having fears? Since your preschooler is in a stage in which reality and fantasy are easily mixed, it's natural that he/she would develop fears. Keep in mind that when understood and handled appropriately, many of these fears will be outgrown as quickly as a pair of shoes. In the meantime, here are some tips for easing your child's fears:

- **Acknowledge the emotion of fear as being real.** Accepting your child's fear rather than ignoring it can help build trust between you and your child. Explain that even grown-ups feel afraid sometimes.

- **Talk about the fear.** Ask your child questions about the fear. Offering a simple explanation about the fear may be all that's needed. In addition, consider describing a time when you were afraid and share how you felt.

- **With your child, develop a solution to the problem or a courageous plan.** Leading your child to solve his/her problem will give him/her an important sense of control over the fear. Be sure to praise your child when he or she displays self-confidence.

- **Model courage.** Remaining calm during frightful incidents will send an important message to your perceptive preschooler.

- **Read books in which the characters face fears.** Look for the books suggested in "The Book Corner" at a library or bookstore. Reading stories about courage can help your child know that he/she is not alone and can give him/her an idea or two for facing common fears.

The Book Corner

Books About
Fears And Courage

Go Away, Big Green Monster!
Simple cut-out pages make a monster appear and disappear at the reader's command.
Written & Illustrated by Ed Emberley
Published by Little, Brown and Company; 1993

Harry And The Terrible Whatzit
Harry loves his mom so much that when she goes into the cellar, he confronts his deepest fear to save her.
Written & Illustrated by Dick Gackenbach
Published by Houghton Mifflin Company, 1979

Franklin In The Dark
Franklin the turtle overcomes his fear of small, dark places.
Written by Paulette Bourgeois
Illustrated by Brenda Clark
Published by Scholastic Inc., 1986

To The Teacher: Duplicate a copy of pages 287 and 288. Complete the information at the top of page 287; then add class-related news to page 288. Trim away these instructions. Duplicate a copy for each child on the front and back sides of a colorful piece of paper.

Together Time

Making Masks

Making masks is a creative way to help your child understand that some scary things aren't really what they seem to be. Enlist the help of your child in gathering several paper plates, markers or crayons, scissors, glue, tape, cardboard tubes, and other items—such as pasta, magazines, construction paper, sequins, or glitter—for decorating masks. Hold a plate in front of your child's face. Gently mark the location for the eyeholes; then cut them out. Encourage your child to use the gathered materials to decorate the mask. Tape a tube to the mask for a handle. If desired, have your child decorate masks for you and other family members as well. When the masks are complete, stand together in front of a mirror, holding the masks in front of your faces. What's so scary? It's just you and me!

Kitchen Capers

Pudding Monsters

No need to be afraid of these delightfully frightful monsters! Have your child assist you in preparing a package of instant pudding. To make pudding monsters, fill small bowls with the pudding; then create monsters' faces using foods such as orange slices, bananas, grape halves, strawberry slices, marshmallows, candy sprinkles, and more. Mmm, monster! Mmm, delicious!

Read All About It!
Our Class News

The ideas in this newsletter are contributed by Jan Brennan, with help from her four-year-old daughter, Kelly.

Building Bridges
Between Home And School

School: _____

Teacher: _____

Date: _____

Building Self-Esteem

It's likely that when you consider the tasks of parenting, you consider fostering self-esteem one of the most important. A child's self-esteem—how your child feels about himself/herself—is a key to success. To develop a positive self-concept, two needs should be met:

- **Your child should feel loved—unconditionally.**
  Find ways to show your child that he/she is loved—not because of what he/she can do, but because of whom he/she is.

- **Your child should know that he/she is special.**
  Remind your child that he/she has value and can contribute something to others. Helping a child see his/her own special qualities is a great way to build self-esteem.

What can you do to continue to foster your child's self-esteem? Here are some tips:

- **Help your child master his/her environment.**
  Provide opportunities for your child to succeed; then praise your child for his/her accomplishments. For example, choose clothing items that are easy to put on and take off, keep frequently used items at reachable levels, and provide toys that are easily manipulated.

- **Encourage your child to initiate activities.**
  Praise each effort, and gently guide him/her by offering some helpful hints. For example, if your child puts a shirt on backwards, praise the effort. Next time guide him/her by pointing out that the shirt's tag goes in the back.

The Book Corner

Books About
Self-Esteem

I Like Me!
The cheerful pig in this bubbly book likes herself in such a contagious way that every reader will see a great example of someone who has a strong self-esteem.
Written & Illustrated by Nancy Carlson
Published by Viking Children's Books

The Mixed-Up Chameleon
An unhappy chameleon wants to be like all of the animals in the zoo. When he gets mixed-up, he realizes that being himself is really best.
Written & Illustrated by Eric Carle
Published by HarperCollins Children's Books

Guess How Much I Love You
Through the characters Big Nutbrown and Little Nutbrown, this book beautifully shows the bond of love between parent and child.
Written by Sam McBratney
Published by Candlewick Press

My Mom And Dad Make Me Laugh
Simon's mom likes spots, but his dad likes stripes. The message of this cute story is that everyone is unique!
Written & Illustrated by Nick Sharratt
Published by Candlewick Press

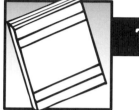

To The Teacher: Duplicate a copy of pages 289 and 290. Complete the information at the top of page 289; then add class-related news to page 290. Trim away these instructions. Duplicate a copy for each child on the front and back sides of a colorful piece of paper.

Your Child's Own Song

With your child, make a list of ways that he/she is special. Then incorporate those traits into this song.

There's Nobody Just Like You
(sung to the tune of "London Bridge")

There's nobody just like you,
Just like you, just like you.
There's nobody just like you,
My sweet [Child's name].

No one [smiles] just like you,
Just like you, just like you.
No one [smiles] just like you,
My sweet [Child's name].

Repeat verse, substituting traits or abilities, such as laughs, paints, sings, *etc.*

No one loves me like you do,
Like you do, like you do.
No one loves me like you do,
My sweet [Child's name].

Do-It-Myself" Dip

Have your child count a designated number of spoonfuls of yogurt into a bowl. Provide him/her with cereal pieces for dipping.

"I'm Super!" Sandwich

Soften a tablespoon of peanut butter by putting it in the microwave for a few seconds. Toast two pieces of bread. Direct your child to spread the peanut butter onto a piece of toast, then sprinkle on sunflower seeds, raisins, coconut, or sprouts. Have him/her top off the sandwich with the second piece of toast, then use a cookie cutter to cut a fun shape out of the sandwich.

Read All About It!
Our Class News

The ideas in this newsletter are contributed by Jan Brennan.

Building Bridges
Between Home And School

School: _____

Teacher: _____

Date: _____

You Can Do It!

"Way to go!" "You did it all by yourself!" "You're a great helper." Sound familiar? If so, good for you! You're already accustomed to celebrating your child's accomplishments. Getting dressed, brushing teeth, performing simple chores—these are just a few examples of things that three- and four-year-olds can do by themselves. Although children become increasingly independent at varying rates, here are some accomplishments you can celebrate with your preschooler.

Celebrate when your child…

… dresses him/herself. Be sure to lavish extra praise for those pesky buttons and tricky zippers!

… washes and dries off. Remember, those big towels are hard for little hands to manage.

… brushes his/her teeth, combs his/her hair, washes his/her own hands. That's some amazing hand/wrist action!

… pours juices and spreads peanut butter and jelly. Lunch is served.

… performs simple household tasks such as setting the table or cleaning his/her room. Who needs a maid with a helper like that?

If you applaud your child's successes, you can be sure that there will be many more to follow!

The Book Corner

"I Can!" Books

Now I'm Big
The youngsters in this photo-illustrated book compare things they are able to do now with their abilities as babies. Read this title and your child is sure to think of lots of things he or she can do, too!
Written by Margaret Miller
Published by Greenwillow Books

Herman The Helper
Herman spends his day happily helping everyone and feeling so good about himself that the reader feels good, too.
Written by Robert Kraus
Published by Simon & Schuster Books For Young Readers

Can I Help?
A wolf pup "helps" his dad with the gardening. Whew! Helping is hard work!
Written & Illustrated by Marilyn Janovitz
Published by North-South Books Inc.

Three Little Kittens
The three kittens that lost their mittens felt very proud when they found them and later washed them all by themselves.
Written & Illustrated by Paul Galdone
Published by Clarion Books

To The Teacher: Duplicate a copy of pages 291 and 292. Complete the information at the top of page 291; then add class-related news to page 292. Trim away these instructions. Duplicate a copy for each child on the front and back sides of a colorful piece of paper.

Now And Then

Celebrate your child's accomplishments by preserving them forever in a book. Together look at photos of your child taken when he/she was younger. Select several of the photos for your "Now And Then" book. Next take pictures of your child doing related activities by him/herself. For example, if you have a picture of your child being fed with a bottle, take a new picture of your child eating at the table. Mount the pictures as shown on tagboard pages. Bind the pages with ribbon or metal rings. Write as your child dictates the text of the book. If desired, decorate the pages with stickers. Title the book; then make sure that the "author" autographs the new publication!

String Of Successes

Keep track of your child's abilities and accomplishments with this successful idea. Cut several sheets of construction paper into two-inch-wide strips. Keep the strips and a marker in a bag or box labeled "I Can!" As you and your child discover tasks that he/she can accomplish by him/herself, write each one on a separate strip. Create a paper chain by connecting the strips together. Hang the chain from the ceiling or along a wall. Continue adding paper links to the chain as your child becomes increasingly independent. While creating this project, your child's self-confidence is sure to grow and grow and grow!

When I was little, I was messy.

Now I can clean up by myself!

I can help set th...
I can fold to wels...
I can make a sand...
I can pick up my...
I can pour my cer...
I can comb...

I can zip my coat!

Read All About It!
Our Class News

The ideas in this newsletter are contributed by Jan Brennan.

Building Bridges
Between Home And School

School: _____

Teacher: _____

Date: _____

Learning Patience

"Are we there yet?" "When will Daddy be home?" "How much longer?" Have you ever found yourself thinking that you just can't wait for your preschooler to learn patience? Here are some fun ways to pass the time when it's necessary to wait:

Storytelling—Tell a story that will capture your child's attention. Share a true story from your childhood or tell a story about when your child was a baby. Begin a story, and then let your child tell or make up the ending. Or take turns telling or making up parts of a story.

Songs—Sing favorite songs together or sing along with your favorite tapes. Make up a silly song that relates to the situation.

Word Games—Play a game of I Spy. Look for items that begin with the first letter of your child's name. Describe items by their location, size, or color. Or describe how an item is used.

Preschoolers have difficulty understanding time because it is intangible and invisible. Make waiting easier by making a tangible and visible helper.

- Make a simple **calendar** with a box that represents each day or event that must pass. Let your child mark through or add a sticker to each box until the anticipated time arrives.
- Make a **paper chain** that includes a link for each day. Cut off one link each day until the big day.
- **Lay out an outfit** or piece of clothing for each day that must pass. When all the clothes have been worn, the day has come!

Be a patient role model, and your little one will learn the virtue of patience in no time!

The Book Corner

Stories About Patience

The Carrot Seed
A little boy plants a carrot seed and proves that he has more patience than anyone else in his family.
Written by Ruth Krauss
Published by HarperCollins Children's Books

Sunflower
This simple story is about planting a sunflower seed and watching it grow and grow and grow.
Written by Miela Ford
Published by Greenwillow Books

Blueberries For Sal
Sal goes blueberry picking with her mom to gather berries to can for winter eating. But Sal has a tough time waiting to eat the berries.
Written by Robert McCloskey
Published by Viking Children's Books

Not Yet, Yvette
Yvette and her dad prepare a birthday surprise for her mom. Is it time? Not yet, Yvette!
Written by Helen Ketteman
Published by Albert Whitman & Company

To The Teacher: Duplicate a copy of pages 293 and 294. Complete the information at the top of page 293; then add class-related news to page 294. Trim away these instructions. Duplicate a copy for each child on the front and back sides of a colorful piece of paper.

Patience With Plants

As your child waits for plants to grow and bloom, his/her patience will grow as well. Just follow these steps for growing an indoor herb garden:

Purchase packages of herb seeds or small herb plants. Dill, basil, and cilantro can be grown from seeds. Other herbs that grow well indoors but should be purchased as plants include bay, chives, oregano, parsley, rosemary, sage, and thyme. Plant the seeds or plants in pots that have drainage holes and water saucers; then place the pots near a sunny window. When the plants are about four inches tall, harvest them by cutting the tips with scissors. Store the herbs in a dry place. When they are dry (about two weeks), crumble them in your fingers. Store them in plastic containers; then use them when you cook!

Worth-The-Wait Ice Cream

1. Pour **1/4 cup milk** into a blender; then sprinkle **1 small envelope of unflavored gelatin** over the milk.

2. Add **3/4 cup scalded milk.** Blend the ingredients for two minutes.

3. Blend in **3/4 cup sugar, 1/2 teaspoon vanilla, and 3 cups cut up fresh fruit** (such as blueberries, strawberries, or peaches).

4. Pour this mixture into a bowl and chill, stirring occasionally until the mixture mounds when dropped from a spoon (about two hours).

5. Whip **2 cups heavy cream** with **2 tablespoons sugar** and **2 teaspoons of vanilla.** Fold this mixture into the chilled mixture.

6. Pour the mixture into a nine-inch square baking pan. Freeze it until it is firm.

Read All About It!
Our Class News

The ideas in this newsletter are contributed by Jan Brennan.

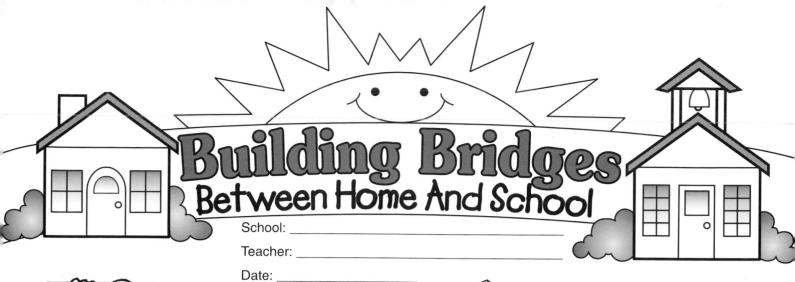

Building Bridges
Between Home And School

School: _____

Teacher: _____

Date: _____

Preschool Pals

It's been a great year! No doubt you have seen your preschooler become more social and develop new friendships. Now, as the school year draws to an end, he/she may experience the anxiety of saying good-bye to some of those friends. But with your help, summertime can offer your child many opportunities to keep in touch with old friends and to make new ones. Here are some facets of preschool friendships to keep in mind:

Aspects Of Three-Year-Olds' Friendships
- Although three-year-olds have the beginning social skills required to play in small groups, twosomes usually work best.
- Threes develop friendships easily; however, these friendships may not be lasting and can change from day to day.
- When participating in an activity, threes are generally more interested in the other children rather than in the activity itself.

Aspects Of Four-Year-Olds' Friendships
- Pairs of four-year-olds develop friendships based on shared activities and are less likely to exclude a third friend.
- Strong friendships are quick to develop in fours. Children start to have best friends.
- By age four, children often play in groups. Play is generally cooperative and is often spent in construction-based or imaginative-play activities.

How Can You Help Your Child Make Friends?
- Using stuffed toys, model conversation starters with your child.
- Provide your child with opportunities to socialize with other children, such as going to the park or participating in a play group.
- When going someplace where your child will encounter other children, bring along some items that can be shared, such as bubble solution or crayons and paper.
- Read books that explore childhood friendships. After reading a book, discuss it so that your own child gains confidence in his/her ability to make friends.

The Book Corner

Books About Friends

My Best Friend
Two best friends discover things about each other that they admire and realize why they are best friends.
Written & Illustrated by Pat Hutchins
Published by Greenwillow Books

My Friends
A little girl tells the wonderful things she has learned from her many animal and people friends.
Written & Illustrated by Taro Gomi
Published by Chronicle Books

Do You Want To Be My Friend?
A mouse seeks friendship from a variety of animals but hasn't any luck until it asks another mouse.
Written & Illustrated by Eric Carle
Published by HarperCollins Children's Books

Making Friends
With photos and conversational text, this book explains the challenges and rewards of preschool friendships.
Written by Fred Rogers
Published by The Putnam & Grosset Group

To The Teacher: Duplicate a copy of pages 295 and 296. Complete the information at the top of page 295; then add class-related news to page 296. Trim away these instructions. Duplicate a copy for each child on the front and back sides of a colorful piece of paper.

Postcards To Pals

Making and sending postcards is a creative way for your child to keep in touch with his/her preschool friends over the summer break. Encourage your child to draw or paint a design on one side of a 4" x 6" piece of poster board. Turn the card over; then draw a vertical line down the middle. On the left side of the card, write as your child dictates a message to his/her friend. Address the right side of the card; then have your child affix a stamp to the upper right-hand corner. Take your child to a mailbox or post office to send this special delivery on its way!

Dear Tammy,
...am having fun. My ...ommy and daddy ...ok me and my ...ther to the beach. ...ade a sand castle. It was big. The water is fun!

Your friend,
Kyle

Tammy Sullivan
105 Park Place
Lyons, NY 12345

"Friendchip" Cookies

Make a date for your child and a friend to prepare a batch of "Friendchip" Cookies. Provide each child with a resealable plastic bag filled with 2 1/2 cups of potato chips. Encourage the children to squeeze their bags until all the chips are crushed into small pieces. Set the bags aside.

To prepare the cookie dough, each child places a stick of softened butter into one mixing bowl. Each child then adds 1/8 cup of sugar and 3/4 teaspoon of vanilla to the butter mixture. While one child stirs, his/her friend gradually adds 1 3/4 cups of flour. The children then add their bags of crushed chips and take turns stirring the mixture. Next, one child rolls the dough into small balls, then places them onto an ungreased cookie sheet. His/her friend flattens the balls with a fork.

Bake the cookies for 12 to 15 minutes at 350° until they are golden brown. When the cookies are cool, assist the children in dividing them so that each friend will have half to share with his/her family. This recipe makes approximately 32 cookies.

Read All About It!
Our Class News

The ideas in this newsletter are contributed by Jan Brennan.

Bulletin Boards and Displays

Use this display to invite your excited learners to squirm into preschool. Border a background with construction-paper apple cutouts; then add a friendly apple character. Invite each child to use her fingers to wiggle paint designs onto a personalized worm cutout. When the paint is dry, add a wiggle eye to each worm. Then creatively arrange the worms on the display.

Leslie Jeffords, Port Royal, SC

Squirm
Into the
Library

To make this birthday banner, use fabric paints to paint a cake onto a pillowcase. Attach the loop side of a piece of Velcro® to the cake; then attach the loop side of a Velcro® strip below the cake as shown. Fold the top of the pillowcase over a dowel; then secure it with safety pins. Tie a length of ribbon onto the dowel for hanging. For each child, label a tagboard strip with his name and birthdate. Also label each of 12 strips with a month. Attach the hook side of a piece of Velcro® to the back of each strip. Each month attach the appropriate strips to the banner.

Sue DeMoss—Preschool
Maquoketa Head Start
Maquoketa, IA

Get Hooked on Reading

This photo display is sure to make a big splash! Mount blue bulletin-board paper waves on a wall. Add a boating character along with a catchy title. Attach colorful, laminated fish shapes to the water. To the fish, attach photos of your new students taken during the first days of school. Change the photos throughout the year to keep this fishy display fresh.

Kim Paulson—Preschool, Busy Bee Preschool
Windom, MN

Get Hooked On Learning!

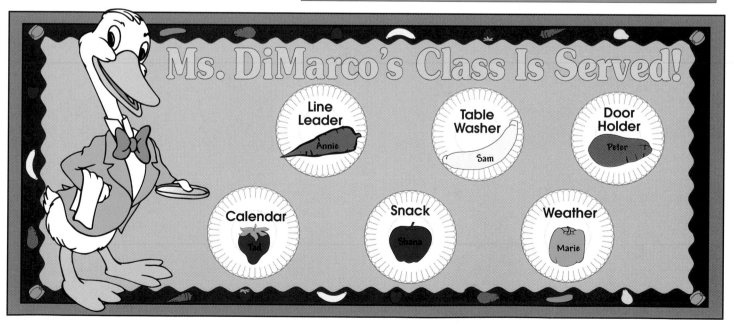

Ms. DiMarco's Class Is Served!

Line Leader — Annie
Table Washer — Sam
Door Holder — Peter
Calendar — Tad
Snack — Shana
Weather — Marie

To create this helpful display, enlarge a waiter character; then mount him on a background. Label a set of plastic plates with your class jobs; then add these plates to the display. From construction paper, cut a class supply of healthful foods, such as fruits and vegetables. Laminate the cutouts; then write a different child's name on each one. Choose your helpers by attaching a food to each plate.

Diane DiMarco—Three- And Four-Year-Olds, Country Kids Preschool, Groton, MA

BULLETIN BOARDS

Invite little ones to get down and dirty when creating this display. Attach a length of bulletin-board paper that has been fingerpainted brown to the bottom half of a blue background. Put students' fingerpainted piggies in the mud (enlarge the pattern on page 308 for use as a tracer). Create a fence by mounting twisted strips of black paper and lengths of yarn to the board. Then accent the display with a title, and sun and cloud cutouts.

Lisa Mole—Four-Year-Olds, Elbert County Pre-Kindergarten, Elberton, GA

Create this eerie bat habitat by attaching crumpled black bulletin-board paper to the wall around your doorway. Prepare a cardboard sign; then insert it into a gravel-filled can. Display student-painted bats around the entrance along with batty facts and/or students' comments.

Barbara Meyers, Fort Worth Country Day School, Fort Worth, TX

Using fabric paint, paint a racetrack on a hemmed piece of fabric. Along the track, attach the hook sides of a quantity of Velcro® pieces. Duplicate a class supply of the race-car pattern and a desired number of the gas-pump pattern (page 308). Laminate; then cut out the patterns. Personalize the cars; then use the loop sides of Velcro® pieces to randomly attach them to the track. Use additional Velcro® to secure the gas pumps at distances around the track. A child moves her car around the track as appropriate behaviors are displayed. When her car stops at a pump, fill 'er up with a treat!

Libby Mackman
Lowell Elementary
Madison, WI

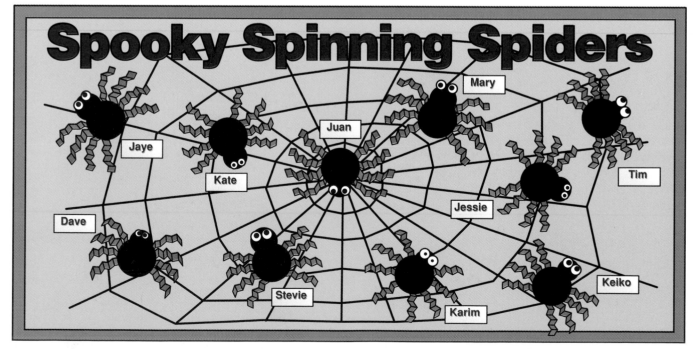

Spin a splendid display by stapling a yarn web onto a background. Then add spooky student-made spiders. To make one, glue together one large and one smaller paper circle. Add cut-out eyes accented with black marker; then glue on accordion-folded paper legs.

Barbara Meyers, Fort Worth Country Day School, Fort Worth TX

BULLETIN BOARDS

Using construction paper and bulletin-board paper, create a fireplace scene. For each child cut a pair of matching stocking shapes from construction paper; then glue the sides and bottom together. Have each child cut out catalog pictures of items he'd like for Christmas, then glue them on his stocking. Provide art supplies for further decorating the stockings. Gently stuff each stocking with tissue paper before adding it to the display.

Ruby Boyatzis, Green Hill International School, Athens, Greece

Decorating this tree will be a creative, cooperative effort! Cut a large tree shape from green bulletin-board paper. Invite students to sponge-paint holiday shapes onto the tree to resemble ornaments. Then have children embellish paper squares and rectangles with craft items so that the shapes resemble gifts. Display the tree and gifts with a holiday greeting from your class.

Tracy Tavernese—Four-Year-Olds
Holy Child School
Old Westbury, NY

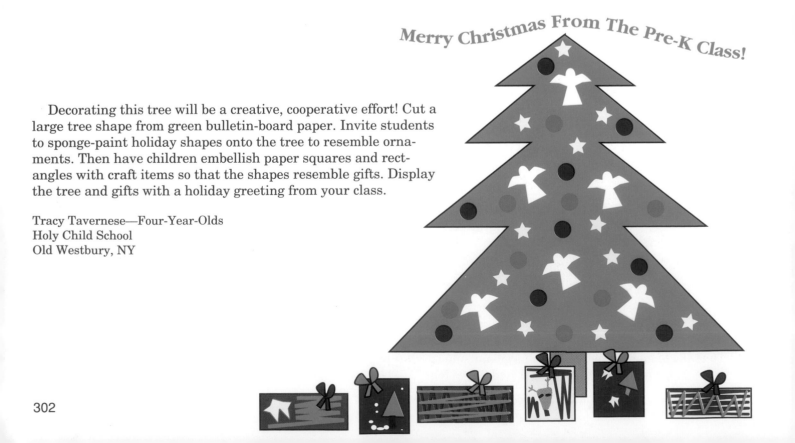

This display doubles as a great gift idea. Invite each child to use red and green ink-filled bingo markers to paint a white paper plate. Take a picture of each child; then trim the developed photos into circles. Glue each child's photo onto the center of his plate. Punch a hole near the top of the plate; then attach lengths of curling ribbon. Arrange the plates in a tree shape on a wall. Just before Christmas vacation, remove the plates from the wall, and send them home to parents.

Joan Johnson—Four-Year-Olds
Columbus School
Bridgeport, CT

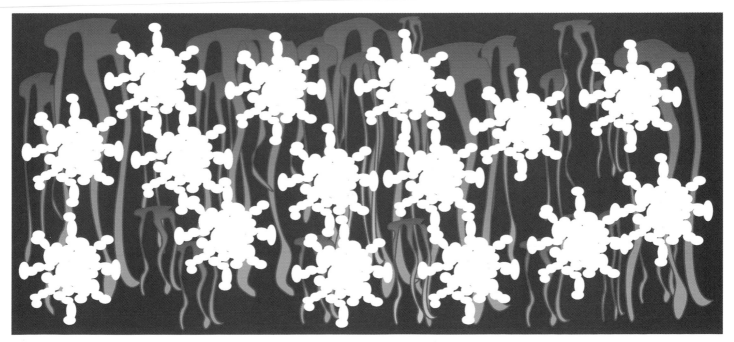

Looking for a cool class display? Look no more! Secure a length of white bulletin-board paper to the lower portion of a wall. Protect the floor with layers of newspaper. Invite students to use small, foam paint rollers to paint the paper blue. Next fill squirt guns with watered-down white paint. Have students sparingly squirt the paint onto the paper. When the paint is dry, direct students to sponge-paint snowflake shapes onto the paper. At winter's end, cut the mural and give a portion to each participant.

Lisa LaLonde—Preschool, St. Mary's School For The Deaf, Buffalo, NY

BULLETIN BOARDS

Celebrate The Young Child!

Promote the Week Of The Young Child with this child-made display. Provide each child with a skin-toned construction-paper doll cutout to decorate with a variety of materials, such as wallpaper, feathers, fabric, yarn, sequins, lace, and markers. Mount each child's project on a personalized piece of construction paper. Display these projects at a location in your community, such as the library, a grocery store, or a school administration building.

Roxanne Rowley—Early Childhood Specialist, Four Stars Preschool, Manistee, MI

Enlarge the bunny pattern on page 309 several times. Color each bunny, creating a unique design on each bow tie and leaving the eggs white. For each bunny, cut four construction-paper eggs that correspond in size to the eggs in the basket. Color each set of four eggs to match a bunny's bow tie. Laminate the bunnies and eggs. Attach the loop sides of Velcro® pieces to the backs of the eggs, and attach the hook sides of Velcro® pieces to the eggs in the baskets. Mount the bunnies on a background, and store the eggs in a real basket. To manipulate the display, a child attaches the corresponding eggs to each bunny's basket.

Donna Austin, St. Matthew's Preschool, Lehighton, PA

Moms will grin with delight at this board and be tickled, too, with the take-home treats! For each child, prepare a head-and-shoulders outline on poster board. Encourage each child to use markers to illustrate the outline to represent his mom. Label the project. Then provide each child with a length of yarn and decorative beads for making a necklace. Punch two holes through the poster board at the shoulders. Thread the necklace through the holes; then tie the ends together at the back. Display the projects and watch for smiles.

Nancy Segars—Four-Year-Olds, First Baptist Preschool, Lawrenceville, GA

Our Classroom Bouquet

Each child contributes to this giant display in a big way! Precut a circle in the center of a paper plate for each child; then personalize the plate. Have each child glue paper petals, a stem, and leaves to the plate. Tape the child's picture to the back of the plate. Arrange the flowers on a wall along with a bulletin-board-paper pot. Add a class photo to the pot and a title to the display.

Theresa Reth—Four-Year-Olds, Little People's College, New Bedford, MA

BULLETIN BOARDS

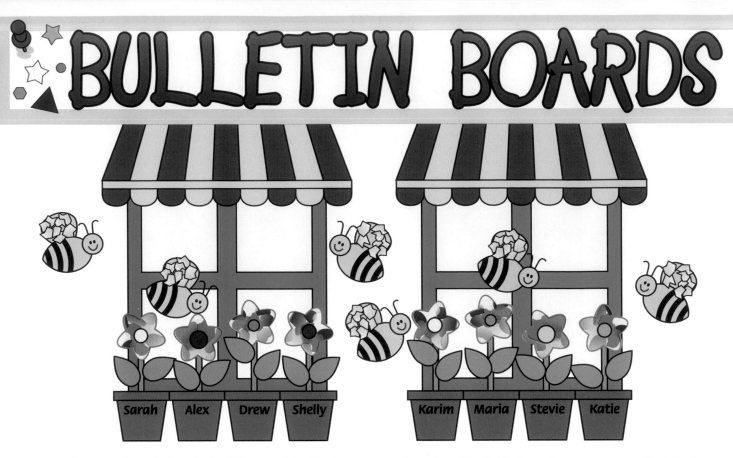

Sarah   Alex   Drew   Shelly   Karim   Maria   Stevie   Katie

To prepare the window look-alikes in this display, mount lengths of bulletin-board paper on a wall. Attach four sheets of construction paper to each length to resemble windowpanes. Cut and color bulletin-board paper to resemble awnings to mount over the windows. Melt crayon shavings between layers of waxed paper; then cut the paper into flower shapes to put in paper pots to line the windows. Glue yellow tissue-paper pieces to paper bee shapes; then randomly arrange them on the wall.

Sharon Mason and Peggy Fuhr—Preschool, Jordan Catholic School, Rock Island, IL

Reel in excitement with this display that reinforces color recognition. Hang a lightweight net—such as a badminton net—in a corner of your room. Each time you focus your studies on a color, make a stuffed bulletin-board-paper fish of that color to put in the net. Watch your net fill up with a rainbow of fish!

Patricia Shemwell—Preschool
Hickory Hills Park District
    Preschool
Hickory Hills, IL

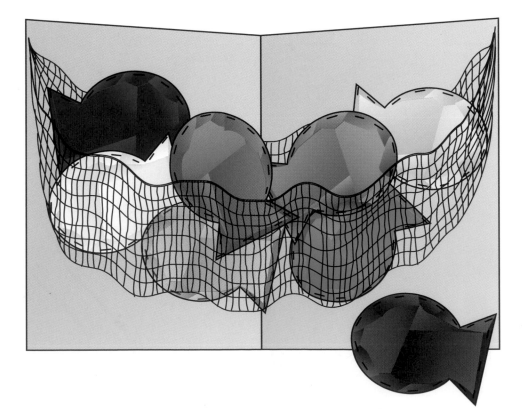

AND DISPLAYS

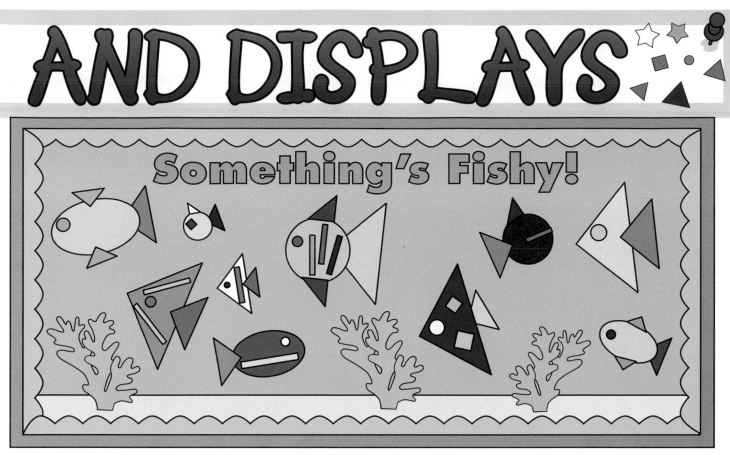

Something's Fishy!

Nothing's fishy about the creativity involved in making these shapely fish! Provide youngsters with glue and construction-paper geometric shapes in a variety of colors and sizes. Have students use the shapes to create colorful fish. Display the fish on a background along with paper seaweed and coral. Yes, that is a new species of triangle fish that you see! Something's Fishy At the Library - Fish Books

Kathy McCauley—Pre-K, St. Patrick Interparish School, Gainesville, FL

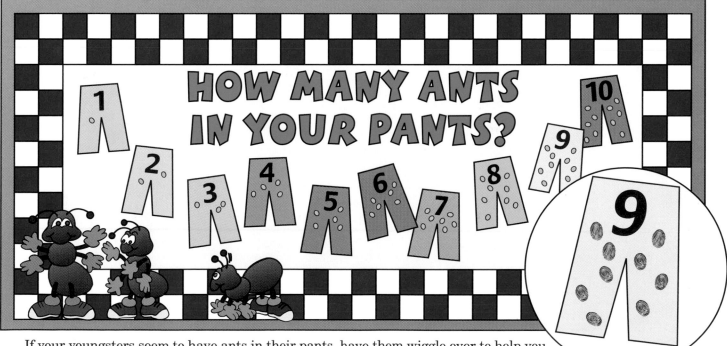

If your youngsters seem to have ants in their pants, have them wiggle over to help you make this summertime display. Cut a class supply of paper pants shapes; then label each shape with a numeral from one to ten. (Write each numeral at least once.) Ask each child to choose a pair of pants and to look at the numeral. Then have him press the corresponding number of fingerprint ants onto the pants. Sequence the pants before mounting them on a titled board along with ant characters.

Pamela Chandler, Clifton Park, NY

Patterns

Use with "Good Day Grand Prix" on page 301.

GALLONS

GAS

Pig Pattern

Use with "Piggies In The Puddle" on page 300.

OUR READERS WRITE

Our Readers Write

Dramatic Dinosaur Duds

Knock your little ones' socks off with these exciting dinosaur duds! To make a dinosaur paw, cut the hook side of a strip of self-adhesive Velcro® to match the width of the toe section of a large tube sock. Attach the velcro to the top of the sock's toe. Cut out three to five colorful felt triangles—the paw's claws—for each dinosaur paw. For dramatic dinosaur play, encourage a child to select a number of claws to attach to a paw's Velcro®. Then direct him to put his hand and arm into the paw. Roar! These paws help little ones grab onto color recognition, counting, sorting, and more!

Helen Honea—Preschool
Prelude Preschool, Prescott Unified District #1
Prescott, AZ

A Good-Bye Game

This game provides just the right amount of comfort on mornings when a child and her parent have a difficult time separating. To prepare a good-bye game, write a different numeral from one to ten on each of ten construction-paper squares. To the back of each square, attach the corresponding number of ministickers. Place the squares in a colorful gift bag. If a child is not ready to say good-bye to a parent, encourage her to select a square from the bag. Show her the numeral; then suggest that she give the parent as many hugs or kisses as there are stickers on the square. One, two, three, four, five, bye!

Paula Greatorex—Preschool
Massachusetts General Hospital Children's Center
Charlestown, MA

Caveman's (Or Woman's) Clothing

The rugged look is in with this year's line of cave-dwellers' clothing. To make a cloak that resembles attire from *years* gone by, fold an old brown, yellow, or tan towel in half. Sew the sides together. Cut away a portion of the top of the towel as shown. Cut along the remaining fold of the towel; then attach a strip of Velcro® to each side of the cut. Use a permanent marker or fabric paint to add dots that resemble animal-skin spots. Now that's timeless fashion!

Charlet Keller—Preschool
ICC Preschool
Violet Hill, AR

Here Comes Tyrannosaurus Rex!

If your little ones are fascinated with dinosaurs, then teach them this fun fingerplay. But don't be surprised if, at the end, they all run away!

Five Huge Dinosaurs
Five huge dinosaurs, looking fierce and mean.
The first one said, "I eat things that are green."
The second one said, "I hatched from an egg."
The third one said, "I have big, strong legs."
The fourth one said, "I can fly through the air."
The fifth one said, "I give everyone a scare!"
THUMP, THUMP came Tyrannosaurus Rex that day,
And the five huge dinosaurs all ran away!

Linda Bockhorn—Four-Year-Olds
Kings Kids Preschool, Kings Local School District, Kings Mills, OH

Rebus Rhymes

Set the stage for some fingerplay fun with these charming charts that reinforce language skills. Use a computer to type each of your favorite fingerplays in a large text size. Cut out the printed phrases; then mount them on tagboard. Locate clip art or magazine photos that illustrate the accompanying action for each phrase of the fingerplay. Cut out, or enlarge and color, the illustrations; then add them to the chart. Punch holes near the tops of the charts; then hang them on a chart stand or around your room. In no time at all, your youngsters will be fingering through their favorite fingerplays.

Lorraine Patterson—Pre-K, Bonham ECDC, San Marcos, TX

312

A shiny, red apple dropped on my nose!

Numbers Tell The Story

This visual cue helps reinforce number recognition and seriation skills. Keep a set of flannelboard numerals handy for use when reading your favorite counting stories, such as *Mouse Count, Ten Black Dots,* and others. Storytime is as easy as 1, 2, 3!

Helen Martinko—Four- And Five-Year-Olds
Brookfield Methodist Preschool
Brookfield, OH

Starry, Starry Night

Help dispel fears of the dark with this activity. To prepare, cut a piece of poster board to match the dimensions of an overhead projector's stage. Then cut a moon and star shapes from the poster-board piece. Lay the poster board on the stage of the projector. During a quiet time, invite your little ones to share their nighttime fears. Then turn the projector on, dim the lights, and tilt the projector's lens so that the moon and stars are displayed on the ceiling of your room. As you gaze at the "night sky," lead little ones in singing the following song to the tune of "Twinkle, Twinkle, Little Star":

When the sun is sinking low,
Night is coming, day must go.
Soon the moon and stars come out,
Shining, shining all about.
I'm so glad these night lights shine;
With their light I see just fine!
There's no need for me to fear;
Soon the next day will be here!

Diane McLoud—Home-School Teacher
Washingtonville, OH

Paint Printers

Put some pizzazz into your art center by making these inexpensive plastic printers. To make one, cut a desired shape from a sheet of plastic grid craft canvas (available at craft stores). Hot-glue an empty film canister to the shape for a handle. Dip the printer into paint, then onto paper to create a perfectly pleasing print.

Anna Majorie—Pre-K
Marrero, LA

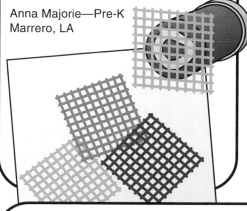

It's A Puzzler

Your youngest learners will be pleased with their problem-solving skills when using these easy-to-make puzzles. To make one, trace the shape of a cookie cutter onto a piece of heavy cardboard; then cut out the shape. Encourage a child to place the corresponding cookie cutter into each puzzle's cut-out area.

Kathie Deann Thornton—Preschool
Home Day Care, Wake Forest, NC

Creative Covers

Shed some light on the creative process by adding inexpensive fluorescent-light covers (available at home-supplies stores) to your art area. Each plastic panel has a textured pattern on one side, and a smooth surface on the other side. Encourage youngsters to make crayon rubbings from the textured sides, and to use the smooth sides as fingerpainting surfaces. Awesome artistry!

Leslie Madalinski—Preschool
Weekday Children's Center
Naperville, IL

Black-Cat Baskets

It's no trick to treat your little ones with these cool cat baskets. To make one, spray-paint two berry baskets black. When the paint is dry, use black yarn to tie the tops of the baskets together along one side. Close the basket. Glue construction-paper eyes and ears to the front of the basket; then attach a pink pom-pom nose and black pipe-cleaner whiskers. Line the completed basket with a piece of black tissue paper; then fill it with Halloween goodies for a treat that will leave your little ones purring.

Lori Parlier—Four- And
  Five-Year-Olds
Hubbard Pre-K
Forsyth, GA

Safe Fishing

Our polls show that this fishing-pole alternative is perfect for preschoolers. That's because it's safe and easy for the youngest of preschoolers to use. To make one for use with your fishing games and centers, simply tie one end of a length of yarn onto a plastic shower-curtain ring. Tie the opposite end around a magnet. Invite a child to hold onto the ring, then go fish!

Carleen Coderre—Preschool And Gr. K
Bright Beginnings Child Care Center
Three Rivers, MA

Ring Around The Rosie

Add variety to this classic chant by asking volunteers to suggest different locomotor movements. *Jump* around the rosie, *run* around the rosie, *stomp* around the rosie—whew! We all fall down!

Elizabeth Graham—Pre-K
Blanchard Elementary
Columbus, GA

Wormy Matching

Make a few of these wormy floor puzzles and your little ones will squirm their way into visual-discrimination skills. To make a puzzle, draw a worm shape onto a piece of green poster board. Visually divide the worm into segments. On both sides of each division, attach matching stickers. Cut out the wormy puzzle; then place it in your games center.

Doris Porter—Headstart-Preschool
Anamosa, IA

Ribbit!

Here's a spring craft worth croaking about—especially if your class is doing a frog unit or learning about the color green. Begin by using a green crayon to color both sides of a small paper plate; then fold the plate in half. Next use a marker to color a wooden ice-cream spoon red. Cut out white paper eyes and green paper legs. Color a black circle on each white circle; then glue the eyes and legs to the plate as shown. For extra fun glue a plastic fly onto the spoon before taping it to the plate. Display the frogs on a blue background, or use them to hop into language fun with your favorite frog fingerplays and songs.

Debi Luke—Four-Year-Olds
Fairmount Nursery School
Syracuse, NY

Our Favorite Colors

Make the most of your youngest preschoolers' paintings with this paint-center idea. Near your easel prepare a display area titled "Our Favorite Colors." When a child paints a sheet of art paper one color, offer to cut the paper into a paintbrush shape when it is dry. Group the paintbrushes by color along with the painters' names.

adapted from an idea by Betsy Ruggiano—Three-Year-Olds
Featherbed Lane School
Clark, NJ

Beth   Ben   Jayne

Take A Guess

Sharpen youngsters' listening and thinking skills with this guessing game. In advance cut simple pictures from magazines; then insert each picture into a separate envelope. On the front of each envelope, write clues about the pictured object inside. Next time you have five minutes to spare, grab an envelope, read the clues aloud, and let the guessing game begin!

Nancy Langhorst—Preschool
Blue Lake Preschool
Carbondale, CO

Ant Cookies

Your little army of ants will be marching to make these delicious cookies that help illustrate ant anatomy. Using the following recipe, prepare cookie balls. To make an edible ant, a child places three cookie balls in a line. He then adds six pretzel-stick legs and two mini chocolate-chip eyes.

Adele Owoc—Four-Year-Olds
The Rainbow Connection
Shelby, NC

Ant Cookies

3 cups of crispy-rice cereal
1/4 cup of honey
1/2 cup of peanut butter

Stir together two cups of the crispy-rice cereal, the honey, and the peanut butter. Roll the mixture into balls. Coat the balls in the remaining cup of cereal. Makes approximately 21 balls.

Ants All Around

Colonize your classroom with these hills that are alive with little ants. Obtain a supply of cardboard cup holders from a fast-food restaurant; then cut each holder into its four sections. Paint the outside of a section brown. Twist three pipe-cleaner pieces together at their centers. Squeeze a large circle of glue onto the top of the section; then place the pipe cleaners on top of the glue. Position three pom-poms on top of the pipe cleaners. Glue wiggle eyes to one pom-pom to complete the ant.

Adele Owoc—
Four-Year-Olds

Tear No More

If you're tired of birthday crowns that tatter and tear, try this helpful hint. Cut a length of corrugated bulletin-board border. Staple a birthday message to the middle of the border; then staple the band to fit the birthday child's head. This easy-to-make crown resists tearing and can be folded flat to take home. What a royal idea!

Susan Ahlhorn—Three-Year-Olds, Wee Wuns Preschool, Cypress, TX

Planning Tip

This timesaving tip will help when planning thematic units. Use a marker to number the spines of your Mailbox® magazines and other resource books. When planning lessons for a thematic unit, write in your lesson plans the names of the ideas you want to use and the numbers of the resource books in which they are located. Then, when you want to teach that same unit another time, simply revisit your plans for the location of the ideas you will need.

Michelle Habrat—Pre-K, La Petite Academy, Glen Burnie, MD

Rider's Permit

Drive home the importance of seat-belt safety with this preschool permit that helps little ones remember to buckle up. After a discussion about seat-belt safety, make a rider's permit for each child by duplicating a permit similar to the one shown. Personalize a copy for each child; then attach the child's photo. Laminate the permits. Send each child's permit home along with a note encouraging his parent to post the permit in the car as a reminder to buckle up for safety!

Amy Rain Monahan—Four-Year-Olds
Evangelical School for the Young Years
Godfrey, IL

Under The Sea

Your little ones will enjoy recycling materials to create these underwater scenes. To make one, cut out a variety of sea-life shapes from construction-paper scraps. Glue the shapes, shredded-paper seaweed, glitter, and sand onto a sanitized Styrofoam® tray. When the glue is dry, wrap the entire tray with blue plastic wrap twice. Tape these little aquariums to windows and watch the sunlight illuminate the scenes.

Karen Mitchell—Preschool, Gretchen's House, Ann Arbor, MI

Preschool Rider's Permit STOP

Rob

Buckle Up
For Safety!

Index

1, 2, 3 To The Zoo, 162
A You're Adorable, 108
Aaron's Shirt, 60
Activity Centers (see Learning Centers)
Alligators
    fingerplay, 211
    reading center, 163
Alphabet
    Chicka Chicka Boom Boom, 114–116
    initial letter, 108, 109, 259
    letter recognition, 108, 109, 114, 190, 253, 258
    matching, 115
    sequencing, 253, 258
Animals
    alligators, 163, 211
    ants, 307, 315
    bats, 300
    bears, 178
    birds, 21, 55, 268–269
    butterflies, 125, 190
    cat, 313
    caterpillars, 81, 106, 125–127
    cow, 216, 248
    crabs, 170, 225
    crocodiles, 217
    dog, 77
    fireflies, 185
    fish, 78, 149–152, 153–154, 225, 306, 307
    flies, 169
    frogs, 314
    insects, 185, 212–213, 307, 315
    kangaroos, 12–17
    metamorphosis, 190
    mice, 130–131, 132
    migration, 55
    moose, 164
    octopus, 225
    peacock, 81
    pets, 199
    pig, 157, 216, 300, 308
    polar bears, 165
    rabbit, 77
    reindeer, 77
    snakes, 85, 167
    spiders, 134–136, 138, 247, 301
    squirrel, 207
    tiger, 81
    turkeys, 195, 219
    turtles, 217
    worms, 314
    zebra, 216
    zoo, 162
Animals Should Definitely <u>Not</u> Wear Clothing, 60
Ants
    bulletin board, 307
    cookies, 315
Appelt, Kathi
    Watermelon Day, 101
Apples
    bulletin board, 298
    fingerplay, 205
Art
    da Vinci, Leonardo, 66
    Matisse, Henri, 65
    Michelangelo, 66
    Mondrian, Piet, 67
    Monet, Claude, 65
    Pollock, Jackson, 67
    thematic unit, 64–69
    van Gogh, Vincent, 64
Arts And Crafts (see also Dough, Fall, Recycling Materials, Spring, Summer, Winter)
    air freshener, 80
    angels, 220
    antlers, 46
    ants, 315
    beads, 40
    bells, 221
    blocks, 230
    bubbles, 233
    buildings, 230, 231
    butterflies, 127
    candle, 140, 257
    candy-cane hearts, 221
    cars, 182
    castle, sand, 120
    cat, 313
    caterpillar, 81, 106, 126, 127
    children, 304
    clay, 99, 120
    clothing, 59, 60, 165
    coconut tree, 116
    collage, 53, 65, 127, 224, 233
    cow, 216
    crabs, 225
    crayons, 232
    crocodiles, 217
    crown, 77, 315
    dinosaur headband, 8
    dog, 77
    dough recipe, 229
    dreidel, 221
    Father's Day, 226
    feet, 102, 103
    fingerpaint, 53, 82, 127, 218, 237, 280, 300
    fish, 78, 150, 225, 307
    flies, 169
    flowers, 64, 82, 88, 119, 144, 254
    frame, 82, 226, 303
    frogs, 314
    hat, 99, 166, 168

headbands, 8, 77, 88
houses, 28
jewelry, 40
kangaroo, 12
kites, 224
Kwanzaa, 40
leaves, 218
marble painting, 74
masks, 31, 288
Mondrian, 67
monsters, 30, 31, 111
moose, 164
mouse, 130
mural, 65, 78, 229
music, 169
ocean scene, 315
octopus, 225
painting, 60, 64, 65, 66, 67, 84, 165, 171, 224, 234, 235, 256, 314
papier-mâché, 98
peacock, 81
pencil cup, 226
pig, 216, 300
pillowcase, 220
pockets, 12, 46
prints, 45, 78–81, 99, 102, 103, 117, 118, 240, 254, 255, 256, 313
pudding painting, 237
pumpkin pie air freshener, 219
pumpkins, 121, 218, 219
puppets, 144
rabbit, 77
rainbow, 229
reindeer, 45–47, 77
rubber stamps, 252, 253
rubbings, 313
sand castle, 120
sculpting, 120
shaving cream art, 236
snakes, 85, 167
snow dome, 52
snow scene, 232
snowflakes, 48, 118
snowpeople, 122, 222
spiders, 301
spin-painting, 235
splatter-painting, 67, 169
sponge-painting, 114, 216, 217, 303
stamping, 71, 252, 253
starch, using liquid, 224
stenciling, 217, 242
stickers, 253
streamers, 253
Styrofoam® creations, 231
sun, 93
suncatcher, paper, 231
sweatshirt, 222
tambourine, 219
tigers, 81
tile, 80
tote bag, 80
turkeys, 219
turtle, 217
vehicles, 182, 240
wand, magic, 278
watercolor, 232
watermelon, 98, 99
white, 53
wraparounds, 104
zebra, 216
Assessment
    portfolios, 276
Attendance
    photo board, 18
    T-shirt display, 18
Auditory Discrimination (see Listening)
Authors
    Appelt, Kathi, 101
    Aylesworth, Jim, 169
    Baker, Keith, 167
    Barrett, Judi, 60
    Barton, Byron, 8
    Borden, Louise, 117–121
    Bunting, Eve, 145
    Carle, Eric, 125–127, 162, 169, 170
    dePaola, Tomie, 166, 170, 188
    Ehlert, Lois, 88, 122–124, 151
    Fleming, Denise, 168
    Freeman, Don, 163
    Gibbons, Gail, 93
    Gould, Deborah, 60
    Herman, Gail, 7
    Hoban, Tana, 26
    Kaye, Buddy, 108
    Kirk, David, 134
    Krauss, Ruth, 168
    Kroll, Steven, 166
    Martin, Bill Jr., 114–116, 165
    Munsch, Robert, 164
    Numeroff, Laura Joffe, 164
    Payne, Emmy, 12
    Peek, Merle, 61
    Raffi, 171
    Reid, Margarette S., 165
    Rogers, Fred, 273
    Sendak, Maurice, 110–113
    Seuss, Dr., 166
    Shaw, Charles G., 171
    Stickland, Paul, 7
    Sturges, Philemon, 185
    Thompson, Carol, 157
    Westcott, Nadine Bernard, 163
    Winthrop, Elizabeth, 162
Autumn (see Fall)
Awards
    friendship, 16
Aylesworth, Jim
    Old Black Fly, 169

Baby Beluga, 171
Back-To-School
    bulletin board, 298
    dinosaur theme, 6–11
Baker, Keith
    Hide And Snake, 167
Balloons
    flour, 229
Barrett, Judi
    Animals Should Definitely <u>Not</u> Wear Clothing, 60
Barton, Byron
    Bones, Bones, Dinosaur Bones, 8
Bats
    door display, 300
Bears
    hibernation, 178
Bedtime (see Night)
Behavior
    motivation, 274, 301
    rules, 8
Birds
    feeders, 55
    learning center rotation, 21
    migration, 55
    nests, 268–269
Birthdays
    bulletin board, 298
    crown, 315
    headband, 77
Blocks (see Learning Centers—Blocks)
Bones, Bones, Dinosaur Bones, 8
Bookmaking, Class
    alphabet, 109
    catalogs, 241
    clothing, 60, 61
    colors, 61, 71, 78
    emotions, 33
    kangaroos, 14
    Mona Lisa, 66
    numbers, 78
    philosophy, 181
Bookmaking, Individual
    colors, 78
    counting, 79
    positional words, 135
    seeds, 86
    valentines, 183
Books
    1, 2, 3 To The Zoo, 162
    A You're Adorable, 108
    Aaron's Shirt, 60
    Animals Should Definitely <u>Not</u> Wear Clothing, 60
    Baby Beluga, 171
    Bones, Bones, Dinosaur Bones, 8
    Button Box, The, 165
    Caps, Hats, Socks, And Mittens: A Book About The Four Seasons, 117–121
    Carrot Seed, The, 168
    Cat In The Hat, The, 166
    Chicka Chicka Boom Boom, 114–116
    Construction Zone, 26
    Dinosaur Stomp!, 7
    Fish Eyes: A Book You Can Count On, 151
    Flower Garden, 145
    Hide And Snake, 167
    House For Hermit Crab, A, 170
    I See A Song, 169
    If You Give A Moose A Muffin, 164
    In The Tall, Tall Grass, 168
    It Looked Like Spilt Milk, 171
    Jamie O'Rourke And The Big Potato: An Irish Folktale, 167
    Katy No-Pocket, 12
    Lady With The Alligator Purse, The, 163
    Making Friends, 16
    Mary Wore Her Red Dress And Henry Wore His Green Sneakers, 61
    Miss Spider's Tea Party, 134
    Old Black Fly, 169
    Piggy Washes Up, 157
    Planting A Rainbow, 88
    Pocket For Corduroy, A, 163
    Polar Bear, Polar Bear, What Do You Hear?, 165
    Shoes, 162
    Snowballs, 122–124
    Strega Nona, 170, 188
    Sun Up, Sun Down, 93
    Ten Flashing Fireflies, 185
    Thomas' Snowsuit, 164
    Time For School, Little Dinosaur, 7
    Very Hungry Caterpillar, The, 125–127
    Watermelon Day, 101
    Where The Wild Things Are, 110–113
    Will You Be My Valentine?, 166
Borden, Louise
    Caps, Hats, Socks, And Mittens: A Book About The Four Seasons, 117–121
Bubbles
    art, 233
Bugs (see Insects)
Building (see Construction)
Bulletin Boards And Displays
    attendance, 18
    back-to-school, 298
    bats, 300
    birthdays, 298
    borders, 22
    Chicka Chicka Boom Boom, 116
    Christmas, 302, 303
    classroom photos, 305
    colors, 306
    crocodiles, 217
    Easter, 304
    feet, 103
    fish, 306, 307
    flowers, 87, 305, 306
    garden, 65, 82

helpers, 299
individualized, 280
It Looked Like Spilt Milk, 171
matching, 304
Monet, 65
Mother's Day, 305
motivation, 301
name recognition, 163
numbers, 307
photos, 299
pumpkins, 218
size, 241
snow, 303
spiders, 301
student information, 7
suns, 92
Week Of The Young Child, The, 304
windows, 306
Bunting, Eve
Flower Garden, 145
Butterflies
movement, 190
puppet, 125
Button Box, The, 165
Buttons (see Clothing)

Calendar Skills (see Time)
Candles
Kwanzaa, 209
manipulatives, 256–257
unit, 139–141, 142–143
Candy
jelly beans, 70–76
Caps, Hats, Socks, And Mittens: A Book About The Four Seasons, 117–121
Careers
construction, 25
Carle, Eric
1, 2, 3 To The Zoo, 162
House For Hermit Crab, A, 170
I See A Song, 169
Very Hungry Caterpillar, The, 125–127
Carrot Seed, The, 168
Cars (see Transportation)
Cat
black, 313
Cat In The Hat, The, 166
Caterpillar
handprint, 81
soda bottle, 106
Very Hungry Caterpillar, The, 125–127
Cause And Effect
squooshy bags, 229
Caves
door display, 300
Centers (see Learning Centers)
Chants (see Songs & Chants)
Chanukkah (see Hanukkah)
Character Education (see also Social Skills)
courage, 287–288
friendship, 14, 109, 273, 295–296
generosity, 181
gentleness, 274
patience, 293–294
Chicka Chicka Boom Boom, 114–116
Christmas
angels, 39, 220
bells, 39, 221
bulletin boards, 302
candy-cane hearts, 221
gifts, 180, 181
manger, 39
reindeer/Rudolph, 44–49, 77, 208
Santa, 38, 43
songs, 181, 196
stockings, 302
tree, 38, 233, 302, 303
Circle Time (see also Flannelboard, Games)
colors, 88, 183
communication, 180
creative thinking, 181
critical thinking, 7
deductive reasoning, 180
emotions, 33
fire safety, 178
flowers, 88
generosity, 181
holiday countdown, 179
letters, 108
listening, 165, 167
management, 19
matching, 162, 185
movement, 188, 189, 190
name recognition, 183, 184
New Year, 196
personal space, 182
play dough, 183
pudding, 180
safety, fire, 178
seasons, 37
seating, 182
self-esteem, 44, 47, 185, 210
shapes, 183
sharing, 37, 178, 182
shoes, matching, 162
Valentine's Day, 210
yarn ball, 189
Circles (see Shapes)
Classifying (see Sorting)
Classroom Management (see also Behavior)
attendance, 18
bingo markers, 259
birthdays, 298
bulletin boards & displays, 22, 277, 280
circle time, 19, 279

cleaning, 23
daily routine, 7
dismissal, 278
field trips, 277, 279
fingerpaint, 280
fishing pole, safe, 314
helpers, 299
learning centers, 14, 20–21, 36, 244
lesson plans, 315
nap time, 278
play dough, 244
portfolios, 276
puppets, 23, 278
puzzles, 22
smocks, 281
snacktime, 20, 279
storage, 22, 23, 276, 277, 281
transitions, 19, 110, 276, 281
Clothing
buttons, 165
international, 56
patterns, 62–63
shoes, 59
theme unit, 56–63
winter, 51
Colors
green, 314
matching, 13, 21, 136, 145, 233, 254, 256, 259
mixing, 78, 228, 231, 237
mural, 229
primary, 67
recognition, 19, 21, 22, 23, 61, 70, 78, 88, 104, 120, 183, 188, 306
similes, 71
sorting by, 39, 72, 88, 258
white, 53
Community
clothing drive, 56
Compare/Contrast
clothing, 51
dinosaurs, 8
leaves, 262
"Little Miss Muffet," 134
people, 7
Computers (see Internet Sites)
Construction
Construction Zone, 26
positional words, 259
thematic unit, 24–29
Construction Zone, 26
Cooking
ant cookies, 315
banana blizzards, 53
caterpillar cake, 126
coconut, 115
"do-it-myself" dip, 290
flowerpot cakes, 87
friendship cookies, 296
fruit, 126
house, 29
ice cream, 294
jelly-bean stew, 74
Kwanzaa kabobs, 40
leafy roll-ups, 263
menorah, 37
pizza pockets, 15
pudding, 180
pudding monsters, 288
puzzle cookies, 286
reindeer "pear," 47
rubber stamp cookies, 252
shakes, cement, 26
snowballs, 223
snowflakes, 223
snowpeople, 123
soda surprise, 73
spider cookies, 134
sun snack, 71
super sandwich, 290
watermelon, 101
Cooperation
cleaning, 23
game, 273
Matisse, 65
size, 241
Coordination (see Fine Motor)
Counting
animals, 162
backwards, 72
balloons, 229
blocks, 246
bookmaking, 79
candles, 256, 257
candy corns, 111
Christmas, 208
clock, 131
Hanukkah, 37
hopping, 14
jelly beans, 72
kangaroos, 13, 14
Kwanzaa, 209
one-to-one correspondence, 256, 257
"One, Two, Three, Four, Five; I Caught A Fish Alive," 149–152, 153–154
reindeer, 208
scoops, 254
snowballs, 123
stars, 184
valentines, 183
Courage (see Emotions)
Cows
bowling, 248
pasting, 216
Crabs (see also Hermit Crabs)
craft, 225
Crafts (see Arts And Crafts)

Creative Thinking
art, 66
clothing, 60
colors, 71
hands, 79
It Looked Like Spilt Milk, 171
monsters, 30
music, 169
philosophy, 181
Creative Writing
storytelling, 253
Critical Thinking
compare/contrast, 7, 8, 51,134, 262
friendship, 273
Crocodiles
craft, 217
Cultures
clothing, 56

da Vinci, Leonardo
Mona Lisa, 66
Days of the Week (see Time)
Deductive Reasoning
animals, 130
boxes, 180
feet, 103
game, 314
ghosts, 179
Dental Health (see Health & Hygiene)
dePaola, Tomie
Jamie O'Rourke And The Big Potato: An Irish Folktale, 167
Strega Nona, 170, 188
Descriptive Writing
catalogs, 241
Differences (see Compare/Contrast)
Dinosaur Stomp!, 7
Dinosaurs
back-to-school unit, 6–11
block area, 245
Dinosaur Stomp!, 7
fingerplay, 312
patterns, 9–11
paws, 312
sand table, 245
Directions (see Following Directions)
Displays (see Bulletin Boards)
Dog
headband, 77
Dough
floral-scented, 87
no-cook squooshy, 229
placemats, 244
sand clay, 120
snow, 54
sparkling, 233
Dramatic Play
clothing, store, 60
clothing, winter, 51
cooking, 37
gentleness, 274
laundry, 60
news center, 249
singer, 255
store, 253
ocean, 248
office, 252
painting, 28
prehistoric, 312
snow, 52
snowpeople, 124
watermelon farm, 98
Where The Wild Things Are, 110–113

Earth Day (see Recycling Materials)
Easter
eggs, 190, 279, 304
jelly beans, 70–76
rabbit, 77
Eggs (see Easter)
Ehlert, Lois
Fish Eyes: A Book You Can Count On, 151
Planting A Rainbow, 88
Snowballs, 122–124
Emotions
fear, 313
thematic unit, 30–35
Eye-Hand Coordination (see Fine Motor, Gross Motor)

Fall (see also Back-To-School, Halloween, Thanksgiving)
apples, 205, 298
fingerplay, 121
leaves, 194, 218, 246
nuts, 121
pumpkins, 121, 179, 218, 219, 246
scarecrows, 194
squirrel, 207
Families
kangaroos, 12
newsletter, 286
Father's Day
air freshener, 80
frame, 226
gift bag, 226
pencil cup, 226
Fear (see Emotions)
Feelings (see Emotions)
Field Trips
bus ride, 279
garden center, 145
home-supply store, 29
safety, 277
Fine Art (see Art)
Fine Motor (see also Arts And Crafts, Learning Centers—Play Dough)
bilateral skills, 28, 232, 235, 246
bimanual coordination, 27, 230, 231

317

cutting and gluing, 65, 105, 168
drawing, 26, 119
dressing, 156
eye-hand coordination, 106, 150, 230, 246, 257
grasping, 27, 189, 230, 235
hammering, 230
obstacle course, fine-motor, 106
pinching, 105, 106
sewing, 59
spoons, 121
squeezing, 104, 183, 228–229
stickers, 104
tearing, 105, 216
tongs, 106, 121, 233
tracing, 216
weaving, 105
wrapping, 104
writing, 59
Fingerplays
alligators, 211
apples, 205
Christmas, 208
dinosaurs, 312
fall, 121
growing up, 211
kangaroos, 13
Kwanzaa, 209
management, 312
mice, 130
positional words, 130
safety, 204, 206
spring, 119
squirrels, 207
summer, 120
winter, 118
Fire Safety (see Safety)
Fireflies
Ten Flashing Fireflies, 185
Fish
Fish Eyes: A Book You Can Count On, 151
fishing pole, safe, 150, 314
handprint, 78
pattern, 152, 153–154
poem, 149–152, 153–154
puppet, 150
shapes, 307
sparkling, 225
Fish Eyes: A Book You Can Count On, 151
Fitness (see Health & Hygiene, Movement)
Flannelboard
bedtime, 155, 157
counting, 184
"Diddle, Diddle, Dumpling," 155–157, 158–159
"Hickory, Dickory, Dock," 130
"Jack Be Nimble," 139–141, 142–143
jelly beans, 72
kangaroos, 13
learning center management, 21
"Little Miss Muffet," 134
"Mary, Mary, How Does Your Garden Grow?", 144
positional words, 130
shapes, 230
stars, 184
Fleming, Denise
In The Tall, Tall Grass, 168
Flower Garden, 145
Flowers (see Plants)
Following Directions
candles, 140
dot-to-dot, 188
hop and seek, 15
Forms
personal information, 9
Freeman, Don
Pocket For Corduroy, A, 163
Friendship
class book, 109
critical thinking, 273
game, 273
learning centers, 14
literature, 295
parent newsletter, 295–296
sharing, 273
song, 273
Frogs
craft, 314

Games
alphabet, 190
bedtime, 157
bowling, 248
cleaning, 23
colors, 73, 88,145
dot-to-dot, 188
egg hunt, 190
fine-motor obstacle course, 106
flowers, 88, 145
friendship, 273
guessing, 179, 314
hop-and-seek, 15
hopscotch, watermelon, 100
I Spy, 241
jelly beans, 73
matching, 33, 136, 185, 258
potatoes, 167
pumpkins, 179
rubber stamps, using, 253
self-esteem, 48
separation, 312
sharing, 182
shoes, matching, 162
valentine, 210
watermelon hopscotch, 100
yarn balls, 189

Gardens (see Plants)
Gentleness
unit, 274
Gibbons, Gail
Sun Up, Sun Down, 93
Gifts
air freshener, 80
bags, 226
frame, 226, 303
holiday songs, 181
pencil cup, 226
pumpkin pie air freshener, 219
tile, 80
tote bags, 80
Gould, Deborah
Aaron's Shirt, 60
Grants
gardening, 88
Graphing
clothes, 57
jelly beans, 70
leaves, 262
left- and right-handedness, 15
names, 109
sun, 93
Green
frogs, 314
Gross Motor
blowing, 256
catching, 120
crawling, 188
eye-hand coordination, 255
hopping, 14, 100,188
jumping, 139, 191
obstacles, 255
rolling a ball, 255
tossing, 38, 120, 229 257
waving, 253
Groundhog Day
song, 198
Group Time (see Circle Time)
Growing Up
fingerplay, 211
Guests
seamstress, 57

Halloween (see also Fall)
bats, 300
black cats, 313
costumes, 194
ghosts, 179
pumpkins, 179, 218, 219, 246
spiders, 134–136, 137–138, 247, 301
Hand-Eye Coordination (see Fine Motor, Gross Motor)
Handwriting (see Writing)
Hanukkah
dreidel, 221
latkes, 37
menorah, 37, 42
Hats
Cat In The Hat, The, 166
watermelon visor, 99
Health & Hygiene (see also Safety)
body awareness, 7, 102, 191, 197
cleaning/soap, 191, 237, 264–265
dental health, 266–267
sunscreen, 94
Heat
absorption/reflection, 95
Helpers, Classroom
bulletin board, 299
Herman, Gail
Time For School, Little Dinosaur, 7
Hermit Crabs
song, 170
"Hickory, Dickory, Dock"
thematic unit, 130–131, 132–133
Hide And Snake, 167
Hoban, Tana
Construction Zone, 26
Holidays (see also Christmas; Easter; Father's Day; Groundhog Day; Halloween; Hanukkah; Kwanzaa; Mother's Day; New Year; St. Patrick's Day; Thanksgiving; Week Of The Young Child, The; Valentine's Day)
collage, 224
countdown to, 179
Home/School Connection
alphabet, 116
art, 68
bedtime, 157
book notes, 172, 173, 174, 175, 176, 184
clothing, 57
counting, 151
emotions, 33
flowers, 146
"Hickory, Dickory, Dock," 131
independence, 291–292
learning centers, 14, 21, 36
"Little Miss Muffet," 136
newsletter, 285–286, 287–288, 289–290, 291–292, 293–294, 295–296
parties, 101
patience, 293–294
self-esteem, 289–290, 291–292
separation, 285–286
summer activities, 92
House For Hermit Crab, A, 170
Hygiene (see Health & Hygiene)

I See A Song, 169
If You Give A Moose A Muffin, 164
In The Tall, Tall Grass, 168
Independence (see also Self-Esteem)
kangaroos, 12, 13
literature, 291
parent communication, 285, 291–292

separation game, 312
Insects
ants, 307, 315
chant, 212–213
fireflies, 185
flies, 169
Instruments, Musical (see Music)
Internet Sites
watermelons, 100
It Looked Like Spilt Milk, 171

Jack-O'-Lanterns (see Pumpkins)
Jamie O'Rourke And The Big Potato: An Irish Folktale, 167
Jobs (see Careers)

Kangaroos
thematic unit, 12–17
Katy No-Pocket, 12
Kaye, Buddy
A You're Adorable, 108
Kirk, David
Miss Spider's Tea Party, 134
Kites
suncatcher, 224
Krauss, Ruth
Carrot Seed, The, 168
Kroll, Steven
Will You Be My Valentine?, 166
Kwanzaa
beads, 40
benderas, 40
harvest, 40
kinara, 209

Lady With The Alligator Purse, The, 163
Language (see also Fingerplays, Literature, and Poems)
adjectives, 109
storytelling, 253
Learning Centers—Blocks
1, 2, 3 To The Zoo, 162
building, 27
counting, 246
dinosaurs, 245
materials for, 230
nativity, 39
signs, 252
Learning Centers—Fine Motor
scooping, 246
sewing, 59
squeezing, 228–229
Learning Centers—Games
carpet puzzle, 244
profile puzzle, 247
Learning Centers—Language
alphabet, 115
reading centers, 100, 163, 245, 255
reporting, 249
writing, 59,109, 244, 252
Learning Centers—Managing
birds, 21
clothespins, 20
cookie cutters, 20
flannelboard, 21
holidays, winter, 36
kangaroos, 14
stickers, 21
Learning Centers—Math
counting, 111, 123, 246, 254
number recognition, 111
sorting, 249
Learning Centers—Play Dough
letters, 259
menorah, 37
placemats, 244
snowballs, 123
watermelon, 98
Learning Centers—Science
observation, 247
Learning Centers—Sensory (see also Sand Table, Water Table)
beads, 248
bubble wrap, 236
cotton, 39
dinosaurs, 245
feet, 103
shaving cream, 38
spiders, 247
Learning Centers—Woodworking
toys, 38
Leaves (see Fall, Plants)
Letter Recognition (see Alphabet)
Listening (see also Following Directions, Senses)
Polar Bear, Polar Bear, What Do You Hear?, 165
potatoes, 167
Literature Lists (see also Authors, Books, Language)
alphabets books, 109
art, 69
birds, 269
clothing, 61
construction, 24, 29
fear, 287
feet, 103
friendship, 295–296
gardening, 89
"Hickory, Dickory, Dock," 131
holidays, winter, 41
independence, 291
kangaroos, 15
monsters, 33
patience, 293
preschool, 285
seasons, 37
self-esteem, 47, 289
separation anxiety, 285
snow, 50
sun, 95

"Little Miss Muffet"
  thematic unit, 134–136, 137–138

Mail
  postcards, 296
  song, 198
Making Friends, 273
Management (see Classroom Management)
Manipulatives
  candles, 256
  candy corns, 111
  cardboard tubes, 254–255
  jelly beans, 72
  "Little Miss Muffet," 136
  magnetic letters and numbers, 258–259
  nuts, 121
  Ping-Pong® balls, 234
  rubber stamps, 252–253
Manners (see Social Skills)
Martin, Bill Jr.
  Chicka Chicka Boom Boom, 114–116
  Polar Bear, Polar Bear, What Do You Hear?, 165
"Mary, Mary, How Does Your Garden Grow?"
  theme unit, 144–146
Mary Wore Her Red Dress And Henry Wore His Green Sneakers, 61
Matching
  bedtime, 157
  colors, 13, 21, 136, 257
  Easter eggs, 304
  fabric, 51
  letters, 259
  mittens, 118
  monsters, 33
  nuts and bolts, 27
  shoes, 59, 156, 162
  socks, 156, 185
  worm, 314
Math (see also Manipulatives, Sorting, Time)
  counting, 13, 14, 111, 123, 131, 149–152, 153–154, 162, 183, 184, 208, 209, 229, 246, 256
  graphing, 57, 70, 79, 93, 109, 262
  measurement, 111
  money, 253
  number recognition, 22, 27, 55, 78, 111, 131, 170, 255, 256, 257, 307, 313
  one-to-one correspondence, 256, 257
  patterning, 252, 257
  shapes, 19, 26, 246
Matisse, Henri
  collages, 65
Measurement
  Where The Wild Things Are, 111
Metamorphosis
  butterflies, 125–127, 190
Mice
  "Hickory Dickory Dock," 130–131, 132–133
Michelangelo
  ceiling paintings, 66
Migration
  birds, 55
Miss Spider's Tea Party, 134
Mona Lisa, 66
Mondrian, Piet
  shapes and colors, 67
Monet, Claude
  garden collage, 65
Money
  store, 253
Monsters
  emotions, 30–35
  Where The Wild Things Are, 110–113
Moose
  craft, 164
Mother's Day
  air freshener, 80
  bulletin board, 305
  frame, 226
  pencil cup, 226
Motivation (see Behavior)
Movement (see also Fine Motor, Gross Motor, Songs & Chants)
  body awareness, 7, 191,197
  circle, moving in a, 73, 131,188, 314
  creative, 93, 140, 171, 254
  follow-the-leader, 111
  locomotor, 15, 73, 90, 140, 188, 259, 273, 314
  obstacles, 255
  reindeer, 46
  running, 56
  song, 196, 197
  spatial, 150
Munsch, Robert
  Thomas' Snowsuit, 164
Music (see also Songs & Chants)
  beat, steady, 94, 189
  bells, 39
  classical, 169
  high/low sounds, 189
  maracas, 101
  movement to, 93
  rhythm, 131, 199, 255
  tambourine, 219
  xylophone, 131

Name Recognition
  attendance board, 18
  class book, 109
  initial letter, 108, 109
  learning center management, 21
  shapes, 183
  socks, 156
  storytime, 184
  spelling, 115, 252, 254, 258
  transition game, 281
Nests (see Birds)
New Year
  song, 196

Night
  bedtime, 155–157, 158–159
  fear of dark, 313
Number Recognition
  ants, 307
  candles, 256, 257
  clock, 131
  fish, 78
  learning center, 27, 255
  literature, 313
  magnetic, 258, 259
  monsters, 111
  puzzles, 22
  snow, 55
  spaghetti, 170
Numeroff, Laura Joffe
  If You Give A Moose A Muffin, 164
Nursery Rhymes (see Poems)
Nuts
  manipulatives, 121

Ocean
  crabs, 225
  dramatic play, 248
  fish, 78, 225
  hermit crabs, 170
  octopus, 225
  scene, 315
Octopus
  craft, 225
Old Black Fly, 169
"One, Two, Three, Four, Five; I Caught A Fish Alive"
  unit, 149–152, 153–154
Opposites
  left/right, 79
  off/on, 155, 156
  watermelons, 96
Outdoors
  hopscotch, 100

Painting (see Arts And Crafts)
Parent Communication (see Home/School Connection)
Parties (see Home/School Connection)
Patience
  literature, 293
  parent newsletter, 293–294
Patterning
  candles, 257
  rubber stamps, 252
Patterns
  beans, 75–76
  bed, 158–159
  book notes, 172
  candles, 41, 142–143,
  car, racing, 308
  clothing, 62–63
  dinosaur, 9, 11
  dinosaur paw, 10
  Easter bunny, 309
  emotions, 34–35
  fish, 152, 153–154
  flowers, 90, 147–148
  frame, 68
  gas pump, 308
  "Jack Be Nimble," 142–143
  jelly beans, 75–76
  kangaroos, 16, 17
  "Little Miss Muffet," 137–138
  marigolds, 91
  menorah, 42
  mice, 132
  monsters, 34–35, 112–113
  pig, 308
  rabbit, 309
  race car, 308
  Santa, 43
  spiders, 138
  tuffets, 138
Payne, Emmy
  Katy No-Pocket, 12
Peacocks
  handprint, 81
Peek, Merle
  Mary Wore Her Red Dress And Henry Wore His Green Sneakers, 61
Personal Space (see Social Skills)
Pets
  song, 199
Phonics (see also Alphabet)
  initial letter, 108, 109
Photographs, Student
  attendance board, 18
  bookmaking, 14, 109
  bulletin boards, 299, 305
  clothing, 61
  Mona Lisa, 66
  plant markers, 86
Physical Fitness (see Health & Hygiene, Movement)
Piggy Washes Up, 157
Pigs
  bedtime, 157
  bulletin board, 300
  fingerpainting, 300
  pattern, 308
  Piggy Washes Up, 157
  sponge-painting, 216
Planting A Rainbow, 88
Plants
  flowers, 64, 82, 84–91, 119, 146, 147–148, 255, 305
  gardens, 65, 82, 84, 145
  leaves, 262–263
  seeds, 96, 168
  watermelons, 96–101
Play Dough (see Dough)
Pocket For Corduroy, A, 163

Poems
  careers, 25
  circle, moving in a, 188
  colors, 120
  construction, 25
  "Diddle, Diddle, Dumpling," 155–157, 158–159
  fear, 272
  feet, 103
  garden, 144
  "Hickory, Dickory, Dock," 130–131, 132–133
  high/low, 189
  "Jack Be Nimble," 139–141, 142–143
  jelly beans, 72, 74
  "Little Miss Muffet," 134
  "Mary, Mary, How Does Your Garden Grow?", 144
  monsters, 32
  off/on, 156
  "One, Two, Three, Four, Five; I Caught A Fish Alive," 149–152, 153–154
  play dough, 183
  snow, 52
  stars, 184
  watermelons, 97
  yarn ball, 189
Polar Bear, Polar Bear, What Do You Hear?, 165
Pollock, Jackson
  splatter-painting, 67
Ponds (see also Animals)
  frogs, 314
Portfolios
  managing, 276
Positional Words
  booklet, 135
  building, 259
  chant, 212–213
  fingerplay, 130
  flannelboard, 130
  song, 7
  spiders, 135
Post Office (see Mail)
Praise (see Self-Esteem)
Pre-Reading (see also Name Recognition)
  color words, 78
  flowers, 86
  shamrocks, 199
Prints (see Arts And Crafts)
Problem Solving (see also Puzzles)
  designing, 26
Pumpkins
  fine-motor skills, 246
  fingerpaint, 218
  game, 179
  milk jug, 218
  tambourine, 219
Puppets
  bear, 178
  caterpillar/butterfly, 125
  dinosaur, 7
  fish, 150
  flower, 144
  letters, 108
  spiders, 135
  storage, 23, 278
Putty (see Dough)
Puzzles
  carpet squares, 244
  Christmas collage, 233
  cookie, 286
  cookie cutter, 313
  dinosaurs, 8
  profile, 247
  storage, 22
  worm, 314

Rabbit
  headband, 77
Raffi
  Baby Beluga, 171
Rainbow
  graphing, 70
Reading Center (see Learning Centers—Language)
Reasoning (see Deductive Reasoning)
Recycling Materials
  appliance boxes, 191
  baby-wipes containers, 106
  bells, 221
  berry baskets, 313
  bubble wrap, 225, 228, 236
  cans, 230
  cardboard tubes, 140, 245, 254–255
  carpet squares, 244
  catalogs, 241
  cereal boxes, 276
  drink mix container, 222
  egg cartons, 119, 217, 225, 245
  film canisters, 71, 101, 313
  garland, 233
  grocery bags, paper, 242
  ice-cream spoons, wooden, 219
  milk cartons, 248
  milk jug lids, 106
  milk jugs, 218
  muffin boxes, 164
  packaging, bulk, 240
  packing materials, biodegradable, 191
  paper bags, brown, 218
  pillowcase, 298
  placemats, vinyl, 242
  plastic bottles, 106, 249
  puzzles, 226
  ribbons, 233
  soda bottles, 106
  spools, 242
  strawberry baskets, 217
  Styrofoam® trays, 240, 315
  tinsel, 233

tissue boxes, facial, 240
towels, 312
valentines, 183
wrapping paper, 233
yogurt containers, 145
Reid, Margarette S.
Button Box, The, 165
Reindeer
headband, 77
Reproducibles (see Awards, Forms, Patterns)
Rhyme (see Poems)
Rhythm (see Music)
Rogers, Fred
Making Friends, 273
Rubber Stamps
manipulatives, 252–253
"Rudolph The Red-Nosed Reindeer"
fingerplay, 208
self-esteem, 44–49

Safety
fire, 178, 206
traffic, 204, 277, 315
St. Patrick's Day
potatoes, 167
shamrocks, 199
Sand Table
cake, birthday, 257
cardboard tubes, 254
construction, 26
counting, 254
dinosaurs, 245
funnel, 249
garden, 145
letters, 259
rubber stamps, 253
snowpeople, 123
Scarecrows (see Fall)
Science (see also Animals, Stars)
heat, 95
observation, 247
plants, 262–263
seasons, 37–43
senses, 37
soap, 264–265
Seasons (see also Fall, Winter, Spring, Summer)
Caps, Hats, Socks, And Mittens: A Book About The Four Seasons, 117–121
Seeds (see Plants)
Self-Esteem (see also Independence)
game, 48
literature, 289
newsletter, 289
song, 290
treasure chest, 185
unit (Rudolph), 44–49
valentines, 166
Sendak, Maurice
Where The Wild Things Are, 110–113
Senses, Five (see also Learning Centers—Sensory)
seasons, 37
Separation (see Independence)
Sequencing
numbers, 313
size, 27, 164, 254, 256
Seriation (see Sequencing)
Sets (see Number Recognition)
Seuss, Dr.
Cat In The Hat, The, 166
Shapes
circles/spirals, 234–235, 255
flannelboard, 230
formation, 259
matching, 246
recognition, 19, 26, 183, 307
rectangles, 67
Sharing (see Social Skills)
Sharing Time (see Circle Time)
Shaw, Charles G.
It Looked Like Spilt Milk, 171
Shoes, 162
Similarities/Differences (see Compare/Contrast)
Size
clothing, 164
long/short, 254, 256
sequencing, 254
sorting by, 233, 241
Snacktime (see Classroom Management, Cooking)
Snake
garden craft, 85
Hide And Snake, 167
Snow (see Winter)
Snowballs, 122–124
Soap (see Health & Hygiene)
Social Skills (see also Character Education)
personal space, 182
sharing, 182, 273
Social Studies (see Character Education, Community, Cultures, Families)
Songs & Chants (see also Music)
"Baby Beluga," 171
bath, 191
bedtime, 155
buddy bear, 178
bug hunt, 212–213
Christmas, 196

clothing, 58
construction, 24
dark, fear of, 313
dental health, 266
dinosaurs, 7
fall, 194
fear of dark, 313
flowers, 85, 88, 146
friendship, 273
Groundhog Day, 198
Halloween, 194
hermit crabs, 170
jack-o'-lanterns, 179
jelly beans, 70, 73
jumping, 139
kangaroos, 12, 13
leaves, 194, 262
mail, 198
"Mary Wore Her Red Dress And Henry Wore His Green Sneakers," 61
monsters, 31, 32
New Year, 196
numbers, 55
pets, 199
restlessness, 110
"Rudolph The Red-Nosed Reindeer," 44–49
scarecrow, 194
seeds, 96
self-esteem, 44, 290
sharing, 182
snow, 52, 124, 197
spiders, 135
stars, 94
summer, 92
Thanksgiving, 195
turkeys, 195
valentines, 183, 210
watermelon, 96, 97
Sorting
angels, 39
balloons, 229
beads, 233
candles, 257
color, 72, 258
fabric, 51
jelly beans, 72
letters, 258
manipulatives, any, 249
numbers, 258
nuts, 121
nuts and bolts, 27
worms, 106
Spiders
bulletin board, 301
thematic unit, 134–136, 247
Spring (see also Birds, Easter, Mother's Day, Plants)
bulletin boards, 306
butterflies, 125–127, 190
fingerplay, 119
kites, 224
mud, 119
Squirrel
fingerplay, 207
Stars
counting, 184
Stickland, Paul
Dinosaur Stomp!, 7
Storage
bulletin boards, 22
crayons, 22, 277
letter templates, 281
puppets, 23, 278
smocks, 281
supplies, 22, 276
Strega Nona, 170, 188
Sturges, Philemon
Ten Flashing Fireflies, 185
Summer (see also Father's Day)
beach, 120
bugs, 185, 307
bulletin boards, 307
feet (bare), 102–103
fingerplay, 120
floats, inflatable, 245
sun, 82, 92–95
sunflowers, 64
watermelons, 96–101
Sun (see Summer, Heat)
Sun Up, Sun Down, 93

Teeth (see Health & Hygiene)
Ten Flashing Fireflies, 185
Thanksgiving (see also Fall)
meal, 195
turkeys, 195, 219
Thematic Units
clothing, 56–63
construction, 24–29
dinosaurs, 6–11
feet (bare), 102–103
fine art, 64–69
flowers, 84–91
garden, 144–146
jelly beans, 70–76
kangaroos, 12–17
spiders, 134–136, 137–138

sun, 92–95
watermelons, 96–101
Thinking (see Critical Thinking, Deductive Reasoning, Puzzles)
Thomas' Snowsuit, 164
Thompson, Carol
Piggy Washes Up, 157
Tigers
handprint, 81
Time
clock, 131, 280
days, 179
Time For School, Little Dinosaur, 7
Timeline
marigolds, 86
Touch (see Learning Centers—Sensory, Senses)
Transitions
any, 276, 281
cleaning, 23
lining up, 19
restlessness, 110
Transportation
car, 308
Triangles (see Shapes)
Turkeys
craft, 219
song, 195
Turtles
sponge-painting, 217

Valentine's Day
hearts, 182, 210
valentines, 166, 183
van Gogh, Vincent
Sunflowers, 64
Very Hungry Caterpillar, The, 125–127
Visual Discrimination (see also Matching)
carpet puzzle, 244
profile puzzle, 247
snakes, 167

Water Table
bowls, 234
bubble wrap, 228
candles, 256
cornstarch, 228
fish, 150
garland, 233
jack-o'-lanterns, 246
laundry, 60
Ping-Pong® balls, 234
plumbing, 27
soap, 237
winter, 51
Watermelon Day, 101
Watermelons
thematic unit, 96–101
Watermelon Day, 101
Weather
snow, 48, 50–55, 122–124, 164, 222, 223, 232, 303
Week Of The Young Child, The
bulletin board, 304
Westcott, Nadine Bernard
Lady With The Alligator Purse, The, 163
Where The Wild Things Are, 110–113
White
collage, 53
Will You Be My Valentine?, 166
Winter
clothing, 51, 118
fingerplay, 118
snow/snowmen, 48, 50–55, 118, 122–124, 164, 197, 222, 223, 232, 303
Winthrop, Elizabeth
Shoes, 162
Worms
puzzle, 314
Writing
adjectives, 109
creative, 169
descriptive, 241
name, 163, 252
storytelling, 253

Yarn Ball
games, 189

Zebra
painted, 216
Zoo
1, 2, 3 To The Zoo, 162